KISS IT GOODBYE

**SHELBY
WHITFIELD**

GOODBYE

ABELARD-SCHUMAN

NEW YORK

An Intext Publisher

Library of Congress Cataloging in Publication Data

Whitfield, Shelby.
  Kiss it goodbye.

  1. Texas Rangers (Baseball club)   I.   Title.
GV875.T4W45   796.357′64′09764531   72–12071
ISBN 0–200–04007–3

Abelard-Schuman Ltd., 257 Park Avenue South, New York, N.Y. 10010

Published on the same day in Canada by Longman Canada Limited.

Printed in the United States of America.

DEDICATION

To Dolores for suggesting that I write this book, and to Lora for her understanding and tolerance.

CONTENTS

ACKNOWLEDGMENTS

I would like to thank *Sports Illustrated, The Sporting News, The Baseball Guide,* and *Washingtonian* magazine for permission to excerpt quotes from their publications.

A special acknowledgment of thanks is in order to Senator J. Glenn Beall, United States Senator from Maryland, for his help in obtaining information about the Interstate Commerce Commission investigation into certain Robert E. Short business practices.

I would also like to thank the *Baseball Register,* published by *The Sporting News,* from which I obtained the statistics used in this book.

INTRODUCTION

"Why don't you write a book about it? You could blow the whole thing wide open!" So said Dolores Williams, the pretty, vivacious, and outspoken wife of Ted Williams, when I first told her that I probably wouldn't continue as "The Voice of the Senators." I didn't give it much thought then, but as time passed and other friends urged me to write about the Bob Short-Ted Williams era, I began to take the idea seriously.

With the completion of Short's plan to move baseball out of the nation's capital, it became apparent to me that this period might be one of the most important in baseball history. And with a cast of characters like Bob Short, Ted Williams, Frank Howard, Denny McLain, Curt Flood, and all the others, it seemed to me that an inside look at this major-league operation, by the club's own broadcaster, could interest fans all across the country.

I wasn't interested in doing a hatchet job, nor in necessarily doing a book that would "blow the whole thing wide open." But the book would have to be honest, accurate, and hard-hitting.

It would probably be controversial. As a broadcaster who worked for a club and then dared to write about it, I would come in for some sharp criticism. To some it would be sour grapes, since I no longer worked for the club. Others might brand it unethical for exploiting friendships and violating confidences. Many told me that the book would kill any chance of my broadcasting baseball again. Some people would hate me.

I decided I could stand the criticism, and I would take my chances on the book ruining my career. As for my owing anything to baseball, I decided I didn't. I had worked hard, been loyal, and fulfilled the terms of my contract. And who was to say that an inside baseball book would hurt baseball? It might help it.

So I made the commitment. I would do the book.

Ted Williams seemed to like the idea. "Go ahead and write it," he said. "Just tell the truth."

Maybe he didn't understand just how truthful I planned to be. In the 1969 season, Ted had been impressed with Jim Bouton as a relief pitcher with the Seattle franchise. Then Bouton turned author with *Ball Four,* and Ted's feelings changed. Bouton became a sports reporter with WABC-TV in New York, and Williams' Senators were in New York when Bouton made his first trip to Yankee Stadium as a reporter. I told Ted that Bouton was on the field with a camera crew, and getting the brush-off from the Yankees. Ted blurted out, "I guess he'll want to interview me. Well, I won't do it. That's a horseshit book he wrote."

In March, 1972, I had lunch with Stan Bregman, Bob Short's Washington attorney, and we discussed the book. Bregman was so alarmed that he immediately called Short, who asked him to call Williams about it. That was the beginning of a long cooling period in my friendship with Ted.

Ted called me from the Rangers spring training camp and said, "Say, everyone is really getting upset about that damn book. You're not doing a Bouton book, are you?"

"Well, not exactly," I said. "His book was a player's diary about one season. Mine will cover the whole Short-Williams era and the entire operation of a major-league club."

"Geez, buddy," Ted told me, "I sure hope you're not going to do anything to hurt baseball. You could reveal an awful lot of strange things. And don't do anything to hurt your chances of doing the broadcasts when you get a club back in Washington. Baseball could blacklist you."

He added, "A lot of things happen that shouldn't be put in any book."

During our conversations over the next year, Ted continued to express concern about the book. But I stood firm. "Ted, I'm not going to budge. I'm going to write an honest book and I'm not going to leave out material to appease anybody." When it became apparent that he wasn't going to change my plans, Ted finally said, "Hell, go ahead and write anything you want."

Dolores Williams' reaction to the book was pure glee. "Great!" she said. "You'll do a good one. Make it juicy, and don't give a damn what anyone says."

Bob Short reportedly called me a bastard, and indignantly said that maybe I wouldn't be able to get it published.

Stan Bregman was a little more jovial about it. "If everyone who is sweating out your book buys a copy, you'll have a best seller."

About the name of the book, *Kiss It Goodbye*. It's a favorite phrase of mine, which I used on home run calls when I was announcing the Senators games. The old Pirates broadcaster, Rosey Rowswell, often used the phrase years ago, so I certainly don't have a patent on it.

And, too, didn't Washington have to kiss its baseball franchise goodbye, after 71 years? Will the things revealed here make the sports fan kiss his illusions goodbye? And there are those who say that, with this book, I could be kissing baseball goodbye myself.

S.W.

Washington, D.C.
January, 1973

KISS IT GOODBYE

1

ANNOUNCING—
SHELBY WHITFIELD

During the 1968 baseball season, it seemed to me that the Senators' radio and TV broadcasters for eight years, Dan Daniels and John McLean, might be on their way out. WTOP was airing both the television and radio broadcasts of the games, and during that season they auditioned announcers for the job. The auditions were done live during the regular season games, and must have been embarrassing for Daniels and McLean. It's not the biggest vote of confidence for a broadcaster when his boss starts putting other announcers on the air just to see how they do.

Then James Lemon put the club up for sale. With a change in ownership, there frequently is a change in announcers. So I began to make plans for landing the job.

I had never applied for a major-league baseball announcing job, but I felt the time had come. I'd studied radio-TV at the University of Texas. I had worked at several commercial stations in the Southwest, including minor-league play-by-play, live and re-create, in the old Class B Southwestern League. I had worked on hundreds of major-league baseball broadcasts aired around the world on Armed Forces Radio and Television.

I enjoyed my job as a sportscaster-sports director there, and, as a civilian employee of the Department of Defense, I had a job with good pay, fringe benefits, and security. But this Washington opportunity was attractive. At age thirty-two, I was ready to try for a play-by-play job with a major-league club.

Major-league baseball broadcasting is a competitive and select fraternity. (There are one hundred U.S. Senators, but only about sixty major-league baseball broadcasters.) From the monetary standpoint, baseball is the ultimate in major-league sports broadcasting. Sportscasters are paid by the game—162 regular season games, and perhaps as many as 28 exhibition games. When there's an opening, sportscasters from all over the country apply. Most are top-notch professionals, announcers with other major-league clubs, minor-league announcers, or former players who want to make the move to the booth.

The case in Washington was no different. Broadcasting tapes and applications started pouring in. After I was hired, I was amazed at those who had applied. They included announcers like Ned Martin, Jimmy Dudley, and Dave Martin. Former baseball players Jimmy Piersall and Rex Barney applied, and even a former basketball player named Hot Rod Hundley.

I had laid careful plans for an opportunity like this. Much time and effort had gone into my application, résumé, and audition tapes. I knew I could sell myself to whoever did the hiring. Bob Short, who had just purchased the club, had already made it plain that he was going to do the hiring and that the number-one broadcaster on the crew would work directly for the Senators. So I set my sights on one Robert E. Short. I mailed duplicates of applications, résumés, and audition tapes of my broadcasting work to Short's office in Minneapolis, his home in Edina, Minnesota, and to the Senators front office. I contacted friends in broadcasting, sports, government, and private industry, advised them of my plight, and they responded with either a call or a letter to Short.

One morning soon after Short bought the club, I picked up the *Washington Post* and read that he was flying into town in his Lear Jet, and bringing a long-time friend and consultant, Tom Gallery. Gallery, the paper said, was supposed to help Short solve his radio-TV negotiations.

My God, I thought, this may be a helluva break. An entry!

I had never met Gallery, though I certainly knew about him. NBC sportscaster Lindsey Nelson, whom Gallery had hired, once described the guy as "a bluff, friendly Irishman with an almost perpetual grin on his face." Lindsey then went on to tell about one of Tom's experiences in his short–lived movie career in the Rin Tin Tin series of the 1920s. Tom had been the male lead but was frustrated because everybody was so busy pampering the dog they neglected him. The payoff came when Tom, playing the part of a young flyer forced down in flames, was being rescued by Rin Tin Tin. Tom was wearing a shoulder harness with a leather thong that came out of his shirt collar at the back of his neck. The dog was supposed to rush into the flames and pull him out by the thong, but instead grabbed him by one ear. Unable to wriggle loose, Tom finally kicked Rin Tin Tin in the chops, to the horror of everyone on the set. Things were not the same after that.

In those days Gallery was very much a part of the Hollywood scene. He knew all the old-time movie stars and was a member of a rotating poker game that included Red Grange, Adolph Menjou, Johnny Mack Brown, and others. In fact, Grange refused to sign his first movie contract in 1926 until he got the same kind of yellow, custom-built convertible that Gallery drove to dazzle other Hollywoodians. According to the stories, he soon took to promoting fights in Hollywood's Legion Stadium, eventually making Friday night the big "fight night" there. His biggest promotion was probably the Joe Louis-Jack Roper heavyweight championship fight with Bing Crosby doing color commentary on radio.

Gallery later became involved in sports at the front-office level: he was general manager of the Brooklyn Dodgers pro football team under Dan Topping, then he went with the New York Yankees. Later Tom worked for the Dumont Television Network and finally moved to NBC as sports director. Tom Gallery had been in semi-retirement for several years, doing things like part-time radio-TV consultant work for the baseball commissioner at $60,000 a year. (Former CBS executive Tom Dawson now does the job on a full-time basis in the Commissioner's office.) He first met Short when Short owned the Los Angeles Lakers and, although it is not common knowledge, I know he refused Short's offer of a front-office job with the Senators.

Since I didn't know Gallery personally and since he and Short might not be in Washington for long, I had to work fast. I called Curt Gowdy and John Curran to see if they could help.

I got Gowdy at home in Wellesley Hills, Massachusetts, and he said he not only knew Gallery but that the guy had actually hired him at NBC. Gowdy called Burt Hawkins, the Senators press man, found out that Gallery was at the Washington Hilton with Short, and contacted him on my behalf. After a phone call from me, Curran did the same thing.

It was still morning when Gallery called *me* to say that Gowdy and Curran had talked to him already, and he had requested my file and audition tapes from the Senators organization.

"I am putting aside thirty minutes for you this afternoon," Gallery's voice filled my ears. "Can you drop by the Hilton at one-thirty?"

When I put down the phone, I hugged my wife Lora and told her, "This is *it!*"

Tom Gallery turned out to be a warm and friendly man, who did everything to make me feel at ease while skillfully probing for information. We discussed my background, baseball knowledge, broadcast philosophy, and my opinions of other major-league broadcasters. I had a broad knowledge of broadcasters' styles thanks to my experience with Armed Forces Radio-TV. Every day AFRT transmitted different games selected from *all* major-league broadcasts, so I had had a chance, during my twelve years in Europe and Washington, to study the styles of all the broadcasters.

Tom told me that, as a matter of fact, he had hired some of the best, including—besides Nelson and Gowdy—such standouts as Jim Simpson and Joe Garagiola. Garagiola, he said, had come to him complaining that he and his radio partner, Harry Caray, had reached the point of not talking anymore. This is not unusual in major-league broadcasting. As Curt Gowdy once said, it's a long season and a small booth.

Tom Gallery continued talking way past our scheduled thirty-minute interview, into the evening. We hit it off fine.

"Now you'll be great as long as the club is winning," he said in the way of advice. "But when the club is losing, Short may think you are a horseshit announcer." He tipped me off to the kind of rips and knocks to expect from critics, to prepare me for it if I landed the job. "You are getting into a competitive rat race," he warned.

But I wasn't paying any attention to the negative aspects of the job. Tom Gallery was talking so much of the positive assets that I felt more and more confident.

For the next few days, Tom asked me to meet other people connected with the club, which I did. But I didn't meet Short himself until the Friday night red-carpet press conference when he announced the signing of Ted Williams. Tom told me that Short wanted me there—but in the background, silent. Short took a second to tell me that he was impressed with my application, recommendations, and experience. "I think we can do some business," he said. And then added, "We'll talk money later."

I chatted with the incumbent Senators broadcasters, Daniels and McLean, at the cocktail party after the conference. Neither had been told that they would not be rehired. I suppose they wondered why I was there. I had always made it a point to stay out of the scene with writers and broadcasters in Washington, since I figured I'd stand a better chance of getting a job as an unknown in town. A new owner might want a fresh face and voice. And if people didn't know my intentions, they couldn't throw any roadblocks in my way.

At the party, Tom Gallery called me aside, and told me something that exhilarated me. Williams had spotted me in the hospitality room after the press conference and had asked Short who I was. According to Gallery, Short told him I was the new Voice of the Washington Senators.

I felt like a football fan whose team has just won the Super Bowl. I wanted to run onto the field and tear down the goalposts. Instead, I ripped down a few quick drinks, enough to calm me down, went home, and I typed out my resignation.

The next day Gallery called to confirm the evidence: "Bob Short and his associates have bought you lock, stock and barrel. And, Shelby, I want to add that I knew you were the man for the job the first day we talked. Congratulations!"

The day after, Gallery offered me more money than I'd hoped for: twice the minimum major-league player salary.

Was everything too good to be true? Yes. That's the way it usually is when Bob Short's involved.

THE SHORT END
OF THE DEAL

Hustling money from people is undoubtedly Bob Short's greatest ability. His critics, who are numerous (for reasons that will make themselves clear), admit that getting other people to put up money for his causes is the best thing Bob Short does. Even a Minnesota Congressman, who has had his differences with Short, said, "He can get on the phone and raise $100,000. . . . just like that! . . . for the Democrats or for a boys' high school. He knows so many people." You see, it's damned hard to shake a carnival-barker mentally equipped with a sense of power and a WATS line.

In October of 1968, Bob Short was in Washington, as treasurer of the Democratic Party, feverishly trying to hustle funds for Hubert Humphrey's presidential campaign. At the height of his humpin' 'n pumpin' for Humphrey (which, for the record, left the Democratic Party $9.3 million in debt), Short was possessed by one of life's rare moments: a marriage of opportunity and inspiration.

One day Stanley Bregman, a young Washington lawyer, who also worked on the Hubert Humphrey campaign, casually asked Short, "Bob, why don't you buy the Senators?"

"You mean they're for sale?" Short replied enthusiastically. And without hesitating, told Bergman, "Find out who we should talk to."

That leap at Bregman's offhand comment reveals the intensity of Short's desire to control the national pastime in the nation's capital. He had offered to buy the Senators three years earlier, after cashing in on the Los Angeles Lakers basketball ownership for a huge capital gain. Short had approached the late James M. Johnston, then Senators chairman of the board and president, about buying the club. Johnston flatly refused him.

After Johnston died, James H. Lemon had followed as club president, and had quietly put the franchise up for sale in that winter of 1968. In fact, Lemon had already given comedian Bob Hope a verbal option to buy the club.

Bregman called an old friend of the family, *Washington Post* columnist Shirley Povich, who was then in Mexico City covering the Olympics. He told Bregman to contact Norman Frost, attorney for the Johnston-Lemon Estate.

Bob Hope wasn't sure about buying the Senators, but Short intended to press him into a decision and then grab the team if he could. Looking back on it now, I can easily see why "businessman" Short was so excited.

The club could be a tax write-off gold mine for Short, and his extensive other holdings. He owned three hotels in Minneapolis—the Leamington, the Leamington Motor Court, and the Sir Francis Drake. Short owned an interlocking network of trucking companies that spanned the eastern two-thirds of the United States, and he had thirty-four trucking terminals across the country—for one of the nation's largest privately owned motor freight lines. In 1967 the trucking empire grossed $40 million.

And Short owned Gopher Aviation, Inc., a Minneapolis-to-Chicago commuter airline. This gave him access to a private Lear Jet, and two full-time personal pilots, Jim Cunningham and Darold Wilke, quickly got used to flying Short all over the country at any hour. Cunningham once told me that they were on twenty-four-hour call, and Short expected them to drop what they were doing and race to the airport whenever he wanted. When Short first bought the Senators, he said he wouldn't fly the $700,000 Lear Jet much, because it was too expensive to operate. But for the next four years, he seldom used commercial airlines. And what seemed like continual Lear Jet flight expenses somehow appeared as charges to the ball club.

If he was able to obtain the club, Short would have a property he could depreciate at full value over a five-year period. A special tax loophole that Congress grants to owners of professional sports teams permitted him to depreciate the club at his full purchase price of $9 million. The Senators could be a dream corporate tax shelter.

Short was still a little giddy about his first conquest of the pro-sports world, the fattening and marketing of the Lakers. No doubt he figured the Senators franchise would be just as easy to manipulate.

In 1957 he and a group of Minnesota businessmen bought the nearly bankrupt Minneapolis Lakers basketball franchise from Ben Berger and Max Winter for $150,000. Short turned this into a capital gain of $5 million.

Short bought a franchise that had been a dynasty in the NBA, finishing either first or second in the standings the first nine years of the club's existence. He didn't just let it alone.

John Kundla, of University of Minnesota fame, had been the coach of the Lakers since the formation of the club and had enjoyed terrific success. Kundla led Laker teams to 374 victories while losing 240, and won the league championship five times during a nine-year period. Short gently shoved Kundla upstairs, to become general manager, and Short named Laker playing great George Mikan the club's new head coach.

Unfortunately, Short's big move as a rookie club owner was a bomb. The proud Lakers floundered in the basement. Short fired Mikan after half of the season, and moved Kundla back to the coaching spot. But the damage had been done. The Lakers finished in last place with a record of 19 wins and 53 losses. It marked the first time the club had finished lower than second place in the standings, and was the first time that the Lakers had missed the playoffs.

The last-place finish did have one advantage: It gave the Lakers draft rights to a brilliant college star named Elgin Baylor. Even though he had a year of eligibility remaining at Seattle University, Short signed him to a professional contract.

By then, Kundla had had enough of the Bob Short basketball operation, and returned to the University of Minnesota as head coach. Short signed John Castellani, the Seattle University coach. Short hired Castellani because he had been Baylor's college coach, and advertised the hiring as a move to keep Baylor happy. When Castellani proved to be inadequate, Short fired him before midseason and replaced him with Jim Pollard, another ex-Laker playing star. Pollard lasted out the remainder of the season.

Short had been eyeing the lucrative California sports market for some time. Bob could see the general attractions of Southern California's population and growth, and the new arena in Los Angeles, a modern, 14,000-seat arena adjacent to the University of Southern California Coliseum, was a special magnet. Short managed to buy out his Minneapolis partners for a fraction of their investment and a promise to pay off $60,000 in debts. Then he moved the franchise to Los Angeles, and set up shop as an absentee owner.

He also purchased radio station KRHM-FM. He hadn't been able to get a contract he liked for radio coverage of the Lakers, so he bought his own station, for $125,000, and used it to broadcast the games. (He sold the station in 1971, for $800,000.)

Once again, a dismal season record, 25 wins and 50 losses the last year in Minneapolis, was turned into a plus for Short. It gave him the right to select another superstar collegian in the player draft—Jerry West of the University of West Virginia.

Jim Pollard had been a playing star in Minnesota, but his name meant little in Los Angeles, and Short dumped him. He hired Fred Schaus, Jerry West's college coach at the University of West Virginia. Short may have been thinking of keeping his superstar happy again. The move turned out to be a good one. Schaus was an excellent coach in the pros. Short prospered through five years in the fertile Los Angeles market.

In 1965, Short sold the Lakers to Canadian sportsman Jack Kent Cooke, who now also owns the Los Angeles Kings hockey club, the Forum arena in Inglewood, California, and 25 percent of the Washington Redskins. Cooke bought the Lakers for what he thought was going to be a price of $5 million even. But it cost even more. Short had sold $310,000 worth of season tickets for next season, and Cooke was flabbergasted to learn that Short was trying to keep that money, even though he was selling the club. It was Short's contention that once the money came in, it was his, even if the games would be played after he was gone. Cooke was outraged, but wound up in a compromise with Short that saw them split the money fifty-fifty. And so the Lakers were sold for the odd figure of $5,155,000.

The best reason for Short's excitement at the prospect of buying the Senators was the fact he could do it without spending much of his own money. In 1972, two Washington Brookings Institution economists, Roger Noll and Benjamin Okner, analyzed the figures that Short himself provided to his accountants, Arthur Anderson & Co. They discovered that Short's entire cash outlay was just $1,000 to form the corporation! He borrowed the rest of the purchase price—a total of $9 million.

He borrowed $2 million from the First National Bank in St. Paul, Minnesota, $4 million from the American Security & Trust Company in Washington, and $3 million from the Johnston-Lemon Estate. The $2 million loan from the Minnesota bank was the only secured loan. And Short was forced to pay 9½ percent interest, well over the prime rate, on the $4 million loan from American Security & Trust. Short did have to write his own check for $100,000 in December of 1968 when the sale contract was signed, but it was to be returned to him at no loss if he was unable to arrange financing, so even that was a no-risk business venture.

On paper, Short even made money from one of his loans to buy the club. He borrowed $3 million from the Johnston-Lemon Estate to make the deal and then sold back 10 percent of the club to Jim Lemon for $1.1 million—a capital gain of $200,000 in less than a year on just 10 percent of the club! And that's not all. Economists Noll and Okner showed that most of the losses that Short eventually conjured up, for public consumption as a reason for moving the ball club, were bookkeeping losses rather than cash losses. For instance, $1.7 million of the $1.95 million loss Short claimed in 1969 was simply player depreciation and other paper deficits. In 1970, $1.96

million out of $2.87 million in losses were depreciation. And even then Short was not hurting since much of the remaining loss did not represent cash outlay. Short simply did not pay more than $830,000 in operating bills up to the end of 1970. In fact, he finally managed to satisfy creditors and pay off his original loans by mortgaging $7.5 million worth of Texas broadcasting revenues over the next ten years. Now the bulk of his loans are being taken care of by future TV-radio revenues and he virtually owns the club outright—in rich new territory—and still has one more year of tax depreciation left. He swung it all on $1,000 cash and millions in bluster.

Short, of course, scoffs at the $1,000 figure uncovered by economists Noll and Okner. He had to put up securities valued at $2 million to back up the loan from the First National Bank of St. Paul and he calls that his "equity." But can you call loan collateral "equity"? "Maybe some economics professor wouldn't call it equity, but I do," Short told C. C. Johnson Spink, editor and publisher of *The Sporting News*. "I risked that $2 million in assets. If the loan goes bad, I can be out $2 million: if that isn't equity, what is?"

Spink then asked Short about the Washington economists' claim that Short's losses consisted mainly of depreciation write-offs on the Senators' investments in players. "Completely untrue," replied Short. "I absorbed actual cash losses, out-of-pocket losses, amounting to $3 million during the three years I operated in Washington. They came to $600,000 in 1969, $953,000 in 1970, and $1.5 million in 1971. [These figures were later disputed by Washington businessman Joe Danzansky, who offered to buy the Senators.] ... Besides, the depreciation the Senators generated hasn't helped my other companies. For one thing, my other businesses weren't showing enough profit to utilize the Senators' depreciation. For another, my real estate and trucking companies produce considerable depreciation of their own, all I can use, in fact."

Spink summed him up: "Bob Short is not a rogue. He is merely adroit at what a respected Wall Street writer calls The Money Game."

Originally, Short's old millionaire Minnesota friend Jeno F. Paulucci, board chairman of R.J. Reynolds Foods, Inc., was supposed to share the Senators deal with Short. That all fell apart when the representatives of the Johnston-Lemon Estate insisted that Paulucci put his name on the bank note with Short. At that time, they were talking in terms of Short and Paulucci each putting up a million dollars and financing the other seven million. Paulucci said his corporation, Jeno's Inc., would buy half of the club but he refused to put down his signature. So Short decided to do it by himself, and arranged for the loans.

Short called Stan Bregman in Washington and told him that he had the Senators. Bregman drew up a sale contract based on the contract signed when the Johnston-Lemon Estate bought the club. Then Bregman carried the contract to the Washington offices of TWA (a client of Bregman), and they arranged for a stewardess to hand-carry the document to Short in San Francisco.

At the baseball winter meetings in San Francisco, Short arranged a hasty press conference, which conflicted with the official baseball dinner (Short might have wondered why almost everyone at the press conference had a white carnation in his lapel). Short said: "I did not buy the Washington team to move it. I chose Washington for a baseball franchise—I could have invested in several other cities—but I invested in the nation's capital because I sincerely believe it can support a team . . ."

At the same press conference he also said he planned no immediate changes in the team general management. He promptly fired general manager George Selkirk, paying him $100,000 for the last two years on his contract, and he canned

Jim Lemon as field manager, absorbing his $27,500 salary in doing so.

After making money, Short's next favorite hobby is politics.

In 1940, at the age of twenty-one, Bob Short was the youngest delegate to the Democratic Convention which nominated Franklin D. Roosevelt for a third term. That got him started in high-level politics and he has been hot at it ever since. He once said, "Once the political bug hits you, you don't quit until you die."

Some of the Minnesota antagonism toward Short stems back to 1956, when he led an intraparty mutiny that helped Estes Kefauver defeat the Hubert Humphrey-backed Adlai Stevenson in the state presidential primary.

Short's detractors claim he thinks he can buy his way into public office. One veteran recalls that, on arriving at the 1958 state party convention, he was greeted by a bevy of pretty girls, all boosting Short. "All I could hear or see was his name, but nothing about what he was running for. When I ran into him later, I asked, 'Bob, what are you running for?' He answered, 'Well, what's available?' "

In 1966, he ran for lieutenant governor. He won the Democratic nomination, but lost the general election.

Short really wanted to be Governor. In 1969, he told me, "You could run Humpty Dumpty with Humphrey in 1970 and win. And I'd like to be that Humpty Dumpty. I'm available." But Hubert Humphrey had to refuse to support Short's "independent" candidacy for the governorship and instead back the regular Democratic candidate, Wendell Anderson, now Governor. Humphrey faced a tough senate race against Clark MacGregor, President Nixon's campaign manager in 1972, and feared that a deviation toward Short might cost him the election. It cost him a rift with Short.

Despite Short's occasional falls from political grace within the Democratic Party, he always seems to bounce back. Humphrey had chosen him to be national coordinator of his 1964 campaign for the Vice Presidency, and Short was chosen national treasurer of the National Democratic Party and chief fund-raiser for the 1968 campaign. Had Humphrey won the Presidency in 1968, Short probably would have had his pick of several top appointments, though perhaps not the one he wanted—Attorney General.

"People don't think of me as a lawyer, but the Attorney General doesn't have to be a great trial lawyer—as Ramsey Clark showed," Short explained. "It's an administrative legal job, and the man who holds it should have a little flair for PR. I would have liked to try it, or maybe Secretary of the Navy would have been fun, but I wouldn't have taken any other appointment."

No matter what his ambitions or pretensions, Bob Short does pay his dues. "First thing is to work like hell," he has said, and this he has done. He grew up under modest circumstances as one of three children of a Minneapolis fireman. He did not participate in high school or college athletics but he worked his way through College of St. Thomas in St. Paul, where he was a national champion debater. During a six-year career in the Navy, he got to be a Commander on the staff of the Secretary of the Navy during World War II. Afterwards, back in Minnesota in 1950, he scraped up $20,000 to buy half-interest in a small Twin Cities-to-Chicago truckline which was the beginning of his trucking-real-estate empire.

Short's own comments about how much money he is worth are limited to admitting that he owes a lot of money. He modestly proclaimed, "I don't consider myself a millionaire, even though some people do. Sure I am, on paper, but everything I've got is tied up in my business." A conservative estimate of a Minneapolis banker places Short's worth at about $10 million. Short admitted to the *Washingtonian* magazine in 1969 that the figure "was not far off." Short admits that he has had plenty of luck in amassing his fortune. "Luck's a hell of a thing," he said. "If you've got it, you can make bad moves and still come out good."

Just after buying the Senators, Short said, "There are plenty of people who wonder why there are boobs like me who would buy this team, which right now looks like a license to lose money. The team now probably isn't worth what I paid for it, but nobody ever lost money selling a big-league baseball franchise." He went on to tell the *Washingtonian,* "Even if I mismanage the team, it still would be worth close to what I paid for it."

Short is fair-skinned, but has a tendency to add some color to his face when he's angry. It happens frequently. He has a quick temper, and often explodes at his employees. Short admits to being an admirer of former union boss Jimmy Hoffa, though he sometimes says that he has little use for the unions. A long-time friend was quoted as saying, "He's an S.O.B. to work for. He says what he thinks and wants things done and takes no excuses. But he pays very well and seems to inspire great loyalty among his employees. He grates on some people because of an arrogance bred by his intelligence and now by his wealth."

Despite being in his fifties, Short always likes to give the impression that he is "with it." He wears mod clothes and keeps his reddish-blond locks in a long style. One of his employees, Joan Flanagan, secretary to the club's publicity director, states flatly, as do most people, "That man dyes his hair."

He and his family (three sons, four daughters, six horses, two dogs, and a few chickens) are accustomed to his sixteen-hour days, about a quarter of that time spent on the telephone. "He had to give up golf about ten years ago because he didn't have the time," Short's lovely wife, Marian, said when he bought the Senators. "But he's home every week-end and spends as much time as he can with his family."

With his penchant for work, Short has made two other qualities work for him: enthusiasm and stubbornness. With that irresistible enthusiasm, he lured the great Ted Williams out of the Florida keys, back to baseball.

But lurking behind all the smiles is the Short stubborn-ness. Two days after Short announced his purchase of the Senators, a few people noticed a small, one-column headline in the *Washington Star*:

SHORT CHANGES TUNE ON MOVE

In an abrupt change of pace, which is frequently the mark of a quotable celebrity, owner Bob Short of the Senators yesterday said, "I'm not committed to keeping the team in Washington if D.C. Stadium is not made safe for the fans."

In a press conference the previous night, Short had said that he did not buy the club to move it, but that the Nation's Capital was the city of his choice in which to own and run a club.

A month later, Morris Siegel of the *Star* wrote that Short "warns . . . if they don't want the Senators here, if there is no radio, no box office support, Dallas or Milwaukee or some other places do."

Short already was making some people nervous about the destiny of the franchise. That was precisely his plan.

INSIDE
TED WILLIAMS

Ted Williams and I got on the elevator at the eleventh floor of the Executive House in Chicago. The two elderly ladies already there had their eyes focused demurely to the floor.

Suddenly Ted boomed, "Boy, wasn't that a shame about the alligator biting that kid's leg off!"

I didn't hesitate. "Wasn't that something! I just caught it on TV. They think he's going to live."

"Yeah, that sure is strange, an alligator in Lake Michigan."

"I didn't think those things could survive here."

"That's it. They can't. This one apparently escaped from the damn Sportsmen's Show. They oughta be more careful!"

"So *that's* what happened. All I heard was the kid never knew what hit him. He was walking through the park off

Michigan Avenue—you know, not too far from here—and the thing just leaped out of *nowhere* . . . and snapped his leg off !"

"The kid went right into shock, huh?"

"Yeah, a real shame. A real shame. Listen, where should we go to eat?"

"How about Fritzel's? It's just around the corner. I'm hungry as a bear."

Ping! The elevator door opened at the lobby. Ted and I stood aside to let the ladies pass but they just stood there frozen in silent horror. We walked straight out without looking back while Ted mumbled something about the need for a better alligator cage.

Ted Williams loves that little routine. For years he has acted it out with buddies in taxis, airports, hotel lobbies, and hundreds of elevators. All he needs is a good straight man.

I joined the practical jokes and other aspects of the Private World of Ted Williams in 1969, the magical year the Greatest Hitter Who Ever Lived returned to baseball after eight years of fishing and posing for Sears' catalogs. I don't know why, but we hit it off right away. I was a rookie major-league broadcaster that year and Ted was a rookie manager, both of us with the Washington Senators. We sat together for most of the seventy-five hours per season the baseball team logged in air trips in 1969 and 1970 when I was the Voice of the Senators and again in 1971. After team owner Bob Short fired me, Ted and I did a daily "Ted Williams Show." On the road, Ted and I had our favorite restaurants, places to get away for a few hours from the players and the rest of the baseball crowd. At home, we would get together on off days. Ted and his wife, Dolores, together with my wife, Lora, and me, might hit a favorite restaurant like Washington's LaFonda, where Ted invariably got the evening off to a soaring start with two rounds of double margaritas before we even tried to focus on a menu. More often, he and I would end up at the White Tower on Calvert Street near his $1,250-a-month apartment at the Shoreham West Hotel, because that was just about the only place still open for his compulsive early-morning meals. He would burst into the place bellowing, "When does the band start?" Then he'd supervise the grilling of the hamburgers: "Hey, that's enough on mine. Turn that one over. Mine's gotta be medium rare."

Williams has seemed so much larger than life to people around him that over the years he has accrued comic-strip name tags. Maybe it was because he was the biggest presence around. People were awed at his storybook feats as a player, but his actual six-foot-four size always seemed to stun them on a first encounter. His voice could blast out a dugout too, although not always intentionally. Ted had a bad case of bronchial pneumonia as a fighter pilot in Korea and it affected his hearing, so to hear himself talk he sometimes has to shout.

Williams has been called The Kid, The Splendid Splinter —although he began to look more like a chunk than a splinter after his playing days—and Thumpin' Theodore. The players on the Senators usually referred to him as Number Nine, his uniform number, or just plain TW. His good friend and fishing buddy, boxer Jack Sharkey, often calls him Chowderhead, and Johnny Pesky—who, by the way, was recommended to Short by Williams to replace him as manager—lovingly calls him Bush. And a Florida Keys pal, fishing guide Jack Brothers, pinned the name Grumpy on him.

But Teddy Ballgame is his favorite. He loves to use the term to refer to himself in the third person. He got the nickname in his playing days when a Boston photographer asked his young son which ballplayer he wanted to meet that afternoon at Fenway Park. "Why, Teddy," the kid said. "Teddy who?" the father asked. "Uh, Teddy . . . Ballgame!"

the boy replied. Ted loved the youngster's inspiration and he's used Teddy Ballgame ever since.

Ted Williams in the off season is the closest thing on earth to a guy in heaven. During the winter, a baseball person usually relaxes totally, the same way he immerses himself in the game the rest of the year. And Ted is almost as famous for his pursuit of leisure as he is for his intense concentration during the regular season.

By 1970, the free life was even sweeter for Teddy Ballgame. His return to the diamond had been triumphant. He had been named Manager of the Year. Washington had its best won-lost record in twenty-four years. It won ten more games than it lost, a twenty-one-game improvement over the previous year; it rose in the standings from its home in the cellar to within a single game of the first division. It was fourth in batting, fifth in pitching. Individual improvements were practically unanimous. Batting averages soared; pitchers discovered they could throw strikes. Dick Bosman had the lowest earned-run average in the league. Attendance almost doubled. Revenue almost tripled. The national pastime in the nation's capital seemed somehow consecrated by, well, Saint Theodore the Only.

Outside of baseball, Ted's favorite subject when we were talking together was his little son, John Henry. Ted told me he named him John Henry because he thought that sounded "like strength." I always felt that the birth of John Henry to Ted and Dolores in 1968 had filled a gap in Ted's life. John Henry certainly gave ballast to their marriage and I think the little guy came along at the right time for Ted. He made him feel more alive. I don't think it was a total coincidence that when John Henry was born Ted was deciding to get back into baseball at the age of fifty.

John Henry was Ted's first son, but this was his second chance as a father. Ted was always disappointed because he had not been able to spend enough time with his first child, Bobby Jo, a daughter born to Ted and his first wife, Doris Soule, in 1939. From the day she was born Ted seemed to be in the wrong place at the wrong time. Doris gave birth to Bobby Jo prematurely in Boston and caught the twenty-one-year-old Williams by surprise while he was fishing in Florida. Ted probably will never forgive the Boston newspapers for underscoring his own sense of guilt by crucifying him in print for not being there, even though when they asked Doris her feelings about his untimely absence all she said was: "Bobby Jo had Ted's eyes and Ted's mouth." But Bobby Jo came at a time when Ted Williams was not suited to settling down. It was fifteen years before he eventually divorced Doris, but Bobby Jo had a troubled youth, including an abortion, divorce, and suicide attempts. Along the way he *did* teach Bobby Jo how to fish, but she grew up and got away from Ted. I remember Ted telling me how much he wanted to send her to college—maybe he thought that would make up for a lot —but she refused to even finish high school. So you can see how much little John Henry means to Ted. And so does John Henry's little sister, Claudia Franc, born to the Williams family on the eve of the World Series of 1971. With the birth of Claudia Franc, Ted decided to limit the size of his family, and in 1971 he underwent a vasectomy.

Ted Williams has a reputation for being impossible for a woman to hold and about as acclimated to family life as a wounded bear. Fact is, Ted always spoke to me of his former wives with some pride and regret. He described Doris Soule as a "Dorothy Lamour type" whom he met in Minnesota while hunting. They fell in love while he was just starting his baseball career with the Minneapolis Millers. He remembers his second wife, Lee Howard, whom he met in Chicago, as a "good-looking blonde with a hell of a figure." But when he returned from his jet-crashing days in Korea, he and Lee realized there was not much substance to their marriage, so they divorced. When that happened, Ted has said, he gave up on the idea that he could be happy in matrimony.

One thing he doesn't recall favorably is the alimony. Ted thinks alimony laws are unjust. The subject infuriates him.

With that background, people naturally assumed Ted's marriage to Dolores would be short-lived. She was, and is, a full-fledged prima donna in her own right. They met on an airplane when Ted passed her a note that read, "Who are you?" She replied, by note, "Dolores Wettach, a model. Who are you?" And Ted wrote, "Mr. Williams, a fisherman."

Dolores is a tall, dark, striking brunette. Twenty-five years younger than Ted, she was just beginning to get major breaks in a movie and modeling career when they met. She was a cover girl on such magazines as *Vogue* and *Coronet* and she appeared in TV commercials for cars and cosmetics. In one commercial, Dolores has told me, she demonstrated the use of Vaseline in a facial that actually can be burned off the face. "After that," she said, "everyone called me hotlips."

She had just finished the lead in Carlo Ponti's *Women of Affairs*, and she was seriously considered for the role of Pussy Galore in the James Bond classic *Goldfinger*. Paramount Studios had screen tested her and were offering a seven-year contract calling for a minimum weekly salary of $1,000.

Ted could never stand to share the spotlight with a woman ("a goddamn *woman*, for crissakes!"). Throughout their rambunctious relationship, at home and in public, he has loudly and publicly reprimanded her for trying to steal the show, like a playful kitten, from one of the world's greatest living male chauvinists. ("How's the old lady?" "Oh, a pain in the ass. All women are pains in the ass. If you couldn't fuck 'em, they wouldn't be worth a thing in the world. Women have had too much to say for too long. This women's lib is a crock o' shit.")

But Dolores has her own way of pricking Theodore the Terrible for his chauvinistic public stance. She often threatens to write her own sequel to his book, *My Turn at Bat*—to be called *My Turn at Bat Was No Ball.*

In 1971, when Dolores began getting morning sickness during spring training at Pompano Beach and realized she was pregnant, she left abruptly for the serenity of their New England farmhouse. The gossip snipers immediately interpreted the gesture to be an omen for the breakup of the Ted Williams family. Dolores had lived with Ted in Washington during the 1969 and 1970 seasons, so when she didn't show up in 1971, most people concluded the worst. Incredibly, players and baseball writers started ugly rumors about it, almost as if they *wanted* Ted and Dolores to divorce each other. Even Short fanned the glowing rumors with occasional "off-the-record" snippets to writers, which doesn't surprise me because Short actually seemed jealous of people, including Dolores, who were closer than he to Ted. Ted refused to confront the rumors because he didn't feel it was anybody's business.

Knowing all this, I devoted part of "The Ted Williams Show" after the All-Star Game break to Ted's family. Ted talked about what a relaxing time he had had with Dolores and John Henry in New England. He made it sound idyllically American. "They're cutting the hay now," he said. "And I shot some woodchuck. It was a good break for me." And that squelched the story. When Dolores gave birth to Claudia Franc, I broke the news to Washington on my "Sports Round Table" talk show. I had known things were going well when I'd overhear Ted sweet-talking Dolores on the phone most nights before games. He'd say softly, somewhat uncharacteristically, "You take care of yourself and say some prayers for the ball club." Papa Ted was becoming somewhat domesticated, whether he would admit it or not.

One of the most raucous times Ted and I spent together was in the winter of 1970. Ted was in Washington for the Baseball Writers' Association dinner, where I introduced the guests of honor, people like Hank Aaron, Harmon Killebrew, Brooks Robinson, and the previous season's Manager of the Year, Teddy Ballgame himself. Ted postponed his return to the Florida Keys an extra day so we could spend some relaxed time together. The next day we met at 3:00 P.M. at Kennedy Stadium.

Even on that wintery afternoon, Ted Williams was as oblivious to weather as he was to fashion. He could have been en route to a baseball game, in Oakland in August. He wore his usual white polo shirt unbuttoned, baggy pants, heavy brogan-type shoes right out of the farmers' section of the Sears' shoe department, and an old gray, nondescript sports-coat that he wore so often he called it his "million-miler."

We decided to eat at Hall's Restaurant, an unpretentious seafood place in an unfashionable southeast section of Washington, perched atop a knoll on the bank of the Anacostia River very near where it meets the Potomac. (Sadly, it no longer exists, replaced by a high-rise project.) I called for reservations, while Ted was getting a trim on his already short hair.

Ted has never succumbed to the long hair fashions—maybe because Ted always has been a stickler for cleanliness. He has given clubhouse men hell for things like handing him a smelly undershirt or uniform blouse. He sniffs the armpits of every shirt before putting it on. And he never permits any of his clothes to be put in an automatic dryer because "they still smell when you use a dryer instead of hanging them up."

We arrived at Hall's at 5 P.M. all clean-cut, sweet-smelling, and right in the mood to eat, drink, and relax—not necessarily in that order. Hall's dining room was encased in glass, with a beautiful view of the green hills that go into Maryland.

You could watch the sailboats plying up and down the river or the pleasure boat en route to Mount Vernon. On the night we were there, we even caught a glimpse of the Presidential yacht, *The Sequoia*. The view is prettier, perhaps, from the Top of the Mark or in the Bois de Boulogne, but I think Hall's was the only unpretentious restaurant in Washington that offered such a wonderful sense of being *in* nature—as well as great seafood!

Ted and I got there so early that no one was in the restaurant except the help. This delighted Ted, who usually has to contend with self-conscious glances and knowing whispers every time he goes out.

"What the hell did you do, reserve the whole fucking restaurant for us?" he said, beaming.

"What else? We wanted some privacy, didn't we?"

As we walked into the main dining room, the only people in sight were a black waiter and a good-looking white gal, who was the cashier. Neither one saw us. She was seated in a chair leaning over a table with the waiter standing behind her, rubbing her back.

Ted leaned down to my ear and whispered, "Watch this." I gave him a quick, wary glance and, oh-oh, he was shining a big, impish grin.

Ted tiptoed up behind the waiter and tapped him on the shoulder, at the same time holding his finger to his mouth in a don't-let-on gesture. He pointed to himself and plied the air with his hands to let the waiter know he wanted to take over the massage. The waiter smiled, and in a maneuver that couldn't have been better timed if they had practiced it, the waiter stepped back and Ted started rubbing the cashier's back—all this without losing a stroke!

Ted was really enjoying this. He always has been an irrepressible flirt. I stood about fifteen yards away, and Ted kept turning toward me, smiling like a beacon.

Then he decided to see how far he could go. His large, rough hands—weathered by a lifetime of outdoor life, hardened by so many hours of swinging a bat as a youth they used to bleed—moved up the gal's neck and then down her back to her waist. She let out a low, gravelly hum of pleasure. Suddenly—I couldn't believe it—Ted slid his hands around the sides of her rib cage and, easily, as if he were gently testing a couple of ripe mangoes, he cupped her breasts.

By this time, several waiters and the kitchen crew had appeared to catch the show. They roared with laughter when the startled gal wheeled around, saw Ted, and dropped her jaw in one of the most surprised expressions I have ever seen. It was a rude awakening from a state of supreme relaxation. But she recovered some aplomb, apparently recognized *the* Ted Williams, and didn't get angry.

Ted was at ease and laughing—a man thoroughly happy with who he was and where he was. And, like most of us when we feel that good, he wanted to enjoy it. Ordinarily, Ted is not a boozer. But when Ted Williams boozes, he boozes big. So as soon as we selected a table, he decided to baptize the evening with those birdbaths that Hall's called double martinis.

"Don't worry about a thing, ole buddy," he told me. "I'll do the ordering. Let's just relax and have a helluva good time. Okay?"

That was fine with me. Ted likes to order, whether it's in the Marines, on the baseball field, or in a restaurant.

Ted's favorite drink, which he makes himself, he learned from the fishermen in Cuba. He calls it "Bull." "Best after-fishing drink in the world," he says. To make it, Ted takes a third part honey, one-third lime juice and one-third rum. He mixes it in a pitcher with plenty of beer.

While sipping double martinis, we talked about his recent trip to Africa for the TV show, "American Sportsmen." He was delighted that he had bagged a large sable antelope for the show, but he also reveled in recounting the shooting of a reedbuck, a warthog, and one of the prizes of the trip, a Cape buffalo.

"We couldn't get close enough to the buffalo herd so we got on our bellies," he said. "Our *bellies*, for crissake!" He laughed and affectionately patted his ample midsection, a former threat that he was learning to live with. "Geez, my ass was dragging. We crawled for nearly 150 yards like that. My elbows and knees were grinding into elephant tracks. I was lugging my .458 in my right hand and the gun made it even tougher. I was thinking maybe we had made a bad decision." They stopped a hundred yards away from the herd. The Cape buffalo made a bluff charge. Ted was still breathing hard when he put his first shot through the buffalo's shoulder, the second through its septum, the third through the brain under a pair of curlycued horns.

"I never thought I'd want to shoot an elephant," Ted said, "but now I think I'd like to go back for one of those big bastards."

By the time it occurred to us to start eating, we had consumed a half-dozen double martinis. Ted is a tremendous eater and during the season I saw him pack away huge meals just to ease nervous tension. We were hardly tense that night, though.

He started with a dozen cherrystone clams and a dozen oysters. I had a crabmeat cocktail.

"Now, look," he said. "Let *me* order the main course. Let's see, waiter, how much is the jumbo two-and-a-half-pound lobster?"

"That's $12.50, Mr. Williams."

"Can you stuff them with crabmeat?"

"Yessir. But that'll make them $15 apiece," the waiter said. "Is that all right?"

"Yeah, yeah, yeah. No problem, no problem. We're living it up!"

Meanwhile, Ted kept ordering martinis.

"The lousy communists are taking over Africa, that's the thing that griped my ass about the trip," he said. "And that's going to be worse for the natives than facing those lions and crocodiles."

"But you *did* enjoy yourself, didn't you?"

"Sure. Sure. It was great. Great. I'll tell you one thing that took me by surprise. We were in a store—I think it was a five and dime in Zambia—when this Episcopal missionary from Tanzania recognizes me and asks, right out of the blue, 'How did Frank Howard do this year? Is he still swinging at bad pitches?' Says he saw Howard on leave some years back and even *then*, to a goddamn *missionary*, Howard looks like he's swinging from the heels at everything."

"You found out about being named Manager of the Year over there?"

"Yeah. Bob Addie called me all the way from Washington. Jeez, I didn't know what to say. But I'll tell you something. It was just another example of writers who don't know what the hell they're doing. Weaver and Martin deserved it more. I'm happy for myself, but I feel bad for them. Hell, I'm a stranger in this managing business, and those guys won their divisions, and Weaver won the pennant in a breeze. I voted for Weaver."

"Yeah, well, you deserved it too, Ted. What a great year."

"That's true, but I'm worried about next year. We had a fairly established club last year and, because it was our first year together, we had a little extra zing on the bench. But it was an older club and it's hard to keep a thing like that going. And right now we don't have much young talent coming up through the Washington system either. Look, 1968 was an expansion year, right? Well, neither new club drafted a major player out of the Washington organization and that's got to tell you something."

"Hey, we're supposed to be relaxing. Don't get so worked up."

"Yeah, yeah, yeah, yeah. Hey, waiter, two more doubles . . . and, uh, c'mere," Ted said, motioning the waiter to approach the table with an exaggerated swoop of head and arm. "Ask the cashier if she'd like another massage." Ted gave the guy a playful punch in the shoulder. "Go ahead, ask her."

All told, we indulged ourselves for four hours. During this time, Ted kept up a steady flirtation with the cashier by means of the waiter. I think every proposal in the world must have been made to her, all in a light, joking manner, of course. The poor, beleaguered cashier decided we definitely were not gentlemen. By that time we were so happy that my mind was perceiving everything in grand archetypes. In my martini-clouded state, the cashier became the symbol of Womankind Herself. So, maybe a tinge of ginned-up guilt was the reason I came up with this "helluva 'n idea."

"Hey, have you called Dolores today?"

"No. And I was supposed to."

"Well, I have an idea Lora is going to have a little bit of the red ass by the time I get home tonight. So why don't you call and tell her what a great son-of-a-bitch *I* am. Then I'll call Dolores and tell her what a great son-of-a-bitch *you* are."

Such is the reasoning of two carefree buddies after ten double martinis and a lotta lobster.

"Great idea, buddy," Ted agreed. "Let's do it from my place."

I convinced Ted that I could drive and we got into my Oldsmobile. My fast driving was a joke between us, and that night it seemed even more absurd.

"Okay, we're going to take it easy and have a nice safe trip," Ted said.

"Well, fasten your seatbelt, then."

"Look, when I wanna take a plane, I'll use a seatbelt," he explained.

We zipped past the Capitol, shining brighter than usual, then hit Pennsylvania Avenue and zoomed by the White House. "That Nixon is one helluva great guy," muttered Ted.

When we got to Ted's suite in the Shoreham Hotel, he suggested we call from the bedroom because it was closer to the john, which provides a big clue to our condition at the time. And I got a firsthand look at the famous portrait of a scantily-clad Dolores Williams. A photo of the portrait appeared in the *Washington Post* when Ted was first named manager, and it caused furor not only in the nation's capital but also between the Williamses.

Ted called Lora first. While they were chatting about families and the propriety of two married men out on the town, I couldn't help anticipating our call to Dolores.

The thought of Ted carousing, whether or not it be innocent, always seemed to make her nervous. She told me once in a moment of unguarded forthrightness, after champagne and suckling pig at Short's estate in Edina, Minnesota, that she worried that Ted was playing around on the road. She said that Ted got letters from old flames and once some bold broad even sent him her Boston hotel bill. Fact is, Ted doesn't chase (while we were together anyway) but he *is* chased. After all, for three decades as a superstar—a regular American pop/folk hero—he nailed down everything that *moved,* and it must be hard to altogether halt that kind of momentum. Dolores told Lora that she was particularly upset once because, while unpacking Ted's suitcase after a road trip, she found a package of prophylactic condoms. She told Lora (and later also told me), "He must be sleeping with other women because he never uses them with me." When I heard the story I asked my wife, Lora, "How did Ted explain it?" "Well, Ted said they weren't his and besides, he wasn't going to worry about it." Good ole Teddy Ballgame. I told Dolores my theory was that some maid in a hotel probably found them in his room and put them in his suitcase by mistake. Or maybe they were supposed to be balloons for John Henry. Or maybe some damn writer planted them there. Anyway, it was no big thing.

As soon as Ted had finished chatting with Lora, he dialed his number in the Florida Keys, handed me the receiver, and quietly disappeared.

"Hi, Dolores. Ted and I are . . ."

Suddenly from the bathroom came the sound of a walrus that has just become aware of buckshot in its gut. "Bllluu-uaaah."

I didn't say a word to Dolores. I didn't have to. She could hear Ted all the way to Florida.

"Good God!" she shouted into the phone. "Don't let him choke to death!"

So I hollered toward the bathroom, where Ted was bent over the porcelain yawn of the toilet. "Are you okay?"

"Yeah . . . I'm o . . . uaah uaah . . ."

"He's okay," I told Dolores. Then she wondered if I was in any condition to tell.

We talked about ten minutes while Ted barfed everything but his toenails.

But what the heck, we'd enjoyed ourselves—had a good time, and really celebrated our friendship.

The next time we saw each other, in spring training in Pompano Beach, Ted and I laughed about that night. He told me it was the first time that had ever happened to him, so he had called a doctor. The doctor's diagnosis was too much gin on an empty stomach. Even I could have told him that.

Ted and I frequently would kill time together when we were on road trips with the ball club. He loves to walk, and when we weren't drinking and eating, we often would be visiting gun shops and art dealers. Maybe it seems like a strange combination, but Williams has a great appreciation for guns and art. He owns about twenty-five guns, and uses them frequently for hunting. And Ted thinks that a speck of rust on a gun is the worst crime imaginable. He can spend hours at a time cleaning and polishing his guns.

Williams is a great supporter of the National Rifle Association, and a severe critic of proposed stronger gun controls. He often spoke out in support of the NRA in Washington, and almost joined it officially in a public relations capacity. A Washington public relations man, Robert Gamble, was doing some publicity for the NRA and approached Williams about lending his name and support to its efforts. Ted was willing to do it, but outside activities of this nature had to be approved by Sears Roebuck, which had Ted under a million-dollar contract. In this case, Sears felt that Ted's support of the National Rifle Association would be too controversial, so they would not approve the plan.

Ted's love for fishing is legendary, and he claims to be the world's best fisherman. He can spend hours at a time tying flies and talking fishing. He has frequently put on casting exhibitions at sportsmen's shows and thoroughly enjoys it. He can pick up an extra $10,000 for appearing at one of these shows.

When people questioned Ted's temperament for managing a baseball team, he would often use a fishing analogy. He'd say, "Show me an impatient fisherman, and I'll show you no fisherman at all. And don't you ever forget that ole Teddy Ballgame is the best fucking fisherman anywhere."

He'd continue, "Look, I'm the guy who says that the hardest thing to do in sports is to hit a baseball. I know damn well that is true, so how can I be impatient of those who haven't yet learned to do it? No one knows better than me how much time it takes."

Ted would take me to his favorite hangouts on the road. One that he enjoyed most was Jim's Steak House in Cleveland, a nice place in the "flats" section of Cleveland. Ted was an old friend of the owners, Charlotte and Ray Rockey. They were gracious hosts, and broke out some great wines. These dinners often served to take the sting out of a loss to the Indians in cold and dreary Municipal Stadium.

Ted had few close buddies, but he seemed to have at least one or two in every town. He liked to get away from baseball and spend some time with old wartime buddies, old fishing and hunting friends, and on occasion, an old baseball teammate of many years ago.

Williams and I are both students of boxing and we loved to try to stump one another in trivia boxing games. Ted used to get a big kick out of seeing Alfie Wolf, his old navy boxing instructor who would come by Kennedy Stadium to visit. Ted and I always wagered on the big fights—nothing big, ten bucks or maybe a steak dinner. Ted knows a lot about boxing, but he had a knack for consistently picking losers in the big matches.

Ted is a good chef. He loves to barbecue, and cooks with more garlic and spices than any French chef I have ever seen. He loves to grill a good piece of meat, with whole cloves of garlic inserted deep into the meat. And he loves to make bulky salads, with vegetables in huge chunks. He and Dolores like French dishes, and Ted can prepare a fancy sauce or season escargot as skillfully as most professional cooks.

When Ted has spare time, he will always hunt and fish if he can. If not, he enjoys a round of golf. He could be a good golfer with practice. He overpowers the ball, and, as you might expect, is a long hitter. But his short game is erratic due to infrequent play. Ted strongly opposes baseball players playing golf during the baseball season, so some feel that he just doesn't like golf. But he has often said that he wants his son John Henry to be a pro golfer. Ted claims, somewhat sarcastically, that the pay is great, and the only way you can get hurt playing golf is by getting struck by lightning.

Ted seems to enjoy his reputation as one of the all-time most casual dressers. Even for a visit to the White House Ted shuns traditional neckwear for a rarely seen string tie. He owned a tuxedo early in his career, but decided he didn't need it and gave it away. Bob Short claims that he bought a tux for Williams in 1969 and had it delivered to his Shoreham West apartment with the hope that it would give Ted incentive to attend the Commissioner's All Star Game dinner, but Ted says that he never saw the tux and wouldn't have worn it if he had.

Teddy Ballgame has taken a keen interest in politics most of his life, despite the fact that he has little respect for most politicians.

He has said that he considers Herbert Hoover the greatest man of all time, despite the fact that Hoover was a one-term President who bore the cross of the great depression. Ted has said, "Not Lincoln, Washington, Alexander Graham Bell, Julius Caesar, Napoleon, Attila the Hun. Not Jefferson, Wilson, Churchill, not even FDR, but Herbert, by God, Hoover. Every cure of the depression was thought up by Hoover. Here is a man who is blamed for things that were not his fault, yet he never complained, and continued to help his country for the rest of his life. To me, that's a real man."

Along with Herbert Hoover, Ted ranks President Nixon, General Douglas MacArthur, Tom Yawkey, Cardinal Cushing, and Marine General Louis B. Robertshaw, his commander in Korea, as the six men he has respected most. A big picture of Nixon hung on his clubhouse office wall.

He is, in his own words, a "substantial contributor to the National Republican Party." He is an ultraconservative in the tradition of Barry Goldwater and John Wayne (whom he resembles more and more each year). In the same strain, Ted admired that other Hoover, J. Edgar, and is so concerned about attacks on the police establishment that he put on his station wagon a bumper sticker that reads: "If You Don't Like Policemen, The Next Time You Need Help Call A Hippie." He gets a big kick out of Vice President Spiro Agnew when he gives hell to the press. It was no surprise when Nixon sent word to Ted that he agreed with his fifteen-minute press ban after each game.

What *is* surprising, even ironic, is the fact that Ted's boss, Bob Short, the man who talked him back into baseball, is one of the country's big Democrats. But Ted, a pretty natural politician himself, shrugs that off, saying, "There's nothing wrong with Short . . . well, nothing that a change of parties wouldn't cure."

Still, it was a study in anomalies to see Ted charming (at that time) Senator and presidential candidate Eugene McCarthy. After a ball game in 1969, Short asked Ted and Dolores and Dr. Clifford Goodband and his wife, Mary Ellen, to dine with McCarthy. Ted asked me to go along. We went to the politicians' landmark, the old Occidental Restaurant, which has since closed down too, like Hall's.

McCarthy used to be a baseball player and we all spent a pleasant, though uneventful, evening. The next spring McCarthy showed up in Pompano Beach in a Senators uniform, prompting Ted to bellow, "Get that guy off the field. He'll get killed out here."

And Ted can still register his protests against liberal Democrats. During the 1972 season, he urged reporters to quote his feelings about George McGovern, Ed Muskie, and Hubert Humphrey. "As politicians, they make me puke," said Ted.

Though Ted himself has ballooned out of shape in recent

years, he still has great appreciation for the need of athletes to work hard physically and to remain in tip-top shape. Ted used to do fifty pushups a day, and then would do fifty more fingertip pushups.

I remember one night before a game in Minnesota, George Brunet and Jim French were having a little game, trying to lift a chair by the bottom of one leg, with one hand. After watching them struggle for a while, Ted said, "Get out of the fucking way." Then he dropped to his knees and lifted the chair high in the air with one hand. Ted seemed happy that at fifty-two years of age, he could outdo his young players.

Many times, Ted told me this young lot of ballplayers just lacks the determination and dedication to become the best. "Hell, most of them are a bunch of softies," he'd say. "None of them want to take any extra hitting, and few of them even do individual exercises. These young players don't even ask questions. Hell, it seems as if they don't want to learn."

I couldn't help but remember what the late Moe Berg, a brilliant Princeton man who spoke several languages, told me about Ted. During the 1971 World Series, Moe described Ted's arrival in the Red Sox camp in 1939. Berg was a Red Sox catcher at the time. Moe said, "They called him screwy, but he was not any screwier than a college sophomore or any kid of twenty. The kid could hit, and it was apparent at that early time. I could tell that he would never be any DiMaggio in the field, but I knew he'd be better than the average fielder. And the thing that impressed me most was his eagerness to learn. He asked more sensible questions than most kids. I remember him asking me, 'What will Ruffing throw to a lefthanded batter with the count two strikes and no balls?' I knew at that point that here was a kid who had interest, and wanted to learn."

Ted Williams expected the same type of interest and dedication from his twenty-year-old players. The enthusiasm has stayed with Williams, his young players lacked it, and that combination was to lead to some managerial problems for Number Nine.

4

TEDDY BALLGAME
IS WATCHING YOU

". . . all managers are losers; they are the most expendable pieces of furniture on earth."

—Ted Williams, *My Turn at Bat*

Ted Williams wrote this dire view before he himself yielded to the temptation to get back into the game and become the manager himself. After he accepted Short's offer he said, "Okay, okay. That's the truth about managers. And now I'm here to challenge it."

But in four years as Short's manager, Williams went from exaltation to depression—and the team from winner to loser, Washington to Texas, bubbling illusion to cold-cement reality.

Ted was named Manager of the Year his first season in 1969, followed by three slow years of failure, while the magic gradually wore away, until he finally found himself in 1972 with "the worst darn team in baseball."

He told Russ White as he was leaving Washington, "What I didn't realize about it is that there would be so many penny-ass things annoying me. I've had to overlook plenty, not let something that used to bother me bug me anymore. Let them keep on bugging you and you'd go bananas."

If he knew what he was in for, why did he come back?

Williams had already turned down offers to manage contenders like Detroit and Boston. Even his old benefactor, Red Sox owner Tom Yawkey, couldn't talk Ted into managing during his eight-year absence from the game. Not that anybody was really concerned. The notion of a flighty superstar like Williams in the capacity as manager was considered illogical. "Manage 25 men?" wrote one Boston newspaperman. "Heck, he can't even manage himself." Sure, he was the last man to hit over .400—the Kid, the Splendid Splinter, the Thumper, the Big Guy, Teddy Ballgame—but he was also the Great Expectorator, who could "spit to all fields" and Terrible Ted, whose "rude gestures" to Fenway Park fans were legendary, who had even conked an old lady on the head with a thrown bat during a temper tantrum. As a player, Williams was frank to admit that he lacked versatility, that he sometimes found his defensive innings in the outfield a bore. And if the fans got on him, well, he flashed them a rude gesture. The fans and press said TW was an impatient man, someone who wouldn't stick to the program they had in mind for him. Many people simply doubted that Ted had the personal qualities a manager needed to lead the team and work with people, especially with marginal players.

When he showed up at the Washington spring camp in Pompano Beach, he read aloud a letter from a friend who was convinced he was about to make a "terrible mistake." The letter reviewed the situation: "the Senators had the worst organization in the majors, the worst scouting system, the worst minor-league talent." The team didn't draw; the stadium was in a riot area; managing would put him in contact with sportswriters who would bring up "the old bull they always bring up." He would have to do public relations. He would be asked a million stupid questions which would give him an ulcer. He would have a strict schedule—no time off. No escape. He would have to wet-nurse 25 ballplayers, not all adults. Losses would be on *his* record, on *his* reputation as a champion. He would discover at age fifty that he could still hit better than any player on the team and would be tempted to pinch-hit. "The Washington players need years of coaching, not days," Williams quoted the letter. ". . . The Washington boys need to be reborn—not remade."

(The frustration experienced by Washington's football and baseball fans may have been best expressed in a prayer by Father Tom Kane, chaplain for the Touchdown Club, at a banquet. His invocation went, in part: "Dear God: In the past thirty years, we fans have developed a great deal of patience in the discouragement of defeat. This year, we fans would feel privileged and honored if You would teach us to be more humble in the glory of victory.")

In his first meeting with the press after accepting the job with Washington, Williams glared coldly at a reporter who quipped, "I know you well, Ted, and you might chuck this whole thing in ninety days." "You don't know me as well as you think," he replied without a smile.

Short had gone to a lot of trouble and had spent a lot of money to get Williams. Williams had played his last eight years with the Red Sox on deferred salary. His last year of active service with the Red Sox was 1960, so his last year of deferred payment was in 1968. Thus Short was contacting

Williams the first year it was legally possible for him to work for another major-league club.

If the timing was perfect, so was the salesmanship. Short hooked Williams first on his enthusiasm—a sort of hornswogglers' optimism that Williams himself has always possessed and admired in others. "I put it to Ted this way," Short confessed later, " ' You're going to inherit the worst team in baseball. If you don't do any better than last year's last place finish, people'll say it's a lousy team anyway. If you do better than last year, they'll say you're a hell of a manager.' " Short told Williams he had a responsibility toward the game, toward the country, toward Nixon "and the whole bunch of bull you throw into a business proposition." Williams still said no, but Short was persistent. He followed Williams to Atlanta, met with him from noon to midnight, and the next day when Williams had to be in South Carolina, Short flew him there in his personal plane and took advantage of the opportunity to sign him up. Ted said, "I've been sitting around doing very little for eight years except fishing."

Of course, Ted got more than a peppy slap on the back and a good line of talk from Short. He got a five-year contract at $65,000 a year (way under the $100,000 per year leaked to the press by Short) plus a $15,000-a-year apartment in Washington and an unlimited expense account. Ted got the title of vice-president of the ball club, an option to move into the front office whenever he felt like it, and a ten-year preferred stock option to buy 10% of the club at any time. (He has until February 1979 to exercise the option.)

There was another important factor that brought Ted into managing: Ted wanted to teach. He has always been a sort of evangelist about baseball in general and hitting in particular. As a player, he often enjoyed counseling young players in hitting, sometimes scaring them in the process. His eyes would narrow and his voice boom and suddenly he would be in a dead-serious trance locked in battle with some invisible adversary-pitcher. Bob Broeg in *The Sporting News* recalled one such batting seminar Williams put on for an eighteen-year-old rookie named Al Kaline:

"Now, both [Fred] Hutchinson and Kaline would recall later, the pleasantness faded as, gripping the bat, Williams began to discuss hitting with the kid. As intently as though facing a pitcher in a crucial spot, Ted curled his lips in a snarl.

" 'Don't,' he said, taking one hand off the bat and motioning to himself, 'don't let 'em jam you in here.'

"The hand came off the bat handle again to jab Kaline for emphasis. 'Don't, I say,' Williams snapped, 'don't let 'em pitch in on your fists. Get out in front of the ball, boy! Hear me, get out in front of the ball! You've got to have fast hands, quick wrists, Practice! Practice!' " Broeg wrote that Kaline's eyes bugged out like a frog caught in sudden lightshine.

He would start talking hitting with some player in a hotel lobby or an a street corner, using a rolled up newspaper or magazine for a bat, and before you knew it, a crowd of people had gathered to watch the demonstration.

Ted not only tried to teach his own players, but he was zealous in helping the players from any team. Perhaps even overzealous. In his first year he couldn't resist telling Cleveland's Ken Harrelson to put more hip into the ball, and Harrelson paid well enough attention to beat Williams' Senators with a home run the next time they met. The team suggested that their manager be fined for "aiding the opposition" after Ted spent part of a spring training afternoon helping Baltimore Oriole Dave Johnson in 1970. In the ensuing World Series that year Johnson broke out of a slump with three hits in the Fourth game and he credited Williams' previous advice for his success. "He told me to be more aggressive, look for a strike and attack the ball," Johnson said. "But because of all the things to think about in the Series, the pressure, the good pitching, the great desire to win, I guess I had temporarily forgotten about it."

Williams wrote a three-page response to a short winter note from California Angels player, young Jay Johnstone. "I was flabbergasted," said Johnstone. "I couldn't believe that a man of Ted Williams' stature would take time to write in such depth to a player he didn't even know." Williams once even kept the team bus waiting for a half hour past midnight while he gave minor-league player, Denver's Dick Baldwin, a fast consultation.

From the beginning, perhaps especially in the beginning, he was full of theories and rules and "ginegar"—a word Ted invented.

"I'm going to try," Williams said upon arriving in Pompano in 1969. "I may turn out to be a horseshit manager, but I'm going to *try*. I'm going to be the last man out on that field every day if that will help.

"I know my weaknesses. I don't know infield play, that's my special little bugaboo. I don't know how to run a game, at least I don't feel I do. I never even made a lineup card. It's something I don't know about—when to do certain things, when to make changes. Get too interested watching a pitcher or a batter and you're two moves behind before you know it. But I'll have somebody right beside me helping me with that part of the act. The thing I know about, the most important part of baseball, is that game between the batter and the pitcher. I know I'm going to be able to help those hitters. I am sure of that."

Immediately, Williams laid out the ground rules for his team. Joe McCarthy had been TW's favorite manager during his playing days. And now he posted for each player Joe McCarthy's "Ten Commandments of Baseball"—things like "Nobody ever became a ballplayer by walking after a ball" and "Do not alibi on bad hops, anybody can field the good ones." Ted said he hoped to instill McCarthy's "businesslike attitude" in the team. He also ordered a midnight curfew, no serious card playing, no players in the hotel bar, and a three-beer limit on plane flights. Automatic fines included $100 for a missed bedcheck and $1,000 for playing golf during the season. Williams was adamant about golf; he was convinced that a good round of golf definitely tired a player out, reduced his effectiveness the next day to maybe 75 percent. He recommended frequent naps instead. If players were paying attention, they realized that many of these rules were simply Williams' personal secrets of getting the most out of body and soul—personal disciplines that helped him continue in competition until he was forty-two years old.

Williams was most fanatic about sexual abstinence during the season. He enforced celibacy as best he could on the road. He claimed that women were an unnecessary distraction during the season and that the players should save up all that energy for baseball. He thought sex took too much out of the players, especially before a game. Pitchers especially should lay off sex for at least a couple of days before pitching. He also believed that when a player marries he has to go through a period of adjustment that affects his performance on the field, and that sometimes it might take more than a year for a player to get back in the groove.

Actually, Williams' idea about the relationship of sex and performance is not unusual. Boxers, for instance, are often "isolated" from wives and girlfriends for weeks before a fight. In football, long-time professional coach Paul Brown used to have what was called "The Wednesday Rule," which meant no sex for his players from Wednesday until Sunday, the day of the game.

Williams even talked about devising a way of checking on the players in Washington. To my knowledge he never could figure out how to. He wanted to, though.

Before Ted actually quit managing, he was criticized for everything from strategy to choice of coaches. The latter flap was ironic in view of Williams' personal confidence and even pride in his coaching staff. "One day I was reading the papers and I saw a piece about Vince Lombardi and how he was surrounding himself with former head coaches," Williams recalled to me once. "And I said to myself, 'Jeez, this guy is getting the best.' " So Williams too decided to bring together "the best staff in the majors."

Williams inherited Nellie Fox, an All-Star infielder for thirteen years who still holds several major-league glove records. He also inherited pitching coach Sid Hudson, who had been coaching for nearly a decade after winning 104 games as a major-leaguer. Wayne Terwilliger was due to manage Buffalo when Ted came onto the scene, but the guy was so aware of what was going on, so intent on the players, and so full of "ginegar," that Williams snatched Terwilliger for his own staff that first spring training. He became the Ted Williams fixture on third base. Williams then added a couple of old friends—then-sixty-one-year-old George Susce, a former Red Sox coach, and Joe Camacho, who had never played in the big leagues, but who had been a coach at the Williams boys' camp and was spending his winter as an elementary school principal when he got Ted's call. "I couldn't sleep for two nights I was so excited," he said. Camacho was Williams' designate as the man-beside-me.

Williams gave most of the credit for his first and only good year as a manager to the staff. "The smartest thing I did this year, without question, was selecting a good coaching staff," Williams said in the winter of 1969–1970. "I had doubts about how Sid Hudson was going to work out as a pitching coach, but I couldn't get anybody else at that point, so it didn't matter. But after a while I began to realize, gee, Hudson understands me, and I understand him, and we worked together good.

"And Susce—sixty-one years old, been around for years, terrific worker, always in better shape than anybody. And here's the funny thing about old George Susce. He gave me more good ideas, things I should have known but didn't, and he'd put them in a concrete way. I'd say, 'Hey, that's right, that's the way.'"

Toward the end of the Williams regime, of course, the staff became vulnerable to criticism, embroiled in the falling apart of team morale and discipline. Many outright dismissed Susce as senile, and the tension between Susce and Hudson rarely relaxed. Susce always claimed that Hudson was responsible for his getting fired when Jim Lemon became manager of the Senators in 1968. I was seated between the two on the team bus in downtown Boston when they engaged in a bitter argument which almost resulted in blows. The other Senators coaches didn't communicate well with Susce, and there were strong rumors that TW had changed his mind about some of his coaches by the time he decided to call it quits as a manager.

Some players and front-office people criticized the coaches for never differing with Williams, but the fact was TW held conferences with them in private when all kinds of differences of opinion were bandied about.

But while Ted was hiring his own men, he took the opportunity to improve the pension plans of some of his old pals like Del Wilber in 1970 and Al Zarilla in 1971. Williams wanted to use former Red Sox teammate Walter Masterson as a coach part of the 1972 season to improve his pension plan, but baseball started cracking down on clubs who used this practice simply to improve the pension plans of old players. So Masterson lost out.

In 1972, the division between the aging Susce and the rest of the coaches became greater. Susce was continually complaining to Williams that he was the only coach who did any work, that the others were not speaking to him. To further complicate matters, Williams and Camacho had cooled toward each other, and what had been a close, warm relationship for three seasons became strained and unpleasant. Ted's unfading loyalty to Susce, and Susce's devisive effect on the coaching staff were the main reasons for the surprising coolness between Williams and Camacho.

Williams absorbed more criticism for his platooning than anything else. Platooning became a focal point for the dissidence that rose up to suffocate him in the final three years. Ted did not feel that he had a choice in the matter—with thin talent a manager has to platoon. "Hell, it would be great to have a position so solid that you didn't have to worry about it all year," he would say. When he platooned in 1969, when he won, TW had no problems. His platooning was even applauded.He changed Del Unser with Hank Allen in center-field when both were having excellent years. In the rest of the outfield he interchanged Lee Maye, Ed Stroud, Frank Howard, Brant Alyea, Sam Bowens, Gary Holman, Dick Billings, and Dick Smith. He platooned Bernie Allen and Tim Cullen at second base, Paul Casanova and Jim French behind the plate, and Howard and Epstein at first base.

Ted claimed that his critics got the wrong idea about platooning from Casey Stengel, who supposedly popularized the tactic when juggling the New York Yankees to successive championships. Stengel platooned star material in the Yankee organization and theorists since have claimed that platooning will work only with top material. Ted said that this epoch of expansion ball teams has brought in the idea of platooning in order to get the best out of marginal talent.

Mike Epstein, who feuded with Williams and sulked when he was platooned, is a typical example of Williams' predicament. He tried playing Epstein against all opposition, but statistics, not theory, finally showed that Epstein had significant trouble against left-handers. Even Epstein admitted it, though he continued to brood. When the streak-hitting Epstein was going good, he would often claim to reporters that he was being misused and should be playing against all types of pitching. But Williams' statistics proved otherwise. Late in the 1970 season, Ted went to Burt Hawkins and said, "Give me an update on Epstein against left and right-handed pitching." Hawkins' figures supported Williams' beliefs. Epstein was batting .150 against lefthanders, with only 16 hits in 107 at-bats. Against righthanders, Mike had 77 hits in 268 at-bats, for a batting average of .287.

Besides platooning, Williams was most criticized for his handling of pitchers. He often insulted them by calling all pitchers "stupid." He would add, "They are dumb and non-athletes." Ted was insistent that his pitchers throw more breaking pitches, and wanted all to use his pet pitch, the slider. Burt Hawkins used to make the remark, "All the opposition has to do is just wait for the slider. They know that Ted insists on all of his pitchers using it."

Ted never thought much of the spitball and claims that few can be effective with it. He made a close study of opposing pitchers who were using the spitball or doctoring the ball with foreign substances. During the 1972 season, I asked Ted about the many charges that Gaylord Perry of the Indians doctored the ball. Ted replied, "He sure as hell does, and I can tell you what he uses. He uses vaginal jelly, and that's the slipperiest damn stuff in the world."

Ted often was charged with overuse of his bullpen, and with pulling his pitchers too quickly. Ted's critics said that he ruined the arm of Dennis Higgins by pitching him too frequently in 1969 and that he endangered the career of Darold Knowles by working him too often in 1970.

Williams had the theory that with the emphasis on relief pitching these days, all he needed from a starting pitcher was five or six strong innings. This was frustrating for the starters, but Ted insisted that there were few nine-inning pitchers on the Senators-Rangers staff. Especially during the 1972 season, Dick Bosman was bitter at not being left in games longer, but he could not win the argument with Ted.

In 1972, Williams' club set a major-league record for fewest games completed by a pitcher, only 11. He used 16 different pitchers during the season and went to the bullpen 324 times, also believed to be a new major-league record.

Ted was also criticized for not using the sacrifice bunt. It was his theory that it has become increasingly hard to execute the sacrifice successfully, and there were few good bunters on the Senators besides Unser. Even Nellie Fox, perhaps the best bunter of all time, who taught this art to the Senators, could not make much headway.

Williams was frequently criticized for playing percentage baseball to the hilt. He felt it was the only kind to play today, just as it was thirty years ago.

Ted had been involved in perhaps the weirdest case of percentage baseball. Jimmy Dykes tells the story about Connie Mack managing a game against the Red Sox. The old Philadelphia A's had a two-run lead in the ninth inning, with two out and the bases loaded. Williams was at the plate, and Dykes says that Mack never hesitated. He ordered Ted Williams walked to force in a run, cutting the lead to one run. The next batter popped up, and the game was over.

Ted's strategy was never that bold, but he was involved in some real percentage battles with managers like Alvin Dark and Dave Bristol. Perhaps it was Dark who was the wildest in his battles with Williams. Dark once moved left-handed pitcher Sam McDowell to second base to bring in a right-hander to face a right-handed batter. He did this so that McDowell could return to the mound after the relief pitcher faced one man. Dark got quite a scare. With his left-handed pitcher playing second base, a grounder was hit to third, and

Graig Nettles' only play was to second base on a force play. He fired the ball true to the bag, and there was McDowell, awkwardly making the catch to retire the fast-approaching runner. After the game, Williams said that Dark had been lucky—and added that McDowell had "looked like an old whore making the catch."

Ted was always a great competitor, and some people felt that he would go to any length to win a game. Ted and the Senators were accused of attempting to steal signs during a game against the Kansas City Royals at Kennedy Stadium in the 1969 season. The Senators were using films of the games to study various techniques and patterns of play. A cameraman was located in the mezzanine section of center field, and Royals manager Charley Metro objected to this, claiming that the cameraman might be able to read the catcher's signals and in some way might relay the signs to the Senators batters. Metro made a protest to American League President Joe Cronin, and the league ruled that the Senators could no longer have a camerman in the centerfield mezzanine section. The ruling made Ted so mad that he discontinued use of the film.

Such practices have been known to happen in the major leagues. Cleveland groundskeeper Harold Bossard claims that Al Dark once asked him to sit in the centerfield bleachers, steal signs with a set of field glasses, and relay the signs to Indians batters. Bossard refused. And Dark became angry at Bossard when he also refused to "bug" the visiting clubhouse. I was never able to determine if Dark succeeded at that, but he did get a man to steal the signs—batting practice pitcher Frank Keaney. An ex-Indians player, Chuck Hinton, confirms that Keaney would sit in an aisle seat, and steal the signs by using a pair of high-power field glasses. Keaney always wore white baseball stockings, and if the catcher was asking for a breaking pitch, he'd move his leg into the aisle so that the batter could see the white stocking. If the catcher were calling for a fast ball, Keaney would not stick his leg into the aisle. There were rarely people in the centerfield bleachers at Cleveland, and no one ever caught on to the Indians' spy routine. Hinton claims that Keaney was an expert at picking up the signs, and that his stolen information was very helpful to Indians batters, especially Hawk Harrelson, who wound up with 30 home runs after being traded from the Red Sox to the Indians in 1970.

Williams believed in keeping good relations with the umpires, just as he had as a player. Ted was never kicked out of a game. Ted regularly used to pump the umpires for useful information—their opinions on various pitchers (even his own) and the current effectiveness of their pitches. Probably the Commissioner would have put a stop to that, had he known about it.

So Ted Williams embarked upon a career as a manager and his first year brought immediate, perhaps too immediate success. The Senators went from 31 games below .500 in 1968 to 10 games above in TW's first year. It was the team's best percentage in 24 years, the first winning record in 17 seasons. They ended up just a game out of third place, winning 8 of their last 9 games. Batting averages ballooned. The team raised its collective average 30 points over the previous year. Most dramatic were Eddie Brinkman, who went from .187 to .266; Del Unser, from .230 to .286; Hank Allen, from .218 to .279. Frank Howard hit .296 with 48 home runs, and Mike Epstein .278 with 30 home runs—the best ever for both. Attendance doubled and revenue tripled. And to top it off, Williams was named Manager of the Year in the American League.

But Williams also felt an impending letdown. "Who's going to have as good a year as '69?" Ted asked me during the winter. "We have no kids coming up, nobody young who's improving." And he was right. The team slipped into last place in 1970, next-to-last in 1971, and last in 1972 until Ted finally quit.

Ted has since regretted that he didn't step into a front-office job while he was riding high after the 1969 season. It would have been a great move, reminiscent of his career-ending homer off Baltimore's Jack Fisher in 1960.

It is hard to say exactly when Ted began to lose communication with some players on the club. Certainly, it started sometime in the second season when the shine of Ted Williams the Legend began to wear off and the team was losing almost compulsively. Ted was never close to any of the players. In fact, Ted made it a point *not* to socialize or become "buddy-buddy" with the players, the old military concept of leadership maintaining its distance—another idea taken directly from the philosophy of Williams' idol, Gen. Douglas MacArthur. Unrest grew on the Senators faster than Ted could trade the dissidents his last three years, and he had rows with Epstein in 1969, Coleman in 1970, McLain in 1971, and Jeff Burroughs in 1972. TW was rapped hard by a number of players when they left the club.Bernie Allen threatened to quit baseball rather than play another year with Williams after the 1971 season, so he got traded to the New York Yankees.

Tom McCraw added some thoughtful, rather than wrathful, comments about Williams when he was traded to Cleveland in 1971. Prefacing remarks with "personally I like Ted," McCraw reasoned: "When Ted Williams played ball, he was the greatest hitter in the world. That's all he worked on. That's why he was a great hitter. He'll tell you the same thing. The only problem is that when you become manager of a major-league club, you don't have a ball club of Ted Williamses.

"The Rangers have good young players in the organiza-

tion, some of the finest in the league. They just need somebody to develop them. . . . I've never been in their minor-
league organization but the players up there with Williams
now aren't getting the training they need to develop. The
guys gotta have somebody to teach them."

McCraw questioned Williams' ability to handle modern
players and develop rookies. He pointed out that Williams
did not develop a single rookie hitter in his four years as
manager, and Williams himself often admitted he enjoyed
working more with veterans. Indeed his successes as a batting instructor included boosting such veterans as Eddie
Brinkman and Mike Epstein and cutting down the strikeouts
while increasing the walks of the behemoth, Frank Howard.
McCraw too, a thirty-one-year-old veteran, benefitted from
Williams' instruction, he claims.

"Another thing," added McCraw. "Ted tells pitchers to
go out and throw 50 percent curves in their next game and
then says, 'If there *is* a next time.' That's . . . Well, maybe he
thinks he's egging them on. But he's tearing up their confidence. Ballplayers aren't like that anymore."

Tim Cullen and Jim French also knocked Ted for not
devoting enough time in spring training to fundamentals.
After being cut by the Rangers and picked up by Oakland,
Cullen said, "In Washington, all the emphasis was on hitting,
although Ted never said much to me. We never played fun-
damental baseball—throwing to the right base, hitting the
cutoff man and all. My Oakland manager, Dick Williams, is
big on that."

Joe Coleman was a product of Ted Williams' Massachusetts baseball camp. Williams' high hopes for him turned into
frustration when Joe would not throw a slider as Ted insisted.
Ted always had trouble with a slider as a player and therefore
he always urged his pitchers to adopt it and called it baseball's most important pitch. Short traded Coleman that win-

ter to Detroit, where he promptly won 20 ball games the next season.

Sometimes, with distance and time, though, even the most surly have mellowed. Like Mike Epstein, who in 1972, after two seasons away from Williams, admitted, "They keep telling me that if anybody should have ripped Williams, it should have been me. But that's wrong. Sure, Ted and I didn't see eye to eye in some respects but that doesn't make him a bad person. He was like a father to me. . . ."

And it is not unusual that the relief pitchers should appreciate Williams. Horacio Piña and Joe Grzenda have both mentioned publicly that Williams' handling extracted better performances from them.

Ted's reaction to the bickering and complaints of some players was to get tougher and more distant, and fine players more often. But during his second year, Ted began to find he couldn't ignite them with his enthusiasm as he did that first year, nor scare them with fines or yelling. At the end of 1970, after 14 straight losses, Williams gave the team a hot farewell speech, intimating that more than half the team should either search their souls or look for another profession before the ensuing season. Unfortunately, the speech only soured some players against Williams. Marginal talent became malcontent and Williams never regained total cohesion.

After his third year, New York sportswriter Red Smith asked Ted to evaluate himself as a manager.

Williams said of Williams, "If I had to appraise him, I would say he gets as much out of the players as any manager . . . [I try to] instill a belief in [my] fairness. Let them know they're all going to be treated alike, and yet not alike because the manager realizes different personalities respond to different approaches . . . But most important is not their liking you but their respecting you as a manager. Recognizing your position, knowing that you're going to do something for the good of the team, not for any individual, and if you treat this one a little different than that one it's for everybody's good . . . I think anybody would agree we play sound percentage baseball. But the strategy of the game is pretty well set . . . I feel I'm a little bit the enthusiastic type of manager. I might put a little extra zing into the guys. But then, there are managers who've been successful who don't do that. Gil Hodges didn't. Danny Murtaugh didn't in Pittsburgh. Even Walter Alston doesn't."

Shirley Povich responded to Williams' declaration with fury. "After one remarkable season that gained him Manager of the Year honors, Williams was a three-ply flop as game strategist, batting coach and inexpert player-relations expert. The more experience Williams gained as a manager, the worse his teams became. The Senators won 86 games his first season, 70 his second, and 63 in his third. Williams was progressing from Manager of the Year to manager of the degeneration. . . ."

Finally on the last day of September, 1972, Ted Williams quietly announced that he was quitting as a manager. "I'm sure I'm making the right decision for myself and for the club," he said. "It has been quite a little time that this has been settled in my mind. I'm quitting for personal reasons and I don't think I have to go any further than that."

Bob Short made a joke out of it. "Some of the players would have hung themselves if I had announced a new five-year contract for Williams," he said, but nobody snickered.

Williams had become so distant that he didn't even tell the team himself. He just tacked up a notice about his decision.

5

RADIO MOSCOW HAS
MORE FREEDOM

After being hired as the radio-TV Voice of the Senators, I enjoyed a precious few days on Cloud Nine before finding out from his long-time public relations chief, Oscar Molomot, that my boss was an egomaniac who expected me to "learn to lie" on the air. In fact, the contrast between Bob Short's cavalier attitude toward honesty in broadcasting and the actual fairness and accuracy of government media operations struck me as shocking and ironic. Pentagon broadcast executives have often been accused of managing news and censorship, but in eleven years with Armed Forces Radio and TV, I never encountered any of the pressure and distortion that Bob Short wanted to impose on the Senators broadcasting team. Short and his little buddy Molomot (noted for his panty hose promotions at the ball park) actually thought their sportscasters should be propagandists who made up things like weather forecasts. They felt that favorable weather forecasts induced people to attend games, regardless of how the weather turned out. Yes, this *sounds* like Big Brother, but actually it was more like P.T. Barnum without any finesse.

My first lesson about the real Bob Short and the rat race I had just joined came soon after I had flown to Pompano Beach for Washington's spring training. Before I knew what was happening, I was sucked into the vortex of petty speculation about the signing of Washington's 285-pound clean-up hitter Frank Howard. Howard, who had led the majors in home runs the previous season, was holding out for $100,000 and the three highly competitive Washington newspapers— *Post, Star,* and *Daily News*—were jealously seeking clues about the Howard situation. The more prestigious *Post* and *Star* were all the more eager for a scoop on Howard since the feisty tabloid *Daily News* had already embarrassed them by being the first to publish the news of Ted Williams' signing. Since Bob Short was so publicity-oriented, he was maniacally sensitive to such news breaks. And *Daily News* reporter Russ White was infuriating Short by chatting with Howard daily at his home in Green Bay, Wisconsin.

When Short finally agreed to Howard's terms, he arranged for a Saturday-morning conference to announce the signing and loose the press upon the hulking slugger. That way, the *Daily News* would be cut out of the initial impact of the announcement since it did not publish a Sunday edition.

The day before the press conference I was tipped off by Burt Hawkins, the Senators traveling secretary, to line up a TV cameraman. My broadcast partner, Ron Menchine, overheard me call a Miami TV station to arrange for a cameraman, and asked me if the arrangements were for Howard. I told him yes, but cautioned him not to leak the news, especially to his pal Russ White of the *Daily News.* Menchine and White, coincidentally, dined together that night, but Menchine kept quiet about the signing. When they got back to the Surf Rider Hotel, Senators headquarters, White saw Short in the lobby and decided to bluff him.

"Well, you sign the big guy tomorrow, right?" White asked.

Short wouldn't even respond. He just stalked off.

Short really plays these games of pseudo-intrigue and in the middle of the night he began an inquisition. Early the next morning Hawkins called to say that he had confessed to Bob Short that I was the only one he had told about the signing, so whom had *I* blabbed to?

"Burt, I didn't even tell the cameraman what this was all about," I said. Then I added, still drowsy from sleep, "But Menchine heard me make the arrangements and he figured it out, but Ron promised . . ."

I didn't have to say any more.

Short accosted me in the lobby that morning. "Look, that damn friend of yours whom you talked me into hiring has blown this story to Russ White who works for the smallest damn paper in town! The *Post* and the *Star* are going to raise hell with me if that tabloid rag beats them on Howard's signing . . ."

Pure paranoia. Not only did White not write such a story, he didn't even know about the scheduled press conference and only walked in on it accidentally when it was already half over.

But Short was not satisfied. He was so paranoid he was blind to the facts. "If I can prove that Menchine told White," he shouted, "he won't work that game today!"

Short was referring to our Very First Game, our debut as a broadcast team, the first exhibition game to be aired that spring. I was sick. Our launching was about to be ruined by a silly misunderstanding and, even worse, I was discovering that my boss could be a madman.

Later that morning I spotted Ted in the batting cage and asked him if we could record a short interview to be used before our inaugural broadcast that afternoon. Both Gallery and Short had emphasized that my prime function in spring training would be to get to Ted Williams and establish rapport. That, at least, seemed to be working out. Ted and I were laying the foundations for a friendship that transcended our professional relationship and helped me put up with a lot of the Bob Short bullshit. Soon Ted was confiding in me. Maybe he needed someone like me to talk to, to loosen up with and release some of the frustrations and anxieties of getting back into baseball.

It was certainly bothering Short. He was still as flighty as a debutante high on benzedrine. Short spotted me pointing the microphone at Ted, but he couldn't get to me until the interview was finished.

"What the hell are you doing with that damn mike in his face?" Short ranted.

I couldn't believe it. I mumbled some obvious answer but Bob wasn't even listening.

"What were you talking about—Howard?" he raved.

"I didn't ask a thing about Howard," I said. "And Ted only mentioned he would be happy when he arrived in camp. He didn't say when that would be."

"Lookit, Whitfield! Keep that damn mike away from him! He doesn't like to be interviewed! You're going to blow my deal with him! It only cost me $400,000 to sign the man, so just leave him alone!"

Minutes before that opening broadcast, Menchine made a quick but uneasy peace with Short and we went on, dispirited but intact. And in the long run Menchine managed to survive me as a Senators broadcaster, sharing the booth with my replacement, Tony Roberts, in 1971.

He even managed to wreak a little vengeance on Short the last week of the final season, after Short already had perpetrated the move of the club from the nation's capital to a freeway between Forth Worth and Dallas. Menchine bad-mouthed Bob Short so ruthlessly that final week that an apoplectic Short was on the phone constantly with WWDC station manager Bill Sanders, threatening, cajoling, pleading with him to muzzle Menchine.

Short didn't dare show his face in Washington for that final game. Angry Senators fans would have lynched him. So he was listening to the broadcast on his WATS line back in Minnesota. When Menchine took verbal jabs at Short, it drove the club owner up the wall. It had been happening on all of the games since Short had asked for and received permission to leave Washington. And even though he had washed his hands of Washington, he still couldn't stand to hear anyone criticize him. He was continually calling the station management to complain. It was amusing that he refused to talk with the station's program director, Gloria Gibson, just because she was a woman. He would say, "No, I don't want to speak with her. Who's the top *man* there?" If Bill Sanders, the AVCO vice-president and station manager, wasn't there, the other men at the station all came under Ms. Gibson.

It was ironic that Menchine lasted three seasons with the Senators, while I lasted just two. Tom Gallery and Short had more or less let me select the number-two man for the broadcast crew, subject to their approval and subject to the approval of WWDC. The station would actually carry the second broadcaster on its payroll.

Menchine and I had two enjoyable seasons working together. It could have been much better had Short and Molomot stayed out of the broadcast picture. They bothered Menchine less than me. Ron didn't work directly for them, and Ron is a carefree shaggy-dog-type bachelor who is quick to laugh, and is not one to be concerned with a lot of responsibility. Menchine possesses one of the worlds biggest appetites, and a facility to make others laugh. He certainly made *me* laugh once during a broadcast of a Senators-Orioles game from Baltimore. I'll never forget his, uh, Freudian description of a sharply hit ground ball. He called it, just as plain and clear as Orson Welles' diction: "a harply shit groundball." It broke me up so much that I had to leave the booth.

Even though our broadcast debut in the spring of 1969 was marred by Short's disappointing behavior, Ted Williams' Senators broke their eight-game exhibition losing streak with 19 base hits and a 18-5 victory over the Atlanta Braves. The hero of that first win was Cap Peterson, who, with the aid of the Pompano wind, hit three home runs, walked twice, and was safe on a fielder's choice. The memory of that performance was still pretty vivid in everyone's mind a week later when Ted told me he had to cut an outfielder and he couldn't choose between Peterson and Brant Alyea. And while Peterson was having a flashy spring, Alyea was lousy.

Ted asked my advice. I recount this anecdote because it always has occurred to me that this might have been a turning point in our relationship.

I pointed out that Alyea had hit over 50 home runs the previous year in Triple A, American League, and winter competition combined.

"Goddamn, I didn't know that!" responded Ted.

And I pointed out also that Peterson had just one kidney.

"Well, sonuvabitch!" Ted exclaimed. "I didn't know that either. Why'n the hell don't these goddamn people tell me anything around here? Buddy, you and I had better stick close together. You're trying to learn something from *me*, and I'm learning things from *you*."

Ted let Peterson go to Cleveland, where he disappeared after the 1969 season. The streak-hitting Alyea never made it big, but he did remain in the majors considerably longer than did Peterson.

Even though Ted had a strong ego to go with his vast ability, he kept an open mind. Just once do I remember his ego closing up his mind. Soon after the season opened I noticed I was having trouble focusing on some fly balls to the outfield and an eye checkup confirmed a slight near-sightedness. When I started using glasses, Ted tried them on and admitted he could see better with the glasses, especially things at a distance. "Yeah?" remarked Jim French, a borderline player who had been scrutinizing Ted-with-glasses. "And they make you look ten years older." Ted never put them on again.

Bob threatened to fire me in 1969 after I honored a strike by my union, American Federation of Television & Radio Artists (AFTRA), against WWDC. I had no choice, and Short knew that.

The major radio and TV stations in the Washington-Baltimore market are organized by AFTRA and it was mandatory that announcers doing the Senators and Orioles games be active members of that union, even though I was on the club payroll and not working directly for a radio or TV station. So, in 1969 when it seemed likely that negotiations might not avoid a strike, I began advising people like Gallery, Short, Joe Burke, and Stan Bregman. Everyone told me that it would be a serious problem—everyone, that is, except Short, who said, "Don't worry. You work for me, not the union." I thought to myself at the time that Short's attitude was a funny one for a man who was used to dealing with unions in the trucking and hotel businesses.

The union decided to start the strike so as to capitalize on the popularity of "The Whole New Ballgame," the slogan emblematic of the Bob Short-Ted Williams success that first year in Washington. The Senators were due to play the Yankees in New York. The Washington audience would be glued to the radio and the union figured that WWDC would be caught without backup broadcasters. So they called the strike for 8 P.M.—game time.

Evelyn Freyman, executive secretary for AFTRA, had left a message at the Roosevelt Hotel for me to call her immediately, except the message was placed in the wrong room slot. The union subsequently sent me a wire in care of the hotel but it arrived way after I already had left for Yankee Stadium. Just in case, though, I told our engineer, Earl Gordon, studio supervisor for WHN in New York, that we might have a strike problem. When he checked out the broadcast lines and coordinated with the engineer back at WWDC, he heard nothing about the strike since the engineers, who belong to another union, were not affected. But as soon as we went on the air at 7:55, the telephones in the broadcast area started ringing and we knew what it meant: strike! And we were caught in the middle. Menchine and I talked it over during the first commercial break and decided that it would be unprofessional to walk off now that the broadcast had begun. So I asked the engineer not to answer any phone calls until after the game. But Menchine, who did work directly for the station and had no recourse but to strike, panicked in the second inning and answered one of the telephones. It was Earl Robbin, WWDC's all-night disc jockey and shop steward, who told Menchine that the strike was called and that both of us should get off the air. It was the second inning when I grabbed a phone and dialed Short at his sprawling estate in Edina, Minnesota, where I knew he would be listening to the game on his WATS line. During my call our engineer killed our mikes, leaving only crowd noise.

Short was in a rage. "Get your ass back on the air or you have had it," he yelled over the phone. I said I'd try, although the engineer, under the circumstances, might not open up my microphone again.

Finally I told the engineer that I would take the responsibility of announcing the rest of the game alone. I was off the air for half an inning. But the calls kept coming until, later in the game, two union men showed up to personally order me off the air. "Well, gents, you'll have to take me off bodily, because my boss has threatened to fire me if I don't finish this game," I said during a commercial break. So they left me alone to finish the game.

Afterwards, I talked to Evelyn Freyman, the AFTRA executive who was both charming and fair. "Look," she said, "I can understand the spot you were in tonight, but please don't go on tomorrow or we'll be forced to fine you, suspend you, or as a last resort we might have to blacklist you. There is no way you will be able to continue your broadcasting career in any union market if you don't honor this strike."

"What kind of protection can you give me?"

"We'll go all the way with you," she said.

"Okay, put it in writing and I will not broadcast the game tomorrow."

AFTRA sent me a telegram promising full protection.

When I called Tom Gallery about the mess, he couldn't believe Short's stance. He agreed that I had no choice but to strike. As soon as I hung up the phone, club official Ed Doherty called to say that Short was considering firing me for going off the air in the second inning! Later, when Short realized he couldn't prevent the strike, he threatened to sue WWDC unless the station permitted me as a non-employee to work during the strike. It made no sense. WWDC was a union station under union contract and the union had the right to make me strike.

Meanwhile, WWDC had little trouble talking Rex Barney, the old Brooklyn Dodger pitcher, into scabbing the strike. Barney was already on the AFTRA unfair list, as the year before he had scabbed a strike in Baltimore involving Orioles games.

On Short's orders, I sat with Barney for the rest of the Yankee series, and I thought he did a pretty good job. He did seem nervous but maybe that was because of what he was reading in the cascade of angry telegrams from union sympathizers. Ironically, during the final game in the series, the United States landed the first man on the moon. The game was halted, the Yankee Stadium public address man gave everyone the news, and the National Anthem was played. And Barney got the thrill of describing one of the biggest moments in broadcast history. WWDC later cut records of that moment for promotions and Oscar Molomot gave them away as premiums at Senators' games the next season. It was great for Barney but disappointing for Menchine and me.

Short was concerned about the strike, because the union had threatened to picket Kennedy Stadium for home games. But there was a break for the All Star game, the Senators went on the road, and the strike was settled before the club returned home.

The first time I saw Short after his angry telephone blast at me during the game from New York was, of all places, in the White House. President Nixon gave a reception in honor of Baseball's Centennial. Short and I came face to face in the Blue Room as we waited to go through the President's receiving line. Bob is a Jekyll-and-Hyde personality. He can be the most gracious and charming person in the world, or he can be the most belligerent and obnoxious. Thankfully, he was on his good behavior that day, and he said, "Hi, Shelby. How are the strike negotiations coming?"

"Bob, I think they're pretty close to a settlement," I replied.

"Good," he said. "If they don't settle it in the next two days, don't make the road trip to the West Coast with the club. Rex Barney will do the games until the strike is settled."

I moved over to talk with Ted Williams, who surprised

some people by showing up at the White House. Ted had passed up the Commissioner's Centennial Dinner the previous night at the Shoreham Hotel. He had stayed in his Shoreham Hotel apartment, just a few hundred yards away from the banquet room, to visit and tie fishing flies with some old friends. Ted's wife Dolores went to the dinner to accept his award as a member of the all-time All Star team. Ted's critics said he passed up the dinner in a huff because Joe DiMaggio was being named the greatest living player, and he felt he should have received the honor. Ted denied this to me. Hell, he was never big on banquets anyway.

Short really became miffed at Williams the following year when Ted passed up the annual Washington Chapter of Baseball Writers dinner to attend a sportsmen's dinner in New York which was held to support efforts to save the Atlantic salmon.

Ted was in fine spirits that day in the White House. We chatted a little about the torrential rain that was just about to flood the Rose Garden, then we both agreed that the All Star game (in which Williams was to be one of the American League coaches), scheduled to be played under the lights that night, would be postponed until the following day. It was.

I told Ted that I was glad that he had at least worn a tie to the White House. It was a string tie which featured a piece of whalebone; a gift from Joe Camacho.

Ted was in a great mood. Being a Nixon enthusiast, he was delighted that the President was throwing this reception for baseball.

Luckily, the AFTRA strike was settled the next day, and things returned to normal I made the road trip to the West Coast with the Senators.

I was stunned a couple of days later in Seattle, when I was awakened from a sound sleep in the Olympia Hotel. A friend was calling to tell me that the *Washington Post* had reported that I would be replaced by Rex Barney as the Voice of the Senators next season. Nothing about the fact that Barney had scabbed the strike. I couldn't believe my goddamned ears. I called Chuck Lucas, an old friend at the *Post,* to determine the source of this tale. Lucas said that Bob Short himself had given the story to the *Post.*

I called Tom Gallery in Los Angeles and said, "Tom, this guy is an idiot. He knows damn well that I had to honor that strike. Now he plants a story in the newspaper saying that I am going to be replaced. What the hell goes?"

I wanted to call Short and find out. But Gallery said, "No. That's no good. Wait until you see him in person."

That was two days later when Short flew into Seattle. I came face to face with him in Williams' office at Sicks Stadium before a night game with the Pilots. I said, still furious, "What the hell is going on, Bob? The *Post* reports that I will be out next season; replaced by the guy who scabbed the strike."

I was beginning to know the man pretty well, so his reply didn't surprise me much. He said, "Don't worry. The *Washington Post* doesn't run this ball club. I do."

If his object was to shake me up, he sure as hell did it. By planting that story in the *Post,* he opened the door for a lot of people to speculate about my future for the next year and a half while I was still doing the games.

Short's contradictory and ridiculous behavior ceased to surprise or outrage me after my first extensive road trip with the team in 1969. After Ted Williams' Return-to-Fenway-Park in Boston (the Senators won that big game, 9–3), Short approached me on the plane to Cleveland with a Boston newspaper that contained an article about Johnny Pesky, a rookie announcer on the Red Sox crew that season. The main point of the article was that Pesky was going to be a "homer"

—an announcer who openly roots for the home team. "Give this to Warner Wolf with my compliments," he told me. I asked if he was serious and he said yes.

Wolf was my television partner for the Senators games, and he had a reputation for a brusque delivery and controversial opinions. I remember he had a shortlived afternoon talk show on WTOP-TV called "Dear Warner" during which he got into discussions about everything from sports to general news. Once the topic of armed robbery in Washington came up and Wolf, in top form, expounded, "I'll tell you how to stop those robberies. Shoot 'em, man. Shoot 'em. That'll stop 'em." Bob Short got the idea early in the season when Wolf could not resist the temptation to second-guess Ted Williams on a refusal to bunt, and so perhaps Short thought that the Pesky article would be a subtle hint.

Wolf apparently sat right down and wrote Short a good-sized letter agreeing with Bob "100 percent" about Pesky and his ilk and added, toward the end, "Frankly, if I ran a ball-club, there would be one man in the booth . . ." Wonder who he had in mind? Warner went on to second-guess my play-by-play in the letter to my boss, and added that he had patterned his play-by-play after Chuck Thompson, an Orioles broadcaster.

Anyway, Short was well aware of Wolf's general popularity in Washington and the letter seemed to intimidate him. After he got it, including the copy of the Pesky article, Short stormed up to me. "Why did you give that article to Wolf?" he yelled.

I couldn't believe my ears. "You mean the one you gave me on the plane?"

"Yes!"

"Well, you asked me to give it to him, remember?"

"No, I didn't!" said Short all blustery. He added, "Lookit, I don't want a feud with Warner Wolf. He can hurt me."

WTOP-TV had originally planned for Wolf to do the play-by-play, and had even made up sales brochures which promoted Warner as their play-by-play man. But Bob was insistent that his broadcaster do the play-by-play on television. He knew the audiences would be big, and he wanted control of the broadcaster who would have access to that big audience. Besides, Washington newspapermen for the most part were not fans of Wolf, and were bad-mouthing him to Short. Meanwhile, WTOP-TV said it would not approve me if Short refused to approve Wolf. After some haggling, the two sides agreed that I would do the play-by-play on TV and Wolf would do color commentary. It was a bad arrangement. Short had pushed me down their throats, and I was to learn that Warner had employers at WTOP who would stand behind him, something that I didn't have with the Senators.

The fact is that Short wanted to distort reality through the airwaves for his own ends—such as selling the product and, later, moving it to another market. This may be okay for a salesman (*caveat emptor* and all that) but Short did not *own* the airwaves and in my opinion he did not have the right to abuse them so. The radio and television airwaves he used belong to the public. I suggest that some independent ombudsman—perhaps even the government—would be wise in checking out these abuses, not just Bob Short's exploitation, but also those of any professional club.

It was early during the 1970 season that Short's little lieutenant, Molomot, put the whole issue in plain, direct words. Menchine and I had been complaining about the number of phony plugs about the Senators that we were forced to broadcast, especially Short's dictum that we make weather forecasts for upcoming games sound good even if the floodwaters were lapping the sides of RFK Stadium. "You and Menchine just have to learn to be subjective instead of objective," Molomot said. In other words, just preach the BS party line. (Pun intended.)

"Look," I told Molomot, "I've got to draw the line here. I've got a reputation to protect. You just can't expect me to go on and say the weather's going to be great when every forecaster in town, every newspaper, every radio station, and every TV station is calling for a monsoon!"

"No, you don't understand," Molomot said. "One of the first things you have to learn when you work for Short is *learn to lie. I* learned that a long time ago."

Oscar has been with Short since his high school days and Bob seemed to enjoy treating Molomot miserably and paying him the same way. The poor guy probably should never have gotten involved in baseball. The guy had only seen two major-league games in his life before joining the Senators front office.

Despite his lack of experience, Molomot managed to pull some quickies. He became famous in Washington for his pantyhose promotions *("fits any size")*. To me his most deceptive caper was lottery drawings for cars and vacation trips and such. These drawings were held after Senators games. Such lotteries were against the law in D.C. but Oscar found a loophole. He made the drawings legal by arranging them so that a person didn't have to attend a game to enter the drawing, just fill out a form at the stadium. He simply minimized that fact in all of his publicity of the drawings.

Short and Molomot did a lot of little things that added up to "managing the news" by controlling Short's announcers. He and Molomot brazenly emphasized that we should always mention Short's name on the air, and (when on television) flash the cameras on him when he attended a game. He told us that was to let his wife, Miriam, know he had arrived at the game safely. He wanted me to intimidate the Washington fans into coming out to the ballpark. "Tell those damn people in Washington that they had better get their asses out to the park or they won't have a club to watch." I'd balk. "Goddamn it," he'd continue. "I am telling you to say it, and if you don't, I'll get someone who will. I don't care what words you use or how you say it, but do it." He told us not to give National League scores, a sort of quixotic attempt, I suppose, to burn away the memories of former fealties among Washington's transitory, intra-American population.

Short would go into rages if Menchine or I mentioned the temperature or the humidity if either was especially uncomfortable (although it is an important factor in the reporting of the game) and he told us to broadcast that "fans are still filing into the stands" up until the fourth inning even if the trickle stopped at the National Anthem. He felt this encouraged late arrivals. He even objected to such inanities as mentioning the number of men left on base because, he said, that made the club look bad.

But the silliest bitch he had was about attendance. He ordered us not to give out attendance figures for other American League games if the attendance was small. In other words, Short didn't care for anything that let Senator fans know that other clubs had some poor attendance. Any crowd at Kennedy Stadium was never a good crowd. No crowd was ever big enough, and "don't compliment Washingtonians on their attendance unless the house is packed."

We drew Short's wrath early in 1969 because of comments about attendance at a Senators game. The Nats, for some reason, always drew poorly on Saturday afternoons. The first week of May, the Nats drew 12,728 fans for a Saturday afternoon game against a bad Cleveland club. During the eighth inning, Burt Hawkins announced on the media intercom that this was a record Saturday afternoon crowd since the expansion Senators started operation nine years earlier. We duly reported this fact on the air, and Short raised hell. I had a message to call him after the game.

"Look, Whitfield. Don't ever say that a crowd of 12,728 is a good crowd."

"Well, Bob," I said, "by comparative standards . . ."

"Look, goddammit, I said it was a bad crowd! Don't say a thing about the crowd tomorrow if there aren't 25,000!"

The next day 24,411 people came to the stadium and Ron and I kept quiet on the air. We knew that Short was probably dying to hear what kind of a crowd we had.

"We came within 689 of having a good crowd today, Shelby," Menchine chuckled afterwards.

It's a hard fact that clubs won't allow a negative sportscaster to report their games. Club announcers have much less freedom than writers. Red Barber is acclaimed by many as the greatest baseball broadcaster of all time. He was interesting, factual, stylish, and fortunate to have had a great deal of freedom on the air most of his career. But even he was fired. He hit it off great with baseball executives like Branch Rickey and Larry MacPhail, but did not see eye to eye with Walter O'Malley or Mike Burke.

Harry Caray and Bob Neal are a couple of veterans who have been known to second-guess managers and players from the booth. They often have been accused by players of not being fair in their reporting and slanting their reporting to the advantage of club management.

One of the nastiest feuds between player and announcer took place in the 1970 season when Indians announcer Bob Neal and Indians pitcher Sam McDowell had a beauty going. When McDowell failed to win his nineteenth game, Neal, on the air, called it a "national disgrace," and unfavorably compared Sam with Orioles pitcher Dave McNally. Russ Schneider of the *Cleveland Plain Dealer* reported McDowell's reply in *The Sporting News:* "I realize that this will give Neal some much needed publicity, but the other guys on the club feel the same as I do about him." Charged Sam, "Bob Neal is a disgrace to the broadcasting industry . . . there aren't ten percent of the fans in Cleveland who enjoy listening to him. Right now, we have a bush-league announcer, and point out that I emphasize the word now. I sure hope that Neal enjoys his job next year, wherever it is, because I think most of the people—not just the players—are fed up with him. There's such a thing as adding by subtraction in broadcasting, too."

Neal rebutted by saying, "Only an illiterate person uses the term 'bush.' "

It was a nasty situation, but Neal, who has a knack for longevity, was still doing the Indians broadcasts in 1972, long after McDowell was gone. Neal was dropped from the Indians games in 1973, after 22 years of broadcasting.

I couldn't keep from wondering about what would happen to me if I became involved in a feud with a Senators player. My relationship with the players was excellent for the most part. Brant Alyea and Bernie Allen were the only ones to ever complain to me about something that I said on the air. Every player wants to come off good on the air, and some wife, girlfriend, or fan is always ready to report to the player some remark which they feel was critical. Allen falsely accused me of faulting him on a play at second base. I had not done so, and he apologized after I played a tape recording of the action back to him. Alyea was a chronic complainer and was quick to bitch about anything.

Some of the players felt that because I was close to Ted Williams I was always protecting him on the air at their expense. Personally, I was never one who felt Ted Williams needed any protecting. He usually stood up for himself pretty well.

Short always seemed to think that I was a negative broadcaster. He didn't want us to mention losing streaks or any deficiencies in the Senators performance. And believe me, there were plenty of those. Weak hitting by the Senators should never be mentioned. It was always strong pitching by the opposition.

Maybe I did get critical of the Senators' playing some-times, but if I did, it's because there were many opportuni-ties, and I did it in the interest of objectivity and meant nothing malicious. Williams once told me, "You're too hard to please. You're too tough on the players, your wife, every-one." I couldn't believe my ears. Here was Ted Williams telling me this. Ted went on, "Hell, you would have been big in the Gestapo. You're worse than that Howard Cosell guy."

I just laughed and tempered Ted's criticism with the knowledge that he didn't feel writers and broadcasters should *ever* be critical of players and managers.

I point with pride to the Senators attendance figures in 1969 and 1970 when I aired every Senators game. The 918,000 who attended games at Kennedy Stadium in 1969 repre-sented the second-highest-paid attendance in Washington in seventy-one years of baseball, and the 825,000 for a last-place club in 1970 ranks as one of the best years. Don't forget that Short's ticket prices were the highest in the league.

Washington was a one-baseball-team town, and I saw nothing wrong with a little rooting for the home town. This didn't set too well with some critics and fans in a town as sophisticated as Washington. But this is a point that has been argued for decades.

As Short's broadcaster under a "personal services con-tract" to him, I was automatically regarded and scorned by writers as a *houseman*. Now that I'm free of Short it's a little easier to relate with newspaper reporters and vice versa. However, I also feel there is a built-in breach be-tween writers and announcers which may never be bridged. Leonard Koppett put it well in his *Thinking Man's Guide to Baseball.* He pointed out that the salaries of base-ball broadcasters are much higher than those of baseball writers—plenty of cause for resentment. Even more, though, writers demean the role of the announcer as a salesman. Writers will never accept that any more than they would let an editor order them out to sell advertising space for their newspapers.

There was nothing quite like the telecasts during my first season with the Senators. After the big hassle over who was going to announce the games, Short and the WTOP-TV executives did agree on one thing. And, brother, was it ever a bomb. Larry Israel, the president of the Post Newsweek Stations, had the idea that baseball broadcasting had to be "jazzed up" to be interesting. He wanted to have a special guest commentator on each Senators telecast. This was in addition to me as the play-by-play man and Warner as the color man. This third special guest commentator would not be a professional broadcaster, but would be a football player, an entertainer, or a politician. What it amounted to was Wolf's interviewing the celebrity guest during the ball game, and me trying to get something about the game in edgeways whenever I could, which was seldom. Then Baltimore Colts tight end John Mackey (now with the San Diego Chargers) was the first celebrity guest, and I learned that Warner would be talking with Mackey about the difference in a fly ball and a forward pass as someone was sliding into second base with a double. Sonny Jurgensen (Washington Redskins quarterback) was another football player who appeared on one of our games, and the redhead did a pretty good job of discussing baseball and putting Warner down. But the best guest was Flip Wilson, and that was the straw that broke the camel's back. As you can imagine, Flip had Geraldine in the booth with him, and the telecast was chaotic from start to finish. I had been complaining about the format to Short, and he in turn was complaining to Israel. Israel was for continuing the format. Naturally, this didn't make any points with WTOP. Finally, Tom Gallery came East and monitored one of the telecasts, the Flip Wilson game as a matter of fact. Gallery agreed with me, and the pressure was put on WTOP to restrict the guest broadcasters to baseball types. So people like Bob Feller, Billy Pierce, Moose Skowron, and Dizzy Trout came on later games, and it worked out much better.

As a result of the nonbaseball types on the early telecasts, I had been bombarded with protest letters and phone calls. WTOP received the same kind of response, but they were not about to admit that the idea was a bomb. The station executives got mad as hell when the telephone operators at WTOP-TV gave me the number of protest calls they received. It was in the hundreds for each of the first few telecasts.

After having been crammed down the throats of WTOP, and having bucked them on their bizarre format, I knew my stock was not exactly booming there. Furthermore, Short had tried to charge WTOP-TV a talent fee for my services during the 1969 season, which they refused to pay since they were not legally bound to do so under their existing contract with the Senators. Short did force WTOP to pay him a talent fee for the games I did in 1970. Incidentally, he charged WWDC a talent fee for all the games I did both years, so the stations were paying a major part of my salary, but had no control over me.

Anyone could have knocked me over with a feather when I learned that Short expected me to turn over to the ball club all fees and honorariums I received for speaking engagements. To make matters worse, Molomot announced to me he was arranging to book me for frequent appearances during the season. My impression was that I would making these promotional appearances during the off season. I didn't mind an occasional appearance during the season, but a steady diet of them was too much. No baseball broadcaster is expected to do that. But apparently my contract with Short was a little different from the normal contracts given most broadcasters. It not only permitted him to exploit me as a speaker, but the personal services agreement had other drawbacks. I was startled early in the 1969 season to learn from business manager Joe Burke that Short expected me in my office at the stadium during the morning and afternoon before a night game. If I arrived at, say 10:00 in the morning for a night game which started at 8:00 that evening, I would be putting in about a fourteen-hour-day. Now, that's not exactly a schedule that major-league broadcasters are expected to keep. Broadcasting baseball is a lot like *playing* baseball. You should do your homework, get your rest, and get emotionally set up for every game. But Short and Molomot had little appreciation of that. Both told me that they needed my expertise and services during the full work day, and that under my contract, Short could work me around the clock if he so desired. Actually, the contract said nothing about hours, just as a baseball player's contract says nothing about hours, but it did say that I would devote my full time to the best interests of the Washington Senators.

When I told Williams about the hours Short was expecting me to put in, he said, "That's ridiculous. Hell, get you a nap each afternoon. Come down to my clubhouse office and take a nap on my couch." So that I did from time to time, and some front-office characters were amazed that this young brazen announcer had the nerve to sleep on Ted Williams' couch.

Ted agreed with me that spending ten or twelve hours a day with a miserable little guy like Molomot was enough to drive someone up the wall. So Ted suggested to Short that I be permitted to work part of the time out of his executive office and help with some of his paperwork. Short said, "Hell no. I need him more on the other end of the building with Molomot. Oscar doesn't know a basketball from a baseball, and he needs someone to lead him out of the wilderness."

Molomot and his promotions were the subject of an arti-

General Manager George Selkirk, new club owner Bob Short, and field manager Jim Lemon all appear happy the day Short purchased the club. A month later, Short fired Selkirk and Lemon.

Commissioner Bowie Kuhn chats with John McCormack before a Congressional Game at Kennedy Stadium. At the time, McCormack was a Congressman from Massachusetts and Speaker of the House.

Frank Ryan, attorney for Short
(checkered coat), Ed Doherty
(white-haired man), Short, and
Short attorney, Stanley
Bregman (with hand over his
mouth). Ryan and Bregman
were on Nats Board of
Directors.

Shelby Whitfield, Ted
Williams, and Dolores Williams
during a quiet moment at
Kennedy Stadium. Williams
was studying a sheet of
statistics as his Senators took
batting practice.

Shelby and Ted Williams discuss baseball before a Senators game at
Kennedy Stadium.

The onetime Splendid Splinter shows he can still swing the bat despite the excess poundage. This was the last time Williams swung a bat, while managing the Rangers late in the 1972 season at a charity exhibition.

Shelby, Milwaukee Brewers general manager Frank Lane and Ted Williams talk baseball while watching a Senators batting-practice session.

Bud Wilkinson, Ted Williams, Bowie Kuhn, Richard Nixon, Bob Short, Ralph Houk, Joe Cronin. Opening day, Kennedy Stadium, 1969.

David Eisenhower (a Senators front office aide), Bob Short, and Peter Bavasi (recently promoted to general manager of the San Diego Padres) pose together at an annual baseball draft meeting.

In 1969 the fans boycotted the lower section outfield seats after Bob Short raised the ticket price from $1.50 to $3.00. The banner was a jibe at Cleveland's Hawk Harrelson.

ROY HOOPES

Dolores Williams, a former Miss Vermont, is Ted's third wife and the mother of two of his children, John Henry and Claudia Franc.

Ted Williams ponders a question the day after Bob Short gained the necessary approval to move the franchise to Texas.

**Players
Bob Short
traded
away**

Joe Coleman.

Eddie Brinkman.

Ken McMullen.

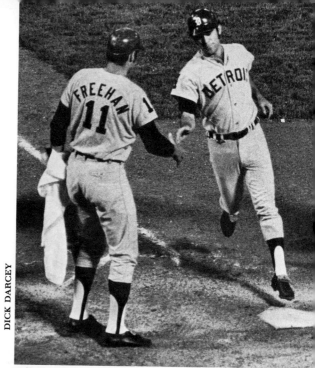

Bill Freehan and Aurelio Rodriguez.

Mike Epstein.

A couple of young Senators players, bonus baby Jeff Burroughs and Larry Biittner, sit with a stewardess in the Senators dugout. The gals took part in an exhibition game before the Senators regular game.

Ted Williams talks to his Senators before a game. From front to back: Paul Casanova, Casey Cox, and Brant Alyea.

PAUL CONKLIN

cle by *Newsweek* magazine during the 1970 season. Oscar admitted that he had a promotion budget calling for $150,000 in premium give-aways, not to mention salaries for a staff of five people. Many fans felt that that money should have been applied toward lowering the ticket prices for baseball fans. Short was quoted in that *Newsweek* article as saying that his surveys showed that the price of tickets had no relationship to attendance. But Short's ticket prices, his trading ability, and his overuse of promotions were the three biggest beefs with the fans.

In the *Newsweek* piece, an aide to Molomot, Ted Rodgers, pointed out that a recent crowd of 14,927 was a result of a Helmet Night promotion, not baseball and the Senators. Molomot pointed to the last day of the 1969 season when a crowd of 17,800 showed up. Oscar claimed that the good turnout, with the Senators having no chance to improve on their fourth-place finish, was a result of Hawaii Night. The fans got free pineapple and a chance to win a trip to Hawaii in a lottery drawing. Oscar didn't think the good turnout on the final day of the season was the fans' way of saying thanks to Ted Williams and the Senators for a good season and the best won-lost record in twenty-three years.

Short, as an absentee owner, didn't communicate very well with most of his employees at Kennedy Stadium, especially during the off season. I met with him shortly after the 1969 season to discuss a new contract. I made my pitch for a salary increase, pointing out the work that I had done and the fact that the 918,000 attendance during my first season had been good. His retort was that he stood to lose $600,000 on the season. He was later to use the same excuse for not giving front-office personnel Christmas bonuses.

But we did agree on a new one-year contract for the 1970 season at the same salary, and I became involved in an off-season promotion program which included making appearances in the District of Columbia, Virginia, Maryland, and Pennsylvania. I booked players for varied appearances and often accompanied them. It was a worthwhile project, but one that Short dropped when he got closer to the end of his stadium lease, which would permit him to move the club. He knew when he bought the Senators that his stadium lease didn't expire until the end of the 1971 season, and that it would be impossible to move the club until that time.

Having agreed on a new contract in October, I didn't worry about the broadcast arrangements for the 1970 season. So you can imagine my surprise when I opened the *Washington Post* one morning at breakfast and saw a story which indicated that Ray Scott would be the play-by-play telecaster for the Senators games next season, and that I would do just radio. That was the first I had heard of it. A typical Short business tactic. Read it in the newspapers first.

I called Tom Gallery and asked what the hell was going on. Tom said that he couldn't believe it, and to take the story with a grain of salt. I said, "Tom, I'm beginning to learn this guy better than you know him."

I was, and still am, a great admirer of Ray Scott as a broadcaster, but I didn't think I should be dumped off TV completely. I called Short, and he said, "Don't worry. You'll be a part of the TV. Scott can do just a few of the games, so you will be just about splitting them." He went on to say that, "WTOP has Scott doing the CBS football games, and they are going to offer him the Redskins Exhibitions games as well." That's the reason they want to use him on some of the Senators games." I realized it was a runaround. I would be on TV only when Scott's busy schedule prevented him from doing the games. I never got to work any games with Scott. I recognized him as a brilliant broadcaster, and I just wanted to move over from the radio side to do, say, three innings with Scott, for the experience of working with him and the continuity of the format. But Short and WTOP couldn't see the logic in that. As it developed, I wound up doing about half of the TV games in 1970, but there is no doubt that it was a putdown for me.

Short didn't agree to the final TV arrangement until spring training when Tom Gallery was in Munich with Los Angeles Mayor Sam Yorty, trying to land the 1976 Olympics for Los Angeles. Gallery would have backed me and insisted on some type of continuity of format for me, but Short wasn't about to.

It was to Short's credit that he was able to get Scott to do some of the games. Short and Scott had been friends for a long time. They were neighbors in Minnesota and were members of the same country club. Short made a dramatic pitch to Scott, saying that he needed him on the TV games. And Scott agreed to work a few as a favor to Short. Short and Scott had been friends socially through the years, and I knew that Ray would get a different type of treatment from Short than I had been accustomed to. Short and Molomot didn't have the gall to go to Ray and give him the line about how necessary it was to push Short's hard-sell policy. I was amused a couple of times when both asked me, "Is Ray pushing tickets on his telecasts?" I told both of them, "How the hell should I know? I'm doing radio when *he* is on TV."

Ray has always been loyal to Short, and has had no reason to be otherwise. After we both ended our relationship with Short's club following the 1971 season, I remarked to Ray that Short and I were just not compatible, that I couldn't get along with him, and vice versa.

Ray replied, "You know, Shelby, I can only judge him by the way he has treated me, and I can say that he has always been very nice to me." I wish I had been as fortunate.

Scott and I remain good friends.

When I was bumped off some of those telecasts in the

spring of 1970, I somehow had the feeling that I wouldn't last long with Short. Most of the 1970 season saw sort of an uneasy calm between Bob and myself, and Ted Williams misconstrued that as an improvement in the relationship. Several times, Ted would say, "I'm glad you and Short are hitting it off better. You guys aren't fighting as much as you did last season." I'd just say, "Yeah, that's true." But by that time, Short and Molomot knew what they could do with me and what they couldn't do. They stopped coming to me with some of the ridiculous demands and requests that could be labeled pure fan-intimidation and fan-deception.

The 1970 season was not much fun. The club did not play good baseball. The same players who were happy and who were winning in 1969 were unhappy and were losing in 1970. The club had finished the season on a fourteen-game losing streak, but I was happy with the way the broadcasts had gone. The attendance for a last-place club was 825,000. The sponsors and station were happy with my broadcasting, and even though there was sort of an eerie calm between Short and myself most of the season, he had complained less about the way we handled the broadcasts. So I felt pretty sure that things would work out okay when it came time to discuss a new contract.

You can imagine my surprise when business manager Joe Burke called me into his office and said, "I just want to let you know that Short has to negotiate a new contract with WWDC and I don't know whether he'll be in a position to push for you to continue on the games next season."

"Now wait a minute!" I told Burke. "Is Short trying to dump me or what?" I knew that if Short wanted me to continue on the broadcasts, he could arrange it, and I knew that if he wanted me off, he would arrange that too.

"Well, no," Burke said. "But he will be negotiating, and I don't want to scare you. But there's a chance you might get squeezed out and that the station will want to use other personnel to broadcast the games."

Okay, I thought, I'm in good with the people at WWDC, and if Short doesn't keep me on his payroll, the station will hire me, and God knows, I'd rather work for them anyway. But I thought I had better get some answers from Short. He was in Washington three days later to announce the signing of Curt Flood. After the signing, I told him I'd like to talk to him about my contract.

I found out that Burke had been setting me up for the kill. Short said that my future didn't look good for next season because the station was going to pay the announcers, and they didn't want to pick up my salary. I thought that was damn funny since they had been paying a big part of it anyway through the talent fees that Short was charging them. So I told Short, "Bob, are you dumping me or not? I am on pretty good terms with the people at the station, and I think they will retain me to do the games."

Short said, "I don't think they will. Now listen to what I am telling you." He added, "I can't afford to keep you on my payroll. I'm going broke as it is." (This was only 15 minutes after Short had conducted his press conference to introduce Curt Flood, who had signed a $110,000 contract.)

"Are you going to reject me, if WWDC wants me?" I asked Short.

"No, I won't."

My next move that same day was to go to WWDC program director Pat Whitley (now the program director at WNBC in New York) and ask about their plans for me. Pat assured me that the station wanted me to continue as the Voice of the Senators. As a matter of fact, Pat even asked that I delay a planned vacation trip until after Christmas so that I might represent the station on "WWDC Day" at Laurel Racetrack.

So I called Short and said, "Bob, the station wants to hire me. So as far as they are concerned, it will be me and Menchine again next season." That's when the truth came out.

"Look, Whitfield," Short blurted. "There's no way you are going to work the Senators games next season, and I'll dump Menchine too if I can." And then he added, "But if you tell this to anyone, I'll deny it."

At that point, I knew that Short was knifing me without getting blood on his hands.

I later learned from Whitley and Bill Sanders that one of Short's pre-conditions in negotiating a new contract was that I would not be the announcer, and that there would be no deal if they divulged this fact.

Three days before Christmas, I got the call from Whitley, telling me that he couldn't go into detail, but that they would not be able to use me on the games. Our four kids didn't get the full meaning of it all, but Lora and I knew the impact. I was fired for the first time in my life. Even at the fairly young age of thirty-four, it was traumatic.

I enjoyed announcing and baseball. And I thoroughly enjoyed my association with Williams. Ted called Short three times on my behalf, much to Bob's irritation.

After Ted gave him the first call, Burke, on orders from Short, came down to my office and threatened me about going to Ted with the truth about my situation. Burke said, "Short wants me to tell you that he wants you to stay away from Williams. Don't call him, because Short is the one person who can help you the most or hurt you most. Short can keep you from getting another job in baseball, or he can help you get another job in baseball."

I didn't want to leave Washington. My family and I enjoyed the area and owned a home in the suburbs. And I did enjoy broadcasting baseball, except the garbage that Short put into it.

That is how Shelby Whitfield Enterprises came to be. I would deal in free-lance sportscasting, sports production, and advertising sales.

The first thing I wanted to do was make arrangements to do a daily Ted Williams program before each Senators broadcast on WWDC. Williams had never done such a program on a regular basis in his entire career. He and I had discussed it before, and Ted was willing to do the show with me before every game back in the 1970 season. It looked like we were all set, until Short said he wanted all the revenue from the program since Williams and I both worked for him. That killed it.

In the spring of 1971, I was not working for Short any more. I flew to Pompano Beach, visited with Ted, recorded some sample pilots, sold the advertising for the show, and bought the air time from WWDC for the broadcasts.

Short did everything that he could to stop me. He flew Tom Gallery in from California to tell Ted the show wouldn't be a good idea but Gallery refused to cooperate. Short even put the word out that he would never permit a Ted Williams-Shelby Whitfield show to get on the air. He even threatened to sue WWDC if they aired the show and he had Joe Burke tell me to forget it. But I didn't scare and neither did Bill Sanders at WWDC. Ted and I were on the air before Short even knew it.

If I had been fired because Short resented my close relationship with Williams, as many felt, then it was even more enjoyable to me that I had a show with Ted on the air. And Ted was great on the money split. He said, "Hell, I'm in a tax bracket where it's not that important to me. The important thing is that it's helping you, that it helps stimulate interest in the club, and that we have fun doing it." We had some fine programs.

At the same time, I started a sports talk show. It was

something that I had wanted to do for several years, but never had the opportunity. I wanted a hard-hitting rap session that involved all aspects of sports. I was amazed that Washington did not have a radio sports talk show. So again, I bought the air time from WWDC, sold the sponsors myself, and started a weekly show, Saturday nights out of Fran O'-Brien's Anthony House Restaurant. Franny had played tackle in the NFL for ten years. His restaurant is a sports-oriented place, which along with Duke Ziebert's, is Washington's answer to Toots Shor's in New York.

I started out with an hour show once a week, and pretty soon it was going so well that we expanded it to two hours. Then the station offered me another sports talk show, one hour each week-night. Now that show has expanded to two hours, which means that I am hosting a two-hour sports talk show six nights per week, plus doing other sportscasts for WWDC.

It was turning out just as Ted Williams said that it would. Ted kept saying, after he saw that he couldn't save my play-by-play job, "It will turn out for the better. They are making a mistake, and you will do well in anything that you choose."

At least now I know what it's like being a manager in the majors. You know when you take the job that, sooner or later, you are going to be fired. A baseball broadcaster has to please the club, the station, the advertising agency, the sponsor, the fan, and the press, not necessarily in that order. There's no way you can please all of them. In my case, no one was able to overrule Bob Short, and in retrospect, it was good for me that it happened that way.

6

THE FIFTEEN-MINUTE BAN—AND KUHN, NIXON AND JESUS CHRIST CAN'T CHANGE IT

Ted Williams had little use at all for the press. As a result, Ted had freedom with the mediamen. Bob Short, on the other hand, was concerned only with the power of the press and its ability to influence the public—especially for his own advantage.

Both showed a personal disdain for the press, but Short never took the same liberties Ted took with newspapermen. For instance, Short would have never embarrassed Jim Murray, nationally prominent *Los Angeles Times* syndicated columnist, the way Ted did. Sportswriter of the year in 1972, Murray was in Minnesota, along with a group of other writers from around the country, to cover the U.S. National Open golf championship. Murray and this group were gabbing in the lobby of Short's Leamington Hotel in Minneapolis when

Ted walked up to them. In his all but timid voice, and with a slight smirk on his face, he quizically roared, "Hey, Murray. Good to see you. Say, what are you doing these days? Still writing?" Murray was slightly pissed off, to put it mildly. When Ted told me about the incident he laughed like hell.

Ted thought it even funnier when the next time the Senators were in California to play the Angels, Jim Murray called and invited him out to lunch. Ted accepted, and it turned out to be a very pleasant lunch, as well as a profitable one for Ted. The next day Murray wrote a highly favorable piece about Ted. Ted amusedly commented, "You know, that's the best thing he has ever written about me."

This type of handling mediamen was a "no-no" with Short. He seemed to subscribe to the old Harry Wismer philosophy that any publicity is good publicity. And he made it work, manipulating the media in any way he could. Besides, no other owner of a sports franchise could generate publicity like Short—first by buying the Senators, then by luring Ted Williams out of retirement, and on through a series of controversial trades including Denny McLain and Curt Flood. Finally he left Washington without baseball, and became the story-of-the-year in Washington sports.

Short paid a price for all this publicity. He possessed a thin skin that couldn't quite protect his inflated ego. He was constantly preoccupied with his image. He subscribed to a national clipping service and each day had Molomot read him articles from the Washington papers over the phone. In 1969, Short called a press conference to urge writers to help him draw a million people into the stadium that year. Short indiscreetly proclaimed, "If this city doesn't draw a million, then it's not a major-league city." Short's *double entendre* didn't fool the press, nor did his treatment of the newpapermen exactly overwhelm them with warmth.

The day after the conference a crippled boy was .visiting

the Senators in the dugout before the game. Short took the opportunity to remark, "Geez, when you see a youngster in that condition, it makes a million in attendance seem insignificant." The *Washington Post* quoted Short the next day. I happened to be in Molomot's office when he called Short and prefaced the reading of the *Post* article by coldly saying, "Hey, Bob. Here's a bit that's great for your image."

When I was doing off-season promotion work for the Senators, I often set up projects to take Senators players out to places like Veterans Hospital and Walter Reed Hospital to visit the crippled and maimed, only to have Molomot criticize my efforts. His attitude seemed to be that hospital patients didn't buy tickets, so why worry about them.

Short attempted to endear the press to him, especially in the beginning. He maintained a spread of free liquor and food for the press at the stadium, and often took writers and broadcasters to expensive restaurants or for courtesy rides in his jet. When the team was in Minnesota, Short loved playing the gracious host. He would leave baskets of booze and fruit in writers' hotel rooms with handwritten notes offering them use of his gym and country club.

His first Christmas as club owner he bought over $2,000 worth of gift baskets containing liquor, hams, cheeses, and such for the Washington media personnel. There were about forty baskets altogether at a cost of $60 each. Although some papers had a rule prohibiting employees from accepting gifts worth more than $2.50, Short got around the rule by giving the gifts to the writers' wives. Few writers became beholden, however, and Short never played Santa Claus to the press again.

Every year at the grassy sprawl of his estate in Edina, Minnesota, Short would throw a sumptuous outdoor feast of champagne, roast suckling pig, barbecued steaks, seafood, and so on, for the press and the ball club.

Though Short could not control the criticism made of him and his operation, he was able, on occasion, to use the press effectively. He could plant speculative stories to his advantage. For instance, it was Short who started rumors that he would trade manager Williams to Milwaukee for its manager, Dave Bristol. Of course, Short later denied it, but in the process he got national publicity and managed to give Williams himself a start. Short likes to keep all of his employees on their toes with a little shock from time to time. Both Bob Addie and Russ White are Washington writers to whom Short complained about Ted's managing. Short told them that he thought Williams was a bad manager, and would like to replace him, but feared the bad publicity of doing so.

Short always talked about his desire to hire the first black manager, but he didn't do it when Ted Williams resigned. Frank Robinson, considered to be excellent managerial material, actually applied for the position of manager for the Texas Rangers when Williams quit. Another well-qualified black managerial hopeful, Maury Wills, was also available. As usual, it turned out that what Bob Short said was not what he actually wanted—and he did not want the first black manager in baseball.

Short also used the press to help him negotiate contracts with radio-TV stations, other clubs, and city officials. This became glaringly obvious in those last hectic months when he was using the newspapers daily to help set up his move to Texas. He was playing a game with the newspapers, radio-TV stations, and the stadium officials—and he won.

It didn't take Short long in Washington to gain a reputation as a double-talker who continually contradicted himself. He loved publicity, and was always available to give a statement to the press.

The following are quotes from Bob Short that appeared in Washington newspapers:

"I would not have been interested in baseball in just any city. My choice to own and run a club is in the nation's capital. It should have the best. . . ." (December, 1968)

"If we cannot win with older players, then we had better attempt to get young ones who can win." (December, 1968)

"I'm not going to operate this club on a status quo." (December, 1968)

"I'm not committed to keep the team in Washington if D.C. Stadium is not made safe for the fans." (December, 1968)

"I will not be bashful if changes are needed to make the Senators an artistic and financial success in the Nation's Capital." (December, 1968)

"I never won in basketball with the Lakers but we made the finals six out of eight years. We gave Los Angeles a contender. That's what I want to do with this baseball team. It's a damn poor second-division club. People ask me if I bought the Senators for an investment. Let me say the team will be a challenge." (December, 1968)

"I pledge a pennant and World Series at Kennedy Stadium . . . and throngs, throngs if you please, will see it. And Frank Howard will lead the Senators." (January, 1969)

"There are only three great baseball cities—New York, Washington and Los Angeles." (January, 1969)

"I'll do everything I know how to do to make this a howling success and if I fail, and I don't think I will, no one will be able to say I didn't give it my best shot." (January, 1969)

"Here [in Washington] you have population and here you are depression-proof. But nothing has been done about it all these years. . . . I can round up a girls' team that can draw 500,000. . . ." (January, 1969)

"Bob Short is no fool, but I'm not a carpetbagger, either. There's no place I would rather be operating a franchise than in Washington." (June, 1969)

"I am not going to suggest that Washington will lose its franchise. It's not going to be moved—No way it's going to be moved." (March, 1970, Board of Trade Luncheon, Mayflower Hotel, Washington, D.C.)

"We will give the team what it takes to play the game like champions." (April, 1970, Souvenir Program, Opening Day)

"I'd like to let everybody in for nothing. I just like crowds." (April, 1970)

"There *will* be an American League club in Washington. There *must* be an American League club in Washington. There *will always* be an American League club in Washington. There will be a pennant-winning team in Washington. We will contend." (April 20, 1970, Welcome Home Senators Luncheon, Washington Statler Hilton Hotel)

"In terms of am-I-a-prisoner-in-Washington, I would rather make it work in Washington and break even than make a million dollars annually in Arlington, Texas, because for whatever it's worth, it stirs more genes. The fact that you make a million dollars in Arlington, Texas, who the hell knows about it except your banker, and the hell with him anyway. . . ." (May, 1971)

"I don't want to move to Dallas, that was never my intention, but I will if I have to." (September, 1971)

"If I could roll back these three years I would under no conditions buy this club . . . Washington, except for a few loyal people, is a bad baseball town. . . ." (October, 1971)

"Washington is an awful baseball town. It wouldn't support a little league club. I would like to buy the Redskins and move them out of town." (May, 1972)

In contrast, I think Ted Williams was more concerned with avoiding having the press *use him.* There was little he wanted from the press: a little peace and quiet and a chance to do his job without scrutiny. Generally, he was one of the most accessible managers in the league and I think he liked a lot of media people and vice versa. But he could not stand to be second-guessed—a practice that writers like George Minot of the *Post,* Merrell Whittlesey of the *Star,* and Russ White, then of the *News,* often indulged in.

The first time Ted ever exploded at the press, as the Washington manager, it was especially aggravating for Ted since he was determined to change the ogre image given him by Boston press years ago. Ted Williams' explosions always made the juiciest news and it was inevitable that he be provoked. *Daily News* sports editor Dave Burgin (now sports editor at the *Star*) had instructed Russ White to do just that, and to do it before anyone else did it. So Russ decided to prick Williams' hide after a sloppy exhibition game, by second-guessing his choice of a lead-off batter. The question was just absurd enough to rile Williams, who was edgy anyway after losing his first six exhibition games.

"Why don't you use Stroud in the lead-off spot instead of Unser?" Russ asked.

"What kind of dumb fucking question is that?" Ted roared. "This is the fucking exhibition season, and you're wasting my time with a crappy question like that."

Ted got dressed and walked over to me. "Did you hear that stupid fucking question Russ White asked?"

"Yeah, I heard it. He must have been just trying to get your reaction."

"Well, he got it," Ted replied.

Afterwards, Williams asked me to ride back from West Palm Beach with him, Nellie Fox and Ed Doherty. Ted went past the Pompano Beach turnoff on the Sunshine Parkway at about 80 miles per hour. All the way back to Pompano Beach, Ted kept fussing about Russ White's question.

Williams had respect for the power of the press, despite his prideful conduct toward them. He often advised me to "butter 'em up 'cause they can help you or hurt you, buddy." He did enjoy publicity and media exposure, especially when his book *My Turn at Bat* was published.

Ted didn't have any real feuds with writers during his managerial days, but Clif Keane of Boston got under his skin more than anyone else. Occasionally, if Ted saw Keane coming across the field toward the dugout, he'd say, "See you later," and speedily remove himself from the dugout.

The following notice, written on Senators stationary, was posted in the Washington home clubhouse:

TO ALL MEMBERS OF THE PRESS:

You are welcome to enter the clubhouse of the Washington Senators fifteen minutes after the completion of a single game or after the completion of a doubleheader. This gives the players and manager a chance to relax whether victorious or defeated and will result in more rational statements or interviews. Because we like to meet each day to discuss our strength and that of opposing

teams, we will halt all interviews and visiting twenty minutes before we go onto the field. We will not permit any
visitors, press or otherwise, in the clubhouse between
games of doubleheaders. Thanks for your cooperation in
this matter.

                                        Ted Williams

Certainly this was the most notable chapter in Ted Williams' relations with the press. His theory was that those
fifteen minutes would not only give the players a chance to
think about what they wanted to say for public record, it
would also give them a chance to cool down.

Naturally, most of the media was opposed to this. Level-
headed quotes don't always make good copy. Ted claimed
the ban was in the best interests of the players who might say
something in a fit of anger that they'd later regret. Williams
always said a good example of this was the time Russ White
quoted Frank Howard after he had been thrown out of a
game by umpire Ron Luciano in 1969. Howard said the umpires were not bearing down. "They were mainly interested
in getting the game finished so they could hit the bars," said
Howard, who is usually so cool-headed that one of his nicknames is "The Gentle Giant." Ted's point is that Howard
would have told White *worse* things during the fifteen minutes immediately following the game and he intimated that
Howard might have even thrown around some furniture.

Dick Young of the New York *Daily News,* president of the
Baseball Writers Association in 1969, was at Boston for Williams' return there. Young went to confront Williams with a
protest over the ban. He asked why such a ban had to be
imposed after a 9-3 win in a relatively big game.

"Lookit," Ted said. "Don't make a project out of that
because it's not going to change."

Young and the Baseball Writers Association of America
made an official protest of the ban to Baseball Commissioner

Bowie Kuhn, who in turn wrote to Short and Williams asking "What can be done about the situation?" Short and Williams just ignored the letter and when President Nixon, who knows the problem of keeping all those pesky correspondents under control, came out in support of the ban, Ted Williams gloated happily, "Neither Kuhn, Nixon or Jesus Fucking Christ could change this goddamn ban." He said he'd quit baseball before he'd give in.

But newsmen will be newsmen and, in Washington, Russ White led the crusade against the ban. He really blew his stack one night after a game in Anaheim. Mike Epstein left the clubhouse during the fifteen-minute ban to be interviewed by the California Angels' broadcasters on a postgame show. Ted permitted this, because he didn't want to deprive the players of the gifts they received for being on this program. Bob Short was in attendance that night in Anaheim, and already in the clubhouse. When the fifteen-minute "cooling off" period was up, White came in storming about Epstein's giving an interview to the radio people during the fifteen minutes.

Bob Short coolly and articulately replied, "Russ, you're a pain in the ass."

Short had been considering running for governor of Minnesota, and White replied, "Governor my ass! I damn sure wouldn't vote for you for governor."

Short's comeback was, "I have more friends than you do."

"Yeah, but your friends are bought. They work for you," replied Russ and stalked off.

Ted later told me that he criticized Short for arguing with White. Ted said, "Why do you want to fight with him? He's a little man and you're a big man."

So Short later apologized to White, by instructing the club to put White in suites in every hotel for the rest of the club's road trip out West, a luxury that a *Daily News* man was not used to. Russ was amazed at this make-up gesture on the part of Short, and accepted the courtesy.

One time Ted Williams actually apologized to a newsman over the fifteen-minute ban. All-time Dodger pitching star, Sandy Koufax, then an NBC game reporter, tried to penetrate the visitors' clubhouse after a game at Yankee Stadium to talk with Williams. Old coach George Susce not only kicked him out but did so in a stream of nasty epithets. Ted was so embarrassed that he immediately apologized to Koufax and also asked me to draft a little note to him, once again saying how sorry he was. Ted felt there was never any doubt about trusting Koufax —after all he was a *baseball* man, wasn't he, not one of those lame writers.

One play triggered the first truly harsh words between Williams and the writers. It was early in his second season and the Senators trailed the Angels, 2-0, in the bottom of the seventh. California pitcher Tom Murphy walked Bernie Allen and John Roseboro with nobody out. Then manager Lefty Phillips walked out for a chat with Murphy, with an eye on the Senators bench. Pitcher Casey Cox was the hitter and he stood halfway between the batter's box and the on-deck circle with his jacket on, looking back toward the bench. Finally, Phillips returned to the dugout and Cox, seeing that no one was batting for him, took off his jacket and tried to bunt. He forced Allen at third and then Ed Brinkman hit into a double play.

Afterwards, the writers got to Williams individually and everyone, independently, had the same question. It sounded to Williams like a conspiracy. "Why didn't you pinch-hit for Cox?"

Ted's reasoning was that Cox was pitching his best game of the season, that he should have been able to bunt the runners around, and that the Senators, of course, were playing for the tying two runs inasmuch as they were playing at home.

The papers made something of it. Wrote Merrell Whittlesey, "Ted's explanation was so much in contrast to his usual thinking that he has Darold Knowles, the best left-handed reliever in the league, and that all he asks of his starters is six or seven good innings."

It was not such a big thing, but Ted stayed angry for days when the papers were filled with second-guessings. "Williams does not know the difference between a second-guess and an analysis of the game—and I told him so," Whittlesey wrote. But Williams was shouting profanity and pounding his desk at the writers the next night and even threatened to refuse to answer questions based on strategy from there on in. He pouted for a couple of days and gave the writers nothing, so they quit coming around. Less than a week later, Williams greeted the writers with a big grin and, "Where have you been?"

More than once, TW told me, "These Washington writers are just as bad as the Boston writers: a bunch of second-guessers. . . ." And I remember two or three instances in that three-year period in Washington that Ted vowed, "I'm not going to talk to them. I'll give them nothing answers." He did that, but it never lasted long, and Ted usually ended shouting sessions with reporters with a chuckle and a smile. And in all fairness, he *did* have to deal with some eccentrics.

Ted had problems only with writers, never photographers. Photography is one of his favorite hobbies. In Washington, one of Ted's buddies has always been Dick Darcey, sports photographer for the *Post.* Darcey told me back in the 1950s when Ted was a Leica German equipment booster and Darcey was using a Japanese Nikon, they would kid each other when Ted came to the on-deck circle at old Griffith Stadium. Ted once ducked out of the last part of an exhibition game when he played for the Red Sox to get a guided tour of the Eastman Kodak Company in Rochester, New York. He has $2,500 worth of camera equipment, some of it gifts from *Sports Illustrated* for cooperation in some articles. This includes a $700 Nikon-F motor-drive sequence camera, Nikon 500 milimeter mirror lens, and a complete set of lenses and bodies.

Since Short and Williams either consciously or unconsciously passed themselves off to the press as a team, Williams' relations were always jeopardized by Short's shortcomings. It is safe to say that press relations for both of them went downhill from the date of Short's 1969 press conference that planted the idea that local newspapers had an obligation to help Short attract a million in attendance. In late 1971, when it was obvious that Ted would simply back up Short, and Short was alienating the Washington press so he could claim that "bad publicity" hurt his franchise in Washington, writers concentrated criticisms personally on Short. He countered that the press picked on him because they were afraid to pick on Williams.

Eventually Ted got to the point of complete apathy toward the newsmen in Washington. When George Minot of the *Post* kept bugging him for a quote about the move, once it became official, a weary Williams finally said, "Write anything you want. Who cares?"

7

THREE STRIKES
AND YOU
SHOULD BE OUT

The Underminers Club was founded, fittingly, in the lavatory of the clubhouse at RFK Stadium. One day late in the 1971 season, five Washington ballplayers convened there and dedicated themselves "to the overthrow of Ted Williams and his staff." The founding fathers solemnly inscribed their names above each toilet stall: Tommie McCraw, Tim Cullen, Dick Billings, and leaders Bernie Allen and Denny McLain.

"We lived to get rid of Williams and his gang, or for Williams and his gang to get rid of us," McLain said. "Actually, our anti-Williams efforts were made public late in 1971 in an article by Russ White of the *Washington Evening Star.* We thought we'd have a little fun out of it. And when Ted found out about the Underminers Club, needless to say, he didn't see the humor in it."

But until the spring of the 1972 season, after McLain, Cullen, and Allen had all been traded, Ted Williams never knew everything about the bizarre scene that took place in McLain's suburban Bethesda home one Sunday that August. August had been a bright spot for Denny. He had come back from a 23-day forced-rest on the disabled list and won four of five decisions that month. So Denny was in his finest mood —that I'm-feelin'-fine-'cause-I-don't-give-a-damn mood that has made him the jolliest troublemaker in the history of baseball. He and his wife Sharyn invited members of the Underminers Club and their wives to a special party that night and also asked coaches, front officers, and even Williams.

Williams did not attend, but club vice-president Joe Burke and traveling secretary Burt Hawkins paid their respects. As soon as they left, Denny and the Underminers paid theirs. And you can bet they appreciated the irony of inviting Williams because that was like inviting Stokely Carmichael to a Ku Klux Klan initiation.

"It was one of the funniest and most entertaining moments of my entire career," McLain said later.

In fact, it *was* a spoof of a KKK meeting. Allen was proclaimed grand wizard and McLain was the imperial wizard onlooker. He and Billings served as accolyte wizards and they all wore blue bedsheets. (Blue because they didn't want anyone to get the wrong idea, you see.) Allen donned a cardboard crown and the ceremony began.

Five new Underminers were being inducted—Elliott Maddox, whom Ted personally sought from Detroit in the now infamous trade for McLain; Toby Harrah, the rookie shortstop and baby-faced cynic; Jim Shellenback, borderline lefty pitcher; Jackie Brown, who bounced back and forth from Washington's Denver farm team; and Denny Riddleberger, another borderliner, since traded to Cleveland. Each inductee toted a wooden cross with a coach's name on it. The biggest cross carried Williams' name. They were blindfolded and guided to the throne, where each newcomer had to give a two-minute speech on why he wanted to become an Underminer.

Said McLain, "Harrah, for instance, said he was the youngest utility player in the major leagues who went away to military summer camp hitting .262 and then couldn't get back into the lineup."

Then they burned the crosses, and Dennis the baptist dumped water over each player's head.

After that, players and wives helped the McLains consume $160 worth of liquor (two and a half gallons of booze and six cases of beer) and McLain played some of the tapes upon which he is basing his book, which he hopes to have published. McLain has said that the book will be a defense of his actions during his major-league career, and he promises that "several people will be brutally hurt, but they deserve to be."

"I tell you," McLain said, "we laughed until we cried. It was tremendous fun. Despite all the losing and bad times, the players at last had some unity. We were just trying to erase the memory of a rotten season. . . ."

This was McLain at the end of the 1971 season—after he had called Washington owner Bob Short a "saint in disguise" for taking him out of Detroit, where "things just kept happening to me."

Short had openly coveted McLain from the time he first bought the Washington franchise. In December of 1968—after McLain had won 31 games with Detroit the previous season—Short said in a press conference that he was interested in that Detroit pitcher whose name he could not quite remember. By midseason in 1969, Short not only remembered McLain's name but hinted that he would like to trade for McLain. At the time, McLain was en route to pitching 9 shutouts and winning 24 games for Detroit and, naturally, there was no serious negotiation of such a trade. Short made it a point to get to know Denny at a baseball writers' dinner in Minneapolis after the 1969 season. It's easy to see why they might get along: both are glib, media-hungry extroverts with a taste for the unorthodox and both are known in baseball as "bad boys."

In the 1970 season, McLain won only 3 of 8 games, posted a bloated earned-run average of 4.65 and was suspended three times—all of which made him available, perhaps even attractive, to Short. McLain's season of woe began when *Sports Illustrated* revealed that he had been ". . . a partner in a bookmaking operation during the 1967 season and had become inextricably involved with mobsters." The magazine claimed that McLain was playing the organ at a Flint, Michigan, restaurant (Hammond organ bookings are one of McLain's lucrative sidelines) when he and a friend, Edwin K. Schober, then an executive with a soft-drink company, were persuaded to put up money to back an alleged bookie, Jiggs Gazell, who in turn was "sponsored by members of a Syrian mob with Cosa Nostra connections." But apparently the mobsters were grabbing the winnings and billing McLain and Schober for the losses—in other words, Denny and his buddy were the victims of a con game. Then came the macabre: "Heavy pressure was put on both McLain and his executive friend in August and September of 1967 to make good on a $46,000 loss suffered when a Battle Creek plunger scored heavily on an allowance race at the Detroit Race Course." A year later, the plunger was killed in an auto accident when his car crashed into a tree on a "lonely stretch" of highway. Reportedly, he never collected more than $1,000 of the alleged debt.

Before the plunger died, *Sports Illustrated* continued, he had gone ". . . from mobster to mobster, seeking influence to enable him to collect his money and finally was granted an audience with Tony Giacalone," the so-called enforcer of the Detroit underworld. Then McLain was taken before Giacalone. In this confrontation, the magazine intimated, Giacalone brought his heel down on McLain's foot, dislocating several of McLain's toes, an injury which forced him to miss two or three pitching starts. *Sports Illustrated* admitted it had no proof that this actually happened but offered this as one of five versions of how McLain injured his toes. What confused everything was that McLain himself, in an orgy of contradictions, actually provided three different versions: (1) he first said he had fallen asleep watching TV and so had one of his legs. He awoke, got to his feet and somehow stubbed his toes; (2) then he claimed he hurt his toes chasing raccoons that were raiding his garbage cans; and (3) finally he said he hurt his toes when he kicked lockers in the clubhouse in a fit of anger.

Just before the *Sports Illustrated* story appeared on newsstands, Baseball Commissioner Bowie Kuhn ordered McLain to his New York office. Afterwards, both told the press the story was about 80 percent false but neither ever bothered to tell the public which 20 percent they regarded as true. Kuhn just said: "There is no indication that these activities in any way involved the playing or the outcome of baseball games. When all the pertinent facts and circumstances have been determined and evaluated, I will have a further statement to make."

McLain, meanwhile, appeared voluntarily before a United States Grand Jury investigating an alleged nationwide sports betting ring and walked out free. The next day, after a five-and-a-half-hour session with Kuhn, McLain was suspended from "all Organized Baseball activities" until Kuhn could wrap up his investigation. Kuhn had decided, however, that "McLain's involvement in 1967 bookmaking activities and his associations at that time" were shady enough to warrant an investigation.

McLain immediately went to his home in Lakeland, Florida, and began pounding his chest in remorse. He told Jerry Green of the *Detroit News*, "All I can say is I'm very sorry I've embarrassed baseball to a certain extent. I'm asking for the benefit of the doubt. I apologize to the commissioner. I'm sorry anything like this had to happen." He felt, however, he would be reinstated within a month. "My immedite problem is getting a job. I'm in financial trouble. What am I going to do for money? I've got a family to take care of. Contrary to belief, 99 percent of my problems stem from business. I made a lot of bad investments."

Week after week passed without the promised announcement from the commissioner's office. Nationally syndicated columnist Red Smith warned: "The longer Bowie Kuhn puts off letting the public in on the facts about Denny McLain, the more baseball and everybody concerned will suffer. . . . The commissioner neither denies nor confirms the implications. He does not maintain silence. He says too little, which is worse. . . ."

Marvin Miller, executive director of the Major League Baseball Players Association, said that McLain had been judged guilty before all the facts were in. "McLain is the victim of self-incrimination. Bowie called him into his office for an informal discussion and said, in the manner of a forgiving Dutch uncle, 'Tell me all about it, Denny.' Then Denny speaks and discovers he has incriminated himself."

The commissioner, in the meantime, began touring the Florida and Arizona spring training camps, holding press conferences everywhere he went with the warning he would not discuss the McLain case. Columnist Smith, attending one such "weekly half hour of silence," observed, "Triple ax murders have been solved in less time than has been consumed getting answers to simple questions. Kuhn is determined not to make a final ruling until he has all the facts. This is wise, but weeks go by and delay invites public suspicion."

If nothing else, the length of the investigation indicated how truly entangled was the case of Denny McLain. The McLain financial confusion also was emerging from daily news bulletins at the time. Though he had been earning at the rate of over $100,000 a year, McLain's total debts came to a whopping $400,042, according to a bankruptcy petition later filed in Detroit. Of that, he was contesting some $273,-500 in a variety of court suits. At that time McLain's attorney, William Aiken of Detroit, listed his client's assets at $413, with which he was supposed to pay off eighty-six creditors, ranging from friends who had loaned him money to corporations which honored his credit cards.

And all this at age twenty-six!

Then, a month after McLain's suspension, the Internal Revenue Service seized the furniture in his rented home in Beverly Hills, a suburb of Detroit, to pay off $9,460 in income taxes owed for 1968. The IRS sold the furnishings at an auction which brought $5,852, including $3,400 paid for McLain's Hammond organ. Typically, McLain later said the organ didn't belong to him, but was loaned to him by the Hammond Organ Company.

Nearly seven weeks after Kuhn's temporary suspension, McLain picked up the phone in his Lakeland home and heard Kuhn's decision in his case. He put down the phone, gave a deep sigh that sagged his chest and shoulders, caught his wife Sharyn in a bear-hug, and like a man reprieved, exclaimed, "Till July first, till July first!"

Kuhn had concluded that even though he *thought* he was investing in a bookmaking partnership in Flint, Michigan, in fact he had been duped. "There is no evidence to indicate that McLain ever bet on a baseball game involving the Detroit Tigers or any other team. There is no evidence to indicate that McLain gave less than his best effort at any time while performing for the Detroit Tigers. There is no evidence that McLain in 1967 or subsequently has been guilty of any misconduct involving baseball or the playing of baseball games," Kuhn's ruling read.

However, the ruling continued: "McLain's association in 1967 with gamblers was contrary to his obligation as a professional player to conform to high standards of personal conduct, and it is my judgment that this conduct was not in the best interests of baseball. . . . While it is true . . . that McLain has been irresponsible in his personal financial affairs, and that this is a source of serious concern, I have not in this particular case based my disciplinary action on such irresponsibility. . . ."

So Kuhn suspended McLain for just half a season.

What was the difference in attempting to become a bookmaker, as McLain had done, and actually being one? "I think you have to consider the difference is the same as between murder and attempted murder," explained Kuhn in what has since become a widely quoted statement.

Reaction to the decision was mixed, of course. Detroit officials were delighted. McLain's batterymate, Tiger catcher Bill Freehan, seemed puzzled and said, shaking his head, "Half a season? Funny. It's like saying he almost did something wrong." Dick McAuliffe, veteran Tiger infielder, also expressed surprise. "If Denny's innocent, it should be nothing. If he's guilty, then this is not enough." Jim Price, Tiger player representative and McLain's closest friend on the club, said, "Most of the guys thought Denny would get one or two years, or nothing at all. The three-month suspension is as close to nothing as you could get."

Like the players, most sportswriters regarded Kuhn's penalty as too lenient. Dick Young of the *New York Daily*

News, probably the nation's most widely quoted baseball writer, wrote: "The fans, most of them, will boo the decision of Bowie the Benign. He let them down. This was his chance to be a stern commissioner, a severe commissioner. Baseball is something special in American society because it has a mystique of purity. The seeming paradox of all life is that more money is bet on baseball than on any other sport because it is honest. The people know it is honest. The people want to keep it that way, even if it takes an occasional scalp or two."

Robert Lipsyte of *The New York Times* commented: "McLain, it can be argued, must have considered himself at least a rookie bookmaker. As such, he knew he was violating some of the strictest laws and customs in baseball and endangering his team and the sport as well as his own career. But his venture into crime did not pay off, he was suckered and saved. His intent was criminal, but his technique inept; therefore, he will miss less than three months of the season."

In other words, Denny was just dumb enough. If he had known what he was doing—or had done what he wanted—he'd be out of baseball today.

Theoretically, all Denny had to do was casually work himself into shape for this mid-season debut. However, in the previous two years he had pitched an incredible total of 661 innings to win 55 games. The effort caused or damaged what Denny called "inflamed tendons in my pitching shoulder." So he was paying the price of overwork—occasional cortisone shots to reduce the inflammation and loosen the muscle. A muscle can take just so much cortisone. Halfway through his suspension-extended spring training in 1970, McLain said: "I pulled something in the back of my shoulder. It hurt so bad I couldn't even eat that night. I couldn't even pick up my fork." Even with cortisone, McLain was knocked out after 5 1/3 innings in his July 1 debut against the Yankees. Reliever

Tom Timmerman was the winner when Detroit tied up the game and won it in extra innings, 6–5. The game drew a crowd of 53,863 paid, the largest crowd at Tiger Stadium in nine years. A total of seventy-one writers covered the McLain Debut, giving the scene a World Series atmosphere. The crowd gave him such a warm reception, McLain said afterwards, "I'm not an emotional man. But I thought I was going to cry when I heard those cheers. I didn't know what to expect. I almost had to swallow my tongue to hold myself together."

McLain made four more starts without success, then won two games in a row, both with relief help. It wasn't until his thirteenth start, on August 22 against hapless Milwaukee, that he was able to go the distance and win. That was the third and final victory of his brief season—compiling a 3-and-5 record with an ERA of 4.65.

More than just his arm was bothering Denny. He later recalled, "From everything I was reading I began to think maybe I *was* nuts." With pressures from creditors, newsmen and who knows what else, McLain apparently decided he wanted to be traded. He was smart enough to know the fastest way to convince a general manager to throw you to another team is to desecrate one of the sacred institutions of baseball. Denny has a proven imagination in this field so it didn't take him long to decide. Baseball writers! A perfect target. Not only do these men keep the scriptures of baseball but they also oversee the morals of the game . . . and its players. And what an emotional outlet for his current frustrations with writers who refused to stop picking on momma's little Denny.

Detroit pitcher Joe Niekro agreed to help Denny. August 28 a *Detroit Free Press* rookie writer, pesky Jim Hawkins, went to the clubhouse about an hour before a night game. McLain and he talked, and as Hawkins was about to leave,

Niekro stopped him. "Sit down for a few minutes," Niekro told Hawkins, and the writer did. McLain snuck up behind him and dumped a bucket of warm whirlpool water on Hawkins' head and shoulders.

About half an hour later, dapper and gray-haired Watson Spoelstra of the *Detroit News,* a former president of the sacrosanct Baseball Writers' Association of America, was in the umpires' room, visiting old friend Hank Soar, when he got a message that McLain wanted to see him. Later McLain insisted he had no grudge against Spoelstra and that the veteran writer just happened into an irresistible situation. "That's a lie," Spoelstra contended. "He sent for me." According to Spoelstra, McLain greeted him cordially and then said, "I didn't like the headlines in your paper." The conversation continued for several minutes but ended pleasantly with both men shaking hands. As soon as Spoelstra's back was turned, McLain poured a bucket of ice water over his head. "I could feel the ice cubes hit my head, and I saw them scatter on the floor," Spoelstra said. Spoelstra immediately went to Detroit General Manager Jim Campbell, who apologized for the club and suspended McLain. And McLain pleaded to be traded.

This second suspension, at $500 a day, technically lasted seven days, when Detroit management advised Commissioner Kuhn they were reinstating McLain. But Kuhn asked them to wait until after he met with club officials and McLain and his lawyers on a regular Detroit swing through New York.

In the two-hour session, Kuhn had a surprise for McLain: his third suspension of the year, which is believed to be an all-time record. This time it was for carrying a gun and breaking probation. This time it was for the rest of the 1970 season. Kuhn said McLain had carried a gun during Detroit's recent West Coast trip and that at least once, in a Chicago restaurant, McLain took the gun out of its holster and showed it to several teammates. Cut and dried. Court adjourned.

In the next McLain case, Commissioner Kuhn actually helped McLain upstage the opening game of the World Series. By this time Kuhn had a two-page report from a "very eminent psychiatrist" affirming McLain's mental health, in case anybody was wondering, so he secretly lifted McLain's suspension on the last day of the regular schedule, thus making him eligible for trade.

Bob Short was becoming obsessed with the prospect of landing McLain for his franchise, his gallery of "faces," as he called them. Ted Williams was not opposed to getting McLain, although he felt the key to a deal would be to get him "reasonably." I was with Ted in his clubhouse office when Short called from upstairs the final week of the season, saying he had just been on the phone with Detroit general manager Campbell about a McLain deal.

"Bob, that's too much. And besides, I don't like his pitching *that* much," Ted said. At the time, Short was offering strong, young pitcher Joe Coleman and veteran shortstop Ed Brinkman for McLain. Ted added, "We can't give away our shortstop like that. And even if I have trouble with Coleman, we can't give him away without equal value." Ted was down on Coleman, but he knew a lot of baseball people thought he would win 20 games.

When Ted hung up and told me what Short was trying to do, I was dumbfounded. "If he's going to give away Brinkman and Coleman, for Godssake, get something more than McLain," I said.

Ted mentioned Maddox and McRae.

"Demand Mickey Stanley then," I said. I knew that Ted liked Stanley, a gold glove winner who could hit.

I, like most baseball people, was amazed when Short, Kuhn, and Campbell called their last-minute press conference at the World Series headquarters in Cincinnati before the first game, and announced the details of the trade.

First, Kuhn dismissed McLain's gun-toting. "He was merely manifesting a kind of flamboyance typical of his personality and has been the victim of emotional stress by a conglomeration of problems," Kuhn said. "A change of location might be beneficial."

Then the shocking news: Detroit sent to Washington McLain, McRae, infielder Don Wert, and Maddox in exchange for Coleman, Brinkman, pitcher Jim Hannan, and—incredibly—the man that Ted Williams called his third baseman "for a decade," Aurelio Rodriguez.

Short was ecstatic. "McLain is the greatest pitcher in baseball," he said. "This is *my* trade."

Believe me, Ted insisted that Short remember that. We talked about it a great deal by phone that winter. "The fucking trade has ruined the club," Ted told me. "The only way it could be profitable at all is if McLain wins 20 games for us. And who's going to play shortstop? They think the kid [Harrah] can play it but I don't know. . . . The kid at third [Rodriguez] is going to be the new Brooks Robinson for the next ten years . . . Coleman and I had our problems but we had to get value for him. . . ."

Meanwhile Short told Oscar Molomot, "It was a stroke of genius!" It probably bought Short Detroit's yes vote to move his franchise at the end of that season, and it assured Short of enough disaster to alienate whatever goodwill remained for the team in Washington.

Ted grumbled enough in public about the trade that winter that Short decided to bring him and McLain together for a press conference at his signing in November. Ted went out of his way to welcome McLain, who immediately interpreted his manager's benevolence as a sign of weakness. "We're really happy to have him as a Washington Senator and I can only tell you after talking to Mr. McLain I'm as confident as I ever have been that Mr. McLain wants to regain his form as the greatest pitcher in baseball," Ted said. Ted even told McLain that the writers, Ted's usual enemies, were "a pretty damn good bunch so I don't think you'll have any problems."

"That's not what he told me twenty-five minutes ago," McLain joked. And McLain brought up for the first time the bugaboo which he always would use as an excuse for his bad relations with Williams: his insistence on pitching every four days instead of every five, as Ted eventually ordered.

"If Ted comes around to my way of thinking, we'll be all right," McLain said.

Spring training had to be better than that. McLain called it his best ever, and Ted agreed he was one of the hardest workers in camp. One thing was puzzling: why did he weigh in at 215 when he was listed at 185 on the Detroit roster during his two big years?

"I've always pitched between 210 and 215," McLain retorted.

"Well, he's a little overweight," Ted told me in Pompano Beach. "But he's really trying. I can tell he's been used to asking a lot of special favors and I'll tell you he's not going to get those here with us. He's a fun-loving guy but he has to get more *serious*."

McLain wasted no time in regaining his form as a prima donna in his first start of the season by bitching when Williams removed him in the tenth inning for a pinch hitter. He changed his tune abruptly when Tom McCraw, who pinch hit for him, won the game with a home run.

He balked home a crucial run in his next start, a 5–3 loss to Boston, but bounced back to shut out Cleveland, 4–0, on a three-hitter. In that game, however, he began an argument with umpire Art Frantz over some close calls on balls and strikes and five days later picked up the hassle again with

Frantz against Milwaukee. He had a no-hitter for four innings until he began questioning Frantz's eyesight. After complaining vigorously to Frantz over calls on Roberto Peña, he lost his concentration and Peña got a two-run single.

"Those are your two runs. You're a shit!" he yelled at Frantz, according to the umpire's report to the league office.

"Watch your language!" Frantz yelled back.

"Go fuck yourself," Denny replied. After Frantz threw him out of the game, McLain rifled the ball into the stands, which is a rules violation.

Ted, who never has been thrown out of a game as a player or manager, lectured McLain on the sure self-defeat in baiting umpires. McLain resented Ted's advice.

Ironically, McLain's next start was his best pitching effort of the year. It came on the day that tormented Curt Flood jumped the team and flew to Spain. McLain shut out Minnesota that day and ended April with a 3–2 record, two shutouts and a 3.00 earned-run average. Writers were calling it the Denny McLain Comeback and they asked Ted to comment. "Well, he's a big favorite here and he's certainly popular on our ballclub," Williams said. "I needle him a little bit to keep him going, keep him heads up." Then he paraphrased what he said in spring training, once again wondering aloud about McLain's attitude. "Our only concern with him is that he should become more businesslike every bit of the time in his workout and his practice and his approach to the game in every regard. And, if we can keep him in that state of mind, there's no way he won't have a good year." This was Ted Williams the Total Ballplayer talking, the "Kid" who used to spend hours on end in hotel rooms practicing his swing in front of a full-length mirror. On the "Ted Williams Show" I asked Ted if everything was okay with McLain, who struck me, at the time, as being a good enough guy. "I get on him a little bit to try to get him not to kid around so much," Ted replied. "Especially with the opposing players." Something was beginning to happen between the two and Ted would not yet put his finger on it.

When the team arrived in Minnesota the first week in May, McLain had lost his last two starts, and the Senators had lost six straight while batting a collective .167 during the slump. Now McLain was beginning to second-guess Williams' lineups. He began to politic openly for his ole Tiger trade-mate Don Wert, who opened the season on the disabled list, to play third base instead of "the nigger"—the words McLain used to describe Joe Foy. McLain also began requesting his buddy Jim French to catch him instead of Paul Casanova, a Cuban black. Ted felt Casanova was the better defensive catcher, with perhaps the best arm in the league. Ted sternly told McLain that the manager, not the pitcher, would designate the catcher.

Four days later McLain lost his third in a row, to Minnesota, although he lasted nine and two-thirds innings. In mid-May he met his old team, the Tigers. Some 18,694 came out to RFK Stadium to see Denny beat Bill Zepp and his teammates on an eight-hitter which Washington won in the ninth, 3–2.

McLain's next start was the beginning of a nine-game losing streak for him and the end of Williams' tolerance of McLain's four-day rotation. In six weeks of working generally with three days' rest, McLain had a 4–6 record, ERA of 3.99, 75 hits in 76.2 innings, 24 walks and 51 strikeouts. At that time his only win in his last five decisions came with four days' rest. Williams also wanted to alter the rotation to make room for Mike Thompson, a strong righthander from Denver, who had just had an impressive start against Baltimore.

The decision to change McLain's rotation habits probably caused more friction between the two men than any other single factor. They had argued about it ever since the press conference at Denny's signing the previous winter. "We keep track of every pitch—what was pitched and what was hit off the pitch," Williams would argue. "And we've gathered conclusive proof that neither Bosman nor McLain could do it that way."

"Williams has figures from six weeks," McLain would retort. "And I have figures from six years."

"Don't forget Mr. McLain isn't 22 or 23 or 24 or 25 or 26 anymore," Williams would say. "Sure, if you've got the personnel that can pitch with three days' rest, fine."

"When I pitch every fifth day, it's like starting all over again," McLain explained after the season. "Every time I pitched that way last year I was stiff and sore the next day. But it wasn't just that. People don't realize how big the mental part of this game is. In a four-day rotation, you're away from the game only one day, the day after you pitch. On the second day you throw and on the third day you watch the hitters, because you're pitching the next day. But in a five-day rotation, you're not involved two days. Even though you go to the ballpark, you don't get involved. You're just not in the game as much. You also don't get as many starts, maybe ten less, which means you can't win as many games."

Using the same logic, some people felt that Denny would have had a shot at thirty *losses* if he had remained in a four-day rotation.

At any rate, McLain lost his second of nine in a row to old Tiger rival Mickey Lolich, 5–0, before 53,337 Detroit fans—the largest crowd in Tiger Stadium since the 53,886 that came out to see McLain debut after his half-a-season suspension the year before. Three weeks later McLain lost his seventh straight in spectacular fashion. In just three innings he gave up five home runs to Oakland, including two to ex-Senator Mike Epstein and two more to Joe Rudi.

About this time, Washington signed young pitcher Pete

Broberg for a $150,000 bonus. He joined the club immediately, and June 20, the day after McLain lost his eighth straight, to Baltimore, Broberg debuted in RFK Stadium, and struck out seven in six and a third innings. When McLain began in the majors he reportedly had signed with the Chicago White Sox for just $17,000. Perhaps that is why I seemed to notice a tinge of jealousy in McLain toward Broberg, whom he called, derogatorily, "the kid." And Broberg got more headlines the rest of the season. McLain, the former 31-game winner, had a lot of influence over some young Washington players like Jeff Burroughs, Toby Harrah, and Mike Thompson, but he failed to impress Broberg with his facetious malcontentedness. "Aw, he ought to be in the minors," McLain would snap.

Not long after Broberg's debut, McLain lost his ninth straight, 4–0 in Yankee Stadium, giving him a loss to all eleven opposing teams by June 26. He was 4–14. McLain, never lacking arrogance, called Short to complain that Williams had taken him out too soon—in the fifth inning after giving up three runs. McLain later claimed he did not pop a fastball the rest of the season and, indeed, he came back June 30 to beat the Yankees, 2–1, on nothing but curves and changeups. This was exactly what Williams tried to get McLain to work on. "He's a craftsman," Ted said on our show once. "He has a good overhand curve, good motion, good changeup and control, and he can spot his fastball. With that he should win quite a few games."

However, right after that showing, Ted yanked McLain after two innings while losing 3–0 to Cleveland. As he walked past the rest of the Senators players on his way to the dugout he muttered, loud enough for most to hear, "I'm going to call Short and get rid of this fucker." He stalked into the Cleveland clubhouse and called Short to complain about another early exit. The next day Short joined the team in Baltimore and, as Short and I were walking and discussing an appearance on my show, McLain pulled Short aside and continued his protestations. When Short tried to intervene with Ted on behalf of Denny, Ted found out about the phone calls and exploded. He said he was disappointed in McLain as a person, accused him of undermining his authority, lying to him, and conniving. Ted wanted to fine or even suspend him but he eventually cooled down about it.

Then, after he lost his next start to Detroit, Joe Falls of the *Detroit Free Press* wrote that McLain had played golf in the afternoon before pitching that night. Ted became irate when he found out. Ted confronted McLain with the story and he denied it, but Falls told me later he even knew who McLain played with that day. McLain himself has admitted that he played golf many times in 1971 in defiance of Ted's rule.

Now, of course, Ted wanted to suspend McLain. But Short was afraid he would be embarrassed by such a move, considering McLain was *his* trade. They compromised by putting him on the 21-day disabled list. Denny used the time to get three deep cortisone shots in his shoulder at Detroit's Ford Hospital. The Senators physician, Dr. George Resta, was trying to get Denny to go easy on the cortisone shots because he had taken so many. Denny said that Resta was a "quack" and he would go to Detroit for the shots.

I learned later that McLain also used some of that rest time to play second base for the charity softball team sponsored by radio station WWDC.

The cortisone was a veritable shot-in-the-arm for McLain. He came back in August to beat Detroit, 4–2, in Tiger Stadium and then win three out of his next four games, including a 4–0 shutout of California. Then he lost six of his last seven to end up the season at 10–22.

On three days' rest his record was 2–7.

On four days' rest, it was 5–13.

On five days' rest, it was 0–2.

He won his opening start, his first start after the 21-day so-called rest and another after six days' rest.

Better than his baseball statistics is McLain's record of run-ins with people in the Washington area. He often seems to be at the vortex of inexplicable and misadventurous forces. Usually, though, he brings things on himself. A good example was an incident he caused in the RFK Stadium parking lot for press, players, and front-office personnel. Each Senator got a season parking pass with a ticket good for each home date. Many players abused the parking privilege by giving passes away to friends and then trying to talk their way into the lot. The D.C. Armory Board, which controls the Stadium, decided to collect the regular $1.00 fee from any player without a pass. Mike Senda has been the attendant at that gate for eight years and says that McLain gave him trouble from Opening Day on. Senda told me that McLain was easily the most obnoxious, disrespectful person he ever had to deal with in eight years at the stadium. Senda said McLain hardly ever had his pass with him. One night McLain nearly ran down Senda while forcing his way into the lot. Not long afterwards, McLain tried to use an old pass to park and Senda, following instructions, refused to let him by unless he paid the dollar fee. So McLain cursed Senda and left his car parked in the middle of the entrance and disappeared into the clubhouse. The Park Police had to call for a wrecker. Security Officer Captain Duane Bowman finally moved the car, but the Senators had to pay a $25 towing charge.

Then McLain tried to get Senda fired over the incident. Denny stormed into the clubhouse in a rage, claiming that Senda was bad for the players, put them in a bad mood, and should be dismissed. The word got upstairs to Short that his "pet" was throwing a fit, and Short came down and immediately agreed with Denny. Tom Whiteford of the Armory

Board, Senda's boss, was called down, and he firmly stood behind Senda. So McLain and Short were frustrated in their demands that the parking attendant be fired.

Senators ex-clubhouse man Fred Baxter, who spent over forty years in the major leagues, claims that McLain is the most difficult player with whom he ever worked. Baxter says that in spite of McLain's $75,000 salary, he never once tipped him during the 1971 season. Fred added that he had to write McLain's business manager to be reimbursed for clubhouse bills owed by Denny.

Despite all these indications, McLain is not entirely nasty. Customers at Fran O'Brien's Anthony House often caught the flighty pitcher in good moods. At the Senators going-away party there at the end of the last season, dashing Denny Dale McLain, dressed like a beach bum—beige Banlon golf shirt, and nondescript slacks, and sockless in tennis shoes—emceed the Senators' "Emmy Awards." He bestowed awards, selected by the players, for the biggest crybaby—Joe Grzenda; worst drinker—Jim Shellenback; best drinker—Frank Howard; worst dancer—Howard; worst poker player —Dick Billings; worst haircut—Casey Cox. McLain presented Bernie Allen with the distinction as "Senator who undermined management most" (although McLain was certainly in the running). Winner of the worst dresser was Howard, who, according to emcee McLain, "owns only one sports jacket—and it's gold." McLain himself got the award for "foulest mouth."

It's interesting to note that the Senators selected Dick Billings as the club's worst card player. Williams had a rule against serious card playing, but some of his players failed to take the rule seriously. Billings and pitcher Jackie Brown were taking part in a card game one early morning in downtown Washington when Dick got caught trying to cheat. Some pretty tough boys were involved in the game and $700 was on the table when Billings got caught trying to slip a card to Brown. The Senators' catcher got off with a reprimand, being lucky enough to finish the season in one piece.

Denny hit it off well with some of the Senators players in his one-year stay. But his six years in Detroit seemed to be more than the Tigers could take. In his controversial book *Behind the Mask*, published in 1970, Denny's battery mate Bill Freehan said, "The rules for Denny just don't seem to be the same as for the rest of us. Most of us have to be at the park two and a half hours before a game. Denny sometimes shows up five or ten minutes before a game. People used to say, before night games, that the best thing about baseball was that you couldn't beat the hours. In Denny's case, anyway, that's still true."

Late in the 1970 season, some of the Tigers requested of manager Mayo Smith a club meeting to discuss some of their problems and, in particular, Denny McLain. Smith granted the meeting, and the first thing one Detroit player said was, "Skip, you have rules. But when you make an exception to the rules for one guy, and you expect everyone else to live by them, it's pretty tough for the club to work together." Another player added, "Right, Mayo. Half the time, McLain doesn't come out here before a game. And he laughs about it. He thinks it's a funny joke. He goes home halfway in the middle of a game. He's never on the bench, never takes batting practice, never shags."

So it's easy to understand the feelings of some of Denny's teammates when he came back from his suspension in the middle of the 1970 season. The night before Denny was scheduled to pitch his first game, teammate Mickey Lolich told newsmen, "Tomorrow night will be the first night I'll have to root against my own team." Tiger outfielder Jim Northrup surveyed the unusually heavy press turnout for McLain's midseason debut and asked, "Are the flies hanging around the garbage, or is the garbage hanging around the fly." When McLain took umbrage at that one, Northrup said Denny must have misconstrued his meaning.

Denny defended his poor relationship with the Detroit players by saying, "I'm a loner. I've been ripped by other players because I don't associate with the guys on the ball club."

Denny continued, "I don't drink [that declaration is going to surprise a lot of people including some bartenders] and I don't smoke and I don't go into bars with the guys because the smoke irritates my contact lenses. I like to go to the hotel or home after a ball game. I have very few close friends."

McLain and I didn't get to know each other well during the baseball season. We had a couple of brief conversations but nothing substantial. After the season we began bumping into each other at Fran O'Brien's. Just before the World Series started, McLain bet me $500 even money that the Pirates would win. He used the money to give a party—which I wasn't invited to.

Ted had once refused to give McLain permission to appear on my "Sports Round Table" show. He was afraid Denny might say something everyone would regret.

, One wonders, in retrospect, just how much method there was to Denny McLain's madness in the winter before the 1972 season. All during that winter he made alienating comments about Ted and the ball club on his three-hour Sunday evening talk show on WWDC. Was McLain a victim of his own uncontrollable indiscretion, or did he carefully plant certain outrageous statements so that he would become *persona non grata* on the Rangers and be traded? After all, look at the results: he was traded from a bad team to a pennant contender in Oakland, a team that could play defense for him and get runs for him much better than Texas.

It would not be the first time McLain has employed such

tactics to be traded. Even he admits that his dousing of two Detroit sportswriters was at least partially calculated to get him out of Detroit. Denny is no raving maniac. Incorrigible, yes, but not uncontrollable. Time and again I've seen him turn on the charm to get whatever he wants out of people. Women have told me McLain brings out the maternal instinct in them and men say they like him because "he just doesn't give a damn." In other words, a free spirit, like a naughty boy.

McLain had started blasting as soon as he started his radio show. He said he wanted to be traded and he openly knocked Ted Williams' managerial policies. He invited anti-Williams pals like Bernie Allen and Jim French to criticize Williams' ideas of platooning and pitching rotation. On December 19, he predicted Williams would retire "during or after the 1972 season." He criticized the winter trades for players like Roy Foster, Rich Hand, Ken Suarez, Ted Kubiak, Hal King, and Mike Paul, thereby burning his bridges with them too. He broadcasted that the Rangers' young players—like Jeff Burroughs, Pete Broberg, Bill Fahey, and Len Randle—were inadequate. "No way this team will be a contender for five years," he said. He referred to the *Washington Post* sports editor, Shirley Povich, as "The Girl." McLain went out of his way to make snide comments about Commissioner Bowie Kuhn. ("I wonder if Bowie Kuhn uses this detective agency.")

Was it guile or garbage? Surely McLain didn't think he was talking to himself for three hours every Sunday.

McLain agreed to be a guest on my Saturday "Sports Round Table" show and he showed up on crutches. He had injured his ankle playing basketball in Florida but it also could have been playing touch football for a club in Ocean City, Maryland, or for the WWDC charity basketball team. Perhaps McLain's sense of competition was his best quality. (Or worst, if you consider the danger of permanent injury killing his career in these off-season sports. In fact, the Uniform Player's Contract does prohibit any baseball player from taking part in any kind of football game.) At any rate, McLain started insulting me on my show from the first time he muttered sarcastically, "I wonder what your buddy Ted will say about this?" McLain loved Short and despised Williams. I played along with him, retorting with sting until it got to a point where I felt the listeners might think I was really trying to do a hatchet job on my own guest. McLain and one of my panelists, Jack Mann, set up a version of the McLain water-dumping on the Detroit writers. McLain and Mann got together after the show and decided to collaborate on McLain's autobiography.

On one of his programs, McLain was asked if he would mind being traded back to Detroit. "Absolutely not," he replied. "I'll even pay my own way back there." When the news broke that Short indeed was talking to Detroit about McLain (Short asked for Rodriguez or Coleman back in exchange for McLain and reportedly Tiger general manager Jim Campbell just laughed), McLain panicked. He called both Short and Ted Williams, told them he wanted to pitch in Texas but if he was going to be traded, please not to Detroit. He said he could not face the writers back in Detroit, but his panic may have had something to do with his creditors in Michigan too.

The news of the McLain-Mann book, which obviously would criticize Ted Williams, and a news article in the *Washington Star* by Merrell Whittlesey both reached Williams about the same time. Whittlesey's article quoted McLain as saying his old manager, Charlie Dressen, and his old pitching coach, Johnny Sain, were so much better than Williams and Hudson. He was also quoted as saying, "The Rangers need Frank Howard and myself, somebody the fans can identify with. Frank and I are major-league baseball players." Undoubtedly the capper in Ted Williams' mind was this McLain quote, in total defiance of his no-golf rule during the season: "I like to play golf. There are some super courses around the Dallas-Fort Worth area. I will be there."

A few days later McLain was on his way to Oakland for minor-league pitchers Don Stanhouse and Jim Panther. Short said he also had to throw in $25,000 to get rid of McLain.

After the trade, McLain said sarcastically of Williams, "We got along great . . . away from the ballpark." Of course that was because they never saw each other away from the park.

When he took off for Mesa, Arizona, the Oakland spring training camp, McLain's absence could be immediately felt at Pompano Beach. Said one of the veteran pitchers, "The morale in this camp went up overnight."

I wonder what Oakland saw in McLain. Was it Charley Finley's infatuation with eccentricity? After all, how could Oakland forget slugging McLain for five home runs in three innings the year before? But Denny has always been plagued by the gopher ball. McLain led the American League in home-run pitches in 1966 with 42, 1967 with 35, and even in 1968, when he won 31 games and gave up as many homers. In 1970 he gave up 19 homers in less than half a season, easily the biggest ratio in the league. And, in 1971, McLain delivered 31 home-run pitches, the third highest in the league.

There are other questions about McLain. Was he too good too soon, winning 20 at age twenty-two and 31 by the time he was twenty-four years old? When he won 31 in 1968, the Tigers gave him an average of 5.8 runs per game. In 1971 with the Senators he complained continuously about lack of support (with much justification) but he failed to notice that 4 of his 10 victories came to him after he had already left the game and a fifth was the result of a relief appearance. The Senators came from behind to win two games for Denny after he was out of the game. On two other occasions, Denny left the game with the score tied, and the Nats scored to give McLain wins. McLain screamed bloody murder to the press when Williams put him in the bullpen once early in the season when Denny was pitching poorly. Denny claimed that he couldn't remember the last time he was sent to the bullpen. Denny's memory is not the best. The record book shows that he made a relief appearance in 1969, when he won 24 games. And he fanned seven consecutive men in relief back in 1965 to tie an American League record. McLain made just one relief appearance for the Senators in 1971.

Is McLain still psychologically tough enough to bear down and concentrate? What is the real health status of a pitcher who depends increasingly on deep cortisone shots in his shoulder, and who on occasion must wear an elastic back support, and who is known to require muscle relaxers to alleviate neck and back problems?

And, more importantly, has McLain learned any lessons from all his past misadventures? Well, the day after his trade to Oakland he accepted delivery of a brand-new airplane, a twin-engine Aero Commander, and, within a week, he invited reporter Russ White to join him on a hop to Las Vegas for a quick betting spree. White declined, but Denny made the trip and bragged to White that he had been a big winner in Vegas.

Flamboyant Denny, who during his salad days drove fancy cars on a complimentary basis, was renting a red Volkswagen for $1 a day at the A's spring training camp in Arizona. And people who had extended Denny credit *after* his bankruptcy were hounding him for money.

The Tigers and Commissioner Bowie Kuhn had been hopeful of getting Denny straightened away financially. The club was well aware that McLain was having trouble handling his money. He had borrowed $46,000 in advance salary from the club in October of 1969. A half year later, when Denny filed for bankruptcy, he had repaid $6,613 to the Tigers. The club was among those unsecured creditors in Denny's bankruptcy suit, and the Tigers were claiming that Denny owed them $39,386.17.

After the 1969 season, the Tigers gave McLain a three-year contract calling for $75,000 per season and advised him to sign up with Mark McCormack's Cleveland-based firm which handles the business and financial dealings of many professional sports stars. Denny did sign up with McCormack, but he refused to follow the firm's advice. Dick Schafrath, who played tackle for the Cleveland Browns for thirteen years, is now associated with Mark McCormack. Schafrath recently told me that they gave up trying to handle Denny's business affairs, calling it "hopeless."

It staggers the imagination when one considers the amount of money McLain has earned and spent. In 1968, when the Tigers won the World Series and McLain won 31 games, his total earnings were $137,611. He made $64,000 in salary from the Tigers, $11,000 in bonuses from the club, and $62,611 from endorsements, entertainment, and other outside considerations. In 1969, Denny earned $72,000 in salary from the club and $43,700 from outside activities for a total of $115,700. McLain had earned $253,311 in those two years, but he spent the money, and when he filed for bankruptcy, claims totaling $400,942.74 in unsecured debts were made against him.

To add to Denny's troubles, he was being sued in seven separate court cases from Florida to Michigan. They included a suit charging breach of contract of an airport lease, one for allegedly violating a preincorporation agreement with a ski resort promotion firm, and one for damaging a building.

Judgments were entered against McLain for not paying two separate flying agencies, for failure to meet payments on a bank promissary note, and in favor of a utilities company in Michigan.

McLain's creditors ran the gamut from airport flying services in a number of cities, to hotels, home improvement services, women's dress shops, banks, hotels, power companies, oil companies, telephone companies, department stores, doctors, hospitals, and lawyers.

Denny lost most of his personal assets in the bankruptcy proceedings which were completed early in 1972. He was able to retain his house in Lakeland, Florida, because it was not in his name and could not be attached by claimants. At the time the bankruptcy proceedings started, Denny still owed $33,341 on the house, which will remain in the name of Scott Kelly until completely paid or resold. Kelly is the man who sold the house to McLain.

In Washington, Bob Short had tried to help Denny get straightened away financially by prorating his salary over a twelve-month period. Baseball players are normally paid only during the six-month season, with pay checks every two weeks.

Denny spent most of his time in the days following the trade bad-mouthing Ted Williams. He should have been concerned with running off some suet, as he reported to the A's camp in Arizona weighing 218 pounds, the heaviest of his career. McLain pitched in three spring training games and was blasted. He blamed his fat 18.2 earned-run average and lack of success on the fact that he contracted the flu shortly after arriving in Arizona.

Once the regular season started, Denny performed a little better but only for a brief period of time. He beat Kansas City, 3 to 2, in his first start, but went just seven innings and permitted eight hits. In his next start, he was beaten by the

Yankees, 4 to 2, on a three-run homer by weak-hitting Gene Michael. Denny was touched for five hits and walked three men in four innings.

Things were not going to get any better. Oakland manager Dick Williams had seen enough. He yanked McLain out of the starting rotation, saying, "McLain hasn't shown me anything and I don't think Denny can help any team the way he is pitching." In five starts, McLain had failed to go the distance, had allowed 32 hits, 17 runs and 8 walks in 22 innings, and had a gaudy ERA of 6.14. The A's manager added, "The figures speak for themselves, McLain doesn't have the velocity he used to have." Dick Williams hinted that McLain would be placed on waivers. After Oakland tried to trade Denny to the other 23 clubs and found no takers, Denny was farmed to Birmingham of the Class AA Southern League. Not to Class AAA Iowa in the American Association, but to a lower classification.

When Denny was demoted, he had his usual supply of alibis regarding his pitching ineffectiveness. He pointed out that he missed one start because of a snowstorm in Minnesota and missed another when he had to fly back to Walnut Creek, California, to be with his wife, Sharyn, who was having complications in pregnancy. (The McLain marriage had been on the rocks in the winter, but the prospects of another baby brought them back together.)

Denny claimed that he was in a weakened condition because of a reaction from diuretic pills which he had been taking for some time before joining the Oakland A's. The A's team physician, Dr. Charles Hudson, said that the pills caused some weight loss along with loss of fluid. Additionally, the drug allowed the kidneys to lose some important chemicals, including potassium.

A check with Rangers team physician Dr. George Resta and Rangers team trainer Bill Ziegler revealed that neither had issued any diuretic pills to McLain. Dr. Resta stated, "If McLain was taking diuretic pills, he was getting them from another source." I mentioned to Dr. Resta that Denny had received another cortisone shot after his first start on April 18. Resta replied, "That is a very dangerous thing for McLain to do. He took cortisone earlier in the spring at Pompano Beach. The body will stand only so much cortisone and Denny had already had too much. He is becoming dependent upon the drug. No one should shoot him with any more cortisone." Dr. Resta tried to discourage McLain from taking cortisone during the 1971 season, but it was useless.

Resta was one of the best needle men in sports and one of the doctors who pioneered the use of cortisone on athletes. And I believed Resta when he said that the drug must be used judiciously.

Denny threatened to quit the game rather than report to Birmingham. And the A's were hoping that McLain would retire. That would have kept the club from paying Denny almost $40,000 of his annual $75,000 salary. Denny even claims that A's owner Charley Finley offered him a $25,000 cash settlement if he would retire, only to renege when he started to accept the offer. After mulling it over, Denny decided that Birmingham wouldn't be so bad after all. It might be ego-busting and insulting to have to hit the long-bus-ride and hamburger-joint trail in the low minors, but, as Denny put it, "It was a matter of eating."

Despite the fact that Denny was getting racked up in Class AA ball, he continued to be his fun-loving self and led his minor-league teammates in silly trivia games designed to pass the time on long bus trips.

In the next few weeks, Denny looked better in some games, but in others he was blasted. After spending six weeks with Birmingham, McLain felt that he was ready to return to the majors. He said, "They sent me down to get

my arm in shape, and I'm ready to go back to Oakland."
So after a 3–1 loss on June 20, Denny jumped the Birmingham club and flew to Oakland to have it out with the A's
regarding his future. When he arrived in Oakland and
talked with A's manager Dick Williams, what he learned
was that he didn't figure in the A's plans. Despite the fact
that the A's had an open spot on their roster, Dick Williams told Denny that he had five starters and needed
only a left-handed reliever. The handwriting on the wall
at last was clear to McLain. The A's didn't want him.
McLain flew back to Birmingham.

Then came the happy news that Oakland was trading
McLain to Atlanta in a deal which saw aging first baseman
Orlando Cepeda go to the A's. Cepeda was in the Braves dog
house, so it was a case of two clubs unloading players they
didn't want.

Despite posting a record of 3 wins and 3 losses with a fat
earned-run average of 6.32 in his stay at Birmingham, Denny
stated, "I'm 100 percent armwise, and my weight's good. I
just want to prove that I can pitch again. The deal is super.
This is a blessing."

McLain made his first appearance for the Braves before
a big Fourth of July crowd of 50,597 fans in Atlanta. The
crowd, hoping the former Cy Young Award winner could
return to his winning ways, gave him a standing ovation
when he went out to the mound to start the game against the
Chicago Cubs. Denny was to describe that ovation after the
game: "I've never experienced anything like that. It was
unbelievable. I was so high in the first inning I could have
gotten the saints in heaven out."

Denny didn't win or lose the game. He went seven innings and gave up seven hits, and the score between the
Braves and Cubs was tied at 3–3 when the game was rained
out. It was an encouraging debut for Denny. He said, "I had

good velocity tonight. I've got myself in super shape and I think I could pitch forever."

But, it didn't take Denny and the Braves long to realize that his Atlanta debut was misleading. Denny finished the season with an unimpressive record of 3 wins and 5 losses with a fat earned-run average of 6.50. In his half season at Atlanta, he completed just two games and allowed 60 hits in the 54 innings that he pitched.

At least Denny was consistent in 1972. His ERA was over six runs at Oakland, Birmingham, and Atlanta. What a decline for a former Cy Young winner. One and 2 at Oakland with a 6.14 ERA; 3 and 3 at Birmingham with a 6.32 ERA; and 3 and 5 at Atlanta with a 6.50 ERA. McLain had the highest earned-run average of any pitcher in the National League who was involved in at least eight decisions.

What was the reason for the fall of Denny McLain? Was it too much cortisone? Did he burn himself out in those big years of 1968 and 1969 when he pitched the staggering total of 336 and 325 innings respectively? Did Denny's off-the-field escapades and problems prevent him from giving his best on the field? Or did Denny simply lack the mental and physical dedication necessary to keep a pitcher on top in a very competitive business? No one can say for sure. But one thing is for sure. Denny had a lot of laughs along the way and hurt a lot of people in the process. Sadly enough, the one person he hurt more than anyone else was himself.

As late as June, 1972, Denny was still hurting himself off the field. The Associated Press reported that instead of staying with his Birmingham teammates at their modest motel, Denny joined with former major-leaguer Hawk Harrelson in accepting a complimentary $75 suite and gourmet dinners at the plush Savannah Inn and Country Club. The generous host was Lou Rosanova, who turned out to be Lou (The Tailor) Rosanova of Chicago gangster fame.

The Braves did some trading over the winter, and it appears they strengthened the pitching staff a great deal, perhaps making it unlikely that Denny will do much pitching in 1973 if he even makes the club.

When Denny was traded to the Senators, he stated that he "had made enough misjudgments to last a lifetime." But, apparently, he had not exhausted his supply.

THE GENTLE GIANT

Every time the 6 foot-7, 285-pound giant came to the plate that cool Indian Summer evening, the crowd rumbled in nervous anticipation. The 14,460 mourners, kids, scene-seekers, and sentimentalists who came together at Kennedy Stadium on September 30, 1971, to celebrate the last event in seventy-one continuous years of American League baseball were all united in the hope that this bigger-than-lifesize Paul Bunyan of a man would punctuate the Baseball Era in Washington with an exclamation point . . . and hit a home run!

Even on the last-place Senators, Frank Howard had continued to be a solid, fan-buzzing attraction in Washington. Though his figures going into that last game were not as sensational as those of his most productive years, he still had 83 runs batted in, 26 home runs, and .279 average. In seven years in Washington he had bloomed into a superstar and become the Senators all-time homer-hitter with a total of 237. He had taken the side of the Washington fans in the controversy over moving the club, and the fans loved him for it. So every time he came to bat that final night of baseball in Washington, the crowd gave him a nervous ovation, ree-nacting collectively, perhaps, the old American classic of "Casey at the Bat."

Frank's first time up, he walked on four straight pitches, and his second time at bat, he popped out to the infield. Finally, in the sixth inning, Frank led off and New York pitcher Mike Kekich did his best to help Howard consecrate himself forever in the history of baseball in the nation's capi-tal. Kekich, a hard-throwing lefty, drilled two straight fast balls, the kind of pitch that Howard prefers. But Frank, in his intense ache to give the crowd this last thrill with a home run, couldn't handle either pitch. It seemed apparent that Kekich was grooving the ball in an effort to help Hondo get the much-wanted home run. This is a practice frowned upon in baseball, regardless of the situation. I couldn't help but think back to the time that Denny McLain grooved a fat pitch for Mickey Mantle's 535th home run, moving him ahead of Jimmy Foxx into third place on the all-time home-run list. But time seemed to be running out on Howard in his effort to give Washington a final homer. The pressure was bearing down on the big right-hander.

Kekich threw another fat straight fast ball when—whooosh! Howard made *partial* contact and rifled a line drive onto the bullpen roof in left field for a home run that Howard later said was his biggest thrill in sports. Howard circled the bases and for the first time in his seven years in Washington he tipped his hat to the crowd. Twice he came back out of the dugout and blew kisses at the crowd. Finally he threw his batting helmet into the stands.

There was good reason for Howard's not tipping his hat before. Washington fans had been known to boo him unmercifully, especially early in his career. The booing had been less frequent in recent years, when Howard developed into a superstar, but Frank had vowed that he would never give the boo birds the satisfaction of seeing him tip his cap after a home run. And he had kept that promise to himself until that blast turned Howard into an emotional giant, crying giant-sized tears of happiness and sadness.

In the ninth inning, after Washington came from behind to lead New York, 7–5, fans stormed the field with two outs and the Senators had to forfeit. But, happily, Frank's homer is still in the record books.

But never mind. "This wasn't my game or the team's game tonight," Howard said afterwards, puffing his postgame stogie. "It was their game. They're the greatest fans in the world, and I ain't kidding."

Howard had good reason to resent his forced removal, as a ballplayer, from Washington. He had arrived in D.C. in 1965 from the Dodgers. Howard had spent five more or less fitful years in one of Walter Alston's platoon patterns after being signed for a $108,000 bonus out of Ohio State, where he was a star basketball and baseball player. After hitting 23 home runs, playing just part-time but good enough to earn the Rookie of the Year award in 1960, Howard became more and more restless with the Dodgers and welcomed the trade to Washington, where he easily fell into the role of a big man in a city of big men. "I had my best years there, made most of my money and a lot of friends," he said later. "You can't turn your back on things like that without regrets."

Indeed, they were great years. Besides hitting 237 homers during that time, the biggest man to ever play in the major leagues also made some reputations as an all-time eater and drinker, as well as a gentle and patient idol for the kids. Though he was listed as 285 (and Williams wanted him at 280 or less), Frank actually displayed 302 pounds in a surprise weigh-in at the close of the 1970 season. Frank's weight seemed to be the source of what little trouble there was between Howard and Williams. Ted was insistent that Hondo keep the weight down and kept a close watch on the big man's weight chart. In the winter of 1970, and again in 1971, Williams let it be known publicly that he was concerned about Howard's weight. Williams told me that he did this to put emphasis on the situation and to issue a public challenge to Howard to keep the weight down in the off season.

Frank would usually report to spring training several pounds overweight, and he would punish himself to take the weight off. His training procedures at Pompano Beach were legendary around the league. Frank would strap ankle weights around both ankles and put lead insoles in his shoes for his workouts. And coach George Susce would be unmerciful as he put Howard through the paces. Frank would often take off ten pounds in one of those workouts, and surely must have gained some of it back when he would stop off for several beers on the way to a health club for a steambath.

Shortstop Eddie Brinkman, a close friend of Howard, used to claim that Frank ate so much it embarrassed him to do it in public. He often ate in his hotel room. Howard would often eat three normal full-course dinners. The people in room service must have thought he was having a party every time he ordered. At least once, he asked for beer by the case in front of Williams when the players were checking into a hotel. That was his indirect protest against Williams' three-beer limit on plane flights, a real sacrifice for Howard.

Despite his capacity to ingest great quantities of food and drink, Howard had no digestion problems. That, says Howard, is a problem that comes with old age. Therefore, it scared the big man in the winter of 1970 at his Green Bay home when he began moaning and groaning about his stomach after a drinking and eating bout with Ed Brinkman and Tim Cullen. Howard continued to get sicker and sicker until finally he asked his wife to call a priest! It turned out that his appendix almost burst, but they operated in time.

Just after the 1971 season, Howard had surgery of a more planned nature. Frank, the father of six kids, underwent a vasectomy.

It's not unusual for parents to name their babies after sports stars. Frank was so honored a number of times in the Washington area. I'll never forget the time I received a wire just before a game against the Orioles in Baltimore. It was from the proud parents of a son born earlier in the day, and they requested that I inform Frank that the baby was being named after him, and would he please hit a home run that night in honor of the infant. I took the wire down to the clubhouse, and Frank broke into a big grin and said, "I'll bust a gut trying to hit one tonight for that kid." I told my listeners about the wire, and I'm sure many people were happy when Hondo unloaded a home run in that game.

Ted Williams often opined that Howard hit the ball harder, and longer, than anyone else who ever played the game. "Mantle and Jimmy Foxx hit it hard," Williams would say, "but you're the strongest guy I've ever seen play this game. I'd have hit a thousand home runs if I'd been as strong as you."

Almost as soon as the two legendary hitters met in Pompano Beach that first spring training, Ted was trying to talk Howard into taking more pitches, being patient for the eventual good pitch.

"I think I can help you," Williams told Howard the first time they met in spring of 1969. "You know, you're the only guy in history of baseball, the only one I've heard of, who ever hit 44 home runs like you did last season and only got something like 50 walks. You should get a hundred walks every year."

"Ted," Howard began in his foghorn voice, "I know that my theory of hitting is certainly in sharp contrast with yours. . . ."

"I know you," Williams exploded. "I've watched you. You're as strong as a bull. But you don't do much thinking up there at that plate. You swing at everything."

Howard smiled. He said later, "When a guy you've never met before tells you things that you know are true about yourself, you have to admit he has a pretty good idea what is going on."

"You can afford to spot a pitcher a strike if it's not the pitch you want," Williams continued, his voice rising now with hitter's-fever. "Spot him *two* strikes if you have to. Sooner or later he has got to give you a pitch that you can handle, in the good hitting zone."

"Sure," growled Howard. "But when you got your pitch, Ted, the one you could handle, you did something with it. Maybe you didn't get a base hit, but you hit it sharply. Me, I don't make that much contact. I have always figured I have got to take three good cuts if I am going to hit the ball hard once."

Williams roared back at Howard, "That's because you're not a disciplined hitter. If you do it my way, I guarantee you'll make more contact, because you will be getting a better ball to hit 90 to 95 percent of the time."

Howard did try it Ted's way, and then decided to spot the pitcher at least one strike, saying, "I just don't feel I make contact often enough that I can afford to spot him two strikes." That season Howard hit 48 home runs and drove in 111 runs, the best record of his career. He also walked 102 times, and struck out less than 100 for the first time in his career.

But Frank also hit them pretty far too. At Kennedy Stadium some of his more gargantuan belts were recorded by white seats painted where the ball landed. The upper deck of the stadium was pockmarked with white. In fact, Howard is the only player to reach the upper deck in dead centerfield in Washington, accomplishing it twice. Among the most memorable homers he ever hit was one against Mickey Lolich at Detroit on May 18, 1968. That blast hit atop the left-field *roof* at Tiger Stadium and bounded out of the park. Without a doubt, his most spectacular hitting exhibition came in 1968 when he connected for 10 home runs in 20 times at bat over six games, a spree that should be recorded as perhaps the greatest exhibition of power in baseball history. Howard hit .600 with 12 hits (the others, a single and double) and batted in 17 runs.

There will always be debates about the hardest ball every hit by Frank Howard. The hardest ball I saw him hit in Kennedy Stadium in three years came in 1971 when he hit a pitch into the exit-way, deep in the upper deck of left field.

Howard hit two of his longest home runs the same day, July 5, 1969, at Fenway Park in Boston. In the first game of a doubleheader, Hondo hit a fantastic shot off Ray Jarvis which cleared the high left-field wall, the high netting atop the wall, and cleared Lansdowne Street in back of the wall. Then in the second game of the doubleheader, Howard hit another gigantic homer off Bill Lee, and that one went over the wall, net, and street at about the same spot.

Mickey Mantle, who has hit some tape-measure home runs of his own, claims that Howard hit the hardest ball he has ever seen hit, in the first game of the 1963 World Series when the Yankees played the Dodgers. Howard blasted a Whitey Ford fast ball off the center-field wall in Yankee Stadium, and Frank was held to a double. Mantle has told Howard that that screaming line drive was the hardest ball he ever saw anyone hit. In game number four of that same World Series, the only one in Frank's career, he helped the Dodgers complete a sweep of the Yankees with a tape-measure homer. Howard sent a Whitey Ford pitch into the upper deck of left field at Dodger Stadium, marking the first time that anyone had hit a fair ball into the second tier of the Dodger Stadium grandstand.

Big Frank took a lot of abuse about his fielding. However, one can't expect a 285-pounder to be the most graceful, and Frank did have good hands. What he could get to in the outfield, he would catch. His arm was not strong when he played with the Senators, but I'm told that he had a good arm when he came up to the majors, only to hurt it. Consequently, many clubs elected to take an extra base on Howard. It sometimes backfired. I remember a game in 1970 when Howard threw out two men who were attempting to stretch singles into doubles.

Frank's speed was not the best, but his hustle was fantastic. He would set a great example for the kids by giving all he had, all of the time. He would thrill at least one or two crowds a season by stealing a base, an unforgettable sight. He has never stolen more than 3 bases in any one season in his entire professional career.

Another strange sight was Frank Howard putting down a bunt. This would happen a couple of times a year when the Senators were trailing by more than one run in the last inning and had no base runners. Frank knew that in that situation, a home run was not enough, and what the club needed was base runners. And when Frank did attempt the bunt, the third baseman was usually playing him so deep that he could beat it out.

Frank Howard is an unselfish ballplayer who is great to have on a team. In his own sort of way, he was the inspirational leader of the Senators. He was unpretentious with everyone, and great to the new kids on the club. When he arrived in spring training, he would seek out the youngsters who were in camp for the first time, would go up to them, stick out a huge hand, and say, "Hi, I'm Frank Howard." And if a rookie made the team, Frank would take him out to dinner a few times on the road trips.

It was only natural, because of Howard's titanic size, that he would be stuck with many nicknames. His favorite and the one used by his teammates, friends, and most fans is Hondo (from the movie *Hondo*). Others are the Gentle Giant, Jolly Green Giant, Bigun, the Washington Monument, and one that came from a newspaper contest, the Capital Punisher.

The adjective "gentle" was often used to describe Howard. Extremely popular with his teammates, he often received a lot of good-natured kidding. Some teammates like Eddie Brinkman and Denny McLain would call him "freak," and less complimentary names.

Frank never lost his enthusiasm and spirit. After a dozen years in the pros, he would lead the Senators in their victory yells following a win. Hondo liked to take his dental bridge out when he led the yells, which gave him the appearance of being something from outer space.

Despite Howard's gentle nature, he could lose his temper. I saw him mad only a few times. Once in Oakland during the 1969 season, he became involved in an altercation with umpire Ron Luciano over ball and strike calls. Frank screamed at Luciano until the latter threw him out of the game, marking the first time he had been ejected in the majors. Both Howard and Luciano were hot in their dispute, and the earth might have trembled had they tangled. Luciano, a former All America tackle at Syracuse, weighed 260 and was not much smaller than Frank.

Frank got mad as the devil twice during the 1970 season. Once was in Baltimore, when the umpires called a long drive down the left-field line foul. Hondo was positive that the ball was fair, and he really let off some steam. The other occasion that season was in Yankee Stadium. Williams had not started him against the Yankees, and that had upset Frank. And when Epstein, who was having a bad game, took himself out of the lineup, claiming some minor ailment, that made Frank even hotter. After the game, Howard blew off steam by throwing around some clubhouse furniture.

Howard had to be miserable with frustration during the 1972 season when the Rangers were platooning him, but he didn't show it in public. Not until the day he was being sold to the Tigers did he display his emotions. After striking out in a game at Yankee Stadium, he returned to the dugout and threw his batting helmet the length of the dugout. I'm sure Frank was irritated that news of his impending sale was in the papers before he was being told, and also that he was coming a day too late for him to be eligible for the playoffs and World Series. Williams said that he "had never seen Frank so mad."

Except for some hassles about sitting out now and then, Howard and Williams got along well. Two legendary hitters from different epochs, they respected each other and sometimes kidded one another. I remember one time in the 1969 season when Ted took a few swings and some of the coaches were getting on him. "You can't hit anymore," someone said.

"What do you mean, I can't hit?" Williams yelled, his face settling into a determined fix. So he began to swing for the fence in right field, but a stiff wind was blowing in. His best shots fell short.

"Skip," yelled Howard, "this ball park is too big for you. You can't reach those fences." Howard was proud of the fact that he had hit home runs in 23 major-league parks in *both* leagues, a feat that Williams, naturally, never had a chance to match.

"CAN'T REACH THOSE FENCES?" Williams shouted

back. "We'll see about *that!*" He was grinning now squarely at Howard. "I bet you that in twenty swings I hit one over."

"You won't reach it in thirty swings," Howard laughed.

"OHHHHHH, I won't?" he yelled.

"In fact, I don't think you can pull anymore, Skip."

"What! What? I can't pull anymore? We'll *see* if I can't pull the ball anymore!"

Williams dug in, swung and swung, huffed and puffed and on the twenty-fifth swing he poked one over the fence.

Things weren't always so happy in the player-to-manager relationship, although Howard always emphasized (in public anyway) that Williams had been fair with him.

Howard is a good competitor and Williams respected that. Ted would ask Howard if he'd like to rest the final inning in a game that was out of reach one way or the other, but Howard would invariably say, "No I'd like to stay in there, Skip, because I might get one more time at bat." Williams even put Howard into the leadoff spot in the final game of 1969 so that the big guy might get an extra chance to go ahead of Harmon Killebrew in the home run race. He didn't, and Frank finished one home run behind Killebrew, who had 49.

Frank and the other Senators players became more and more critical of Ted as a manager during Williams' third year. But Frank kept his feelings pretty much to himself and to his teammates. He was never one to criticize the manager openly, and did not give sensational statements to the press. Frank had a feeling that a good percentage of the media people in Washington had not been fair in their coverage of the Senators down through the years. He felt that much of the coverage had been negative, and often told me, "Look, we are major-leaguers, and the media should give us major-league treatment."

So with his track record in mind, it was a little out of character for Frank when he started speaking his mind toward the end of the season. Williams was resting him more and more toward the end of the 1971 season, to the frustration of Howard, and the big man was very upset that Short had gained approval to move the club to Texas.

I asked Frank if he wanted to appear on my sports talk show as soon as the season was over, and he said, "Yes, I'd be happy to. Maybe it's time that some things were said that should be said," he added. Hondo hit the home run in that sad finale and was the toast of the town. So it was no surprise when Fran O'Brien's restaurant was jam-packed for Frank's appearance on my show.

Frank was not outright critical of Williams on my program, but he did say that he really hadn't gotten to know the man in three seasons. He also said that he didn't believe in platooning and had been very unhappy with the Dodgers under Walter Alston because he had been platooned. He sided with those who were critical of Williams and his "four-day-rest" pitching rotation. Hondo also revealed on my program that he would like to be a manager or coach when his playing career was finished. And he was outspoken in his criticism of Short for moving the club to Texas and of the American League club owners for permitting the move. Hondo went on to say that he "would have to give it serious thought before deciding if he would go to Texas with the club."

He came right out on my show and said that he would like to be traded. He listed Boston, Detroit, and Milwaukee as his sequence of preference for a trade.

I feel sure that Short and Williams were not happy with some of the things Frank said on the show. Williams doesn't like one of his players to be second-guessing his policies of platooning and pitching rotation, and some managers feel uncomfortable when they learn that they have players who want to become or can become managers.

One thing is for sure. Short didn't like someone to whom

he was paying $120,000 to publicly criticize him, and he didn't like his players to state openly that they wanted to be traded.

So their reaction to some of Frank's remarks, coupled with the fact that Short and Howard had their longest and most bitter salary disputes in the upcoming months, really meant that the Texas Rangers and Frank Howard were in for some bad relations. Hondo missed all of spring training because of his holdout. And then when he finally did agree to terms at $120,000, the same salary he had made the season before, the player strike came along and prevented him from getting into shape. Once the strike was resolved, Frank was not ready to play. Williams made plans to platoon him. Ted sat down with Howard at the start of the season and told him, "I know you probably won't like this, but we are stepping up our youth movement, and you won't be seeing action every day."

Frank wound up being sold to the Detroit Tigers with only one month remaining in the season. Short vows that he received nothing more than the $20,000 waiver price, even though many people doubt it.

I'm sure that Howard was plenty happy to leave Short, Williams, and the losing Texas Ranger organization. After all, the Tigers were contending, were a great baseball organization, and Tiger Stadium would be Frank's dream for a home park. And Frank would be rejoining some old teammates in Eddie Brinkman, Aurelio Rodriguez, and Joe Coleman. Howard made the switch from Texas to Detroit like the swell guy that he is. He didn't bad-mouth Short or Williams.

Howard was Detroit's first baseman against left-handers, a platoon job, and he became the team's chief rooter in its drive to the American League East title.

"Sure, for the last month this year I sat and it was a terrific experience," he told Russ White the night Detroit clinched the Eastern Division title. "But I wouldn't want this type of thing for a whole season, especially now. I really think I can still go for a full year. This is what frustrated me so in Texas. I should have played more often with that team. I just can't say how frustrating an ordeal it was.

"At the same time I can't blame Ted Williams for what he did. I tried to understand the man's own frustrations. I was with him four years. He had no easy time, for the most part. It was no surprise he finally said last week that that was all he wanted."

Tigers manager Billy Martin appreciated the part Howard played in the Tigers winning the American League Eastern Division Pennant, so much, in fact, that he requested permission from the playoff opponent, the Oakland A's, and the American League, that Frank be granted permission to play in the playoffs. The request was denied, but Hondo was permitted to suit up and cheer his teammates on. When the regular Detroit first-base coach, Dick Tracewski, an old Dodger teammate, was called back home to Pennsylvania because of illness in the family, Howard became the Tigers first-base coach. And in the deciding game, Frank let his spirit boil over in protesting a call at first base by umpire John Rice and was ejected from the game. Hondo said about umpire John Rice, "Rice gave the play a lackadaisical effort. The players bust their butts and the umpires should too."

The Tigers saw something in Howard they liked. They decided to keep him for the 1973 season, and Billy Martin plans to platoon him as the designated pinch hitter for the pitcher. The Tigers did feel that Hondo should play for considerably less than his $120,000 salary of 1972. Baseball rules don't allow more than a 20 percent salary cut unless the player agrees and special permission is given by the Commissioner's office. That is what happened in Howard's case for 1973, as he agreed to play for $70,000, and Bowie Kuhn approved the contract.

The American League decision to use the designated

pinch hitter for pitchers starting with the 1973 season is expected to prolong the careers of aging players like Frank Howard. They will no longer have to play in the field, but will be able to bat several times in a game.

When I called Frank to chat during the off season, he expressed delight with the Tigers organization and inquired about the prospect of baseball returning to Washington. When I told him that it would return, it was just a matter of time, he blurted out, "I tell you, if they do get a club back and need a nearsighted first base coach, I'm available." (Frank wears fairly strong glasses.) He went on to say that baseball could be a big success in Washington.

"If I had my say in the matter—and this is the truth—I'd get a plot of land out off the beltway and build me this park, sort of like Fenway Park," he said. "Small, with 28,000 seats, just enough to make it tough to get tickets. The people in Washington would love sitting right close to one another and being able to reach out and touch the players. I'd build the fences in close so there would be plenty of home runs. Everyone likes to see the home-run hitters. I'm just sure a team would be successful there . . . very sure." It was apparent that a good bit of Frank's big heart is still back in the nation's capital.

Frank will never have any serious money worries. He has invested his money wisely and deals in real estate development in the off season. As a matter of fact, that November day when I spoke with him, he was getting ready to attend a meeting about plans to open a new supermarket.

Much of the material wealth that Frank Howard enjoys can be traced to his success in Washington. He developed from an average major-league player to a superstar during his days with the Senators. His last four years in Washington, he commanded a total of $400,000 in salary, had averaged 40 home runs per season, had made the All Star game each of those years, and won the hearts of Washington. In the eyes of most Washingtonians, Frank Howard is the biggest man to play in the major leagues in more ways than one.

9

THE GREAT ESCAPE

Things were getting worse for the thirty-three-year-old portrait painter who was trying to make a comeback in baseball. Curt Flood had only three hits during his first 20 times at bat, two of them bunts, and he had not played regularly since the fifth game of the season. Flood's business, a chain of photographic studios in St. Louis, had collapsed into financial ruin. Creditors were suing him. He was subpoenaed in a suit for back alimony. Two days earlier, Flood suddenly settled accounts with Fred Baxter, the Senators clubhouse-equipment man. Baxter thought it was strange at the time, but when Flood showed up the next night, Baxter forgot it.

On April 27, 1971 Flood did not show up. He had checked out of the Anthony House Hotel in the middle of one of Washington's swinging downtown sections, where he had been accustomed to nursing his vodka martinis beginning at noon and wooing his women at all hours.

This night he was supposed to start, in his new limited platoon duty, against Minnesota's left-hander Tom Hall. Two hours before the game, however, Flood was flying to New York to make connections at Kennedy Airport for a flight to Lisbon and then to Barcelona, Spain.

Curt Flood was finished as a baseball player. He was ruined as a businessman. He had no family, and now no team. From Kennedy Airport, he sent a telegram to Bob Short. It read, "I tried. A year and a half is too much. Very severe personal problems are mounting every day. Thanks for your confidence and understanding."

There was still time to stop him, Short thought. He contacted Bowie Kuhn's office. Joe Reichler of the commissioner's office stormed out to Kennedy Airport and managed to board the plane bound for the Iberian Peninsula, and find Flood. He pleaded with Flood to return to the Senators. "I can't man," Flood told Reichler. "I'd go crazy."

That was the end of Curt Flood, except for his $3.75 million suit against baseball.

The idea to sign Flood first hit Short during the spring 1969 meeting of baseball in Montreal after the commissioner's lawyer had counseled the group of owners that the cost of defending the Flood suit could run as high as a million dollars. And the owners would have to pay it. The story goes that when he was nineteen, Flood got a message in Venezuela, where he was playing winter ball, that he had been traded from Cincinnati to St. Louis. The trade shocked him and, according to the Players Association director, Marvin Miller, Flood vowed that he would never allow baseball to do that to him again. So when Flood, at the time a $90,000-a-year superstar with twelve years as a major-leaguer and a member of the three-time-pennant-winning Cardinals, heard about being traded to Philadelphia before the 1969 season, he refused to report and decided to challenge the legality of the reserve clause instead. The clause binds a player to a team *for life* thanks to a 1922 Supreme Court decision handed down by Justice Oliver Wendell Holmes stating that since baseball was essentially a sport and not a business, and therefore exempt from normal anti-trust laws. Flood made this move at considerable personal expense. Philadelphia had offered him a $90,000 salary plus $8,000 in expenses.

In the owners' meeting, Short's line of logic was obviously aimed at pricking Philadelphia general manager and vice-president John Quinn. "If they're the only ones who have a right to sign him, maybe they ought to be the only ones who should pay for not being able to sign him," Short told the group, referring to the expenses of the lawsuit.

After the meeting, Quinn came over to ask Short, not wholly without sarcasm, whether he thought he could sign him. The answer came short and quick.

"Yes."

From that moment, Short was obsessed with the idea he could bring Flood back to baseball, just as he did Williams. "Hell," he boomed, "here's a guy who can do everything: hit, field, run. A natural. And I've got *vacancies*. I've got guys who can't do anything."

When the two baseball leagues met again in joint session that summer, Short pursued the matter with Quinn, stressing the fact that since there was no chance that Flood would ever play for them, anything they could get would be better than nothing. Short offered Quinn one player, Greg Goossen, just for the right to talk to Flood. He would send three more players if he could sign him.

There were plenty of people who felt that Goossen couldn't run, couldn't throw and couldn't hit. But what did the Phillies have to lose? Goossen could play somewhere in the minor-league system, so Quinn said to Short, "Go ahead and talk with Flood."

As soon as he could find Flood, who was painting portraits and trying to make a go of a restaurant-lounge in Copenhagen, Short put through a trans-oceanic call.

"Listen," Short said, after he had introduced himself, "I know you don't intend to play again, but don't say anything more until I talk to you." And then he talked some more.

"Listen," he told Flood, "you've won the battle. The war can continue without you. Do you have to spill all your blood? You've given up $100,000. If there's a cause you're fighting for, the abolition or modification of the reserve clause, who has done more than you?"

By the second call, Short had Flood talking nostalgia. "I'll tell you something," Flood said. "I'm a professional baseball player, and I've discovered that the purpose of a baseball player's life is to play baseball. I never thought I'd miss it this much. I never realized how much I loved it."

The two men met for the first time face to face in the apartment of Flood's lawyer, Arthur Goldberg, at the Pierre Hotel in New York on Saturday, October 24. Goldberg demanded that any contract with Flood have a special clause stipulating that the signing would not prejudice the lawsuit against baseball. Also, Flood wanted a contract which, in effect, would have removed the ironclad reserve clause and placed the player at the bargaining table as an equal, with protective rights.

"I wish you wouldn't ask me to depart from the standard contract," Short told them. "But if you're asking me would I sign that kind of contract if the commissioner's lawyers told me I could, I certainly would."

There was the catch. Commissioner Bowie Kuhn was not about to approve a contract that broke the laws of baseball.

handed pitcher Fritz Peterson, who had posted a record of
17 wins and 16 losses with an impressive 2.55 ERA. Williams
was ready to make the deal on the spot. But Short didn't
approve, and while Ted was trying to convince Short that the
trade was a good one, the Yankees withdrew the offer. Peterson won 20 games the next season.

The Yankees made another effort to land Epstein in the
fall of 1969 when they offered pitcher Al Downing and outfielder Bill Robinson. Downing had posted a 7–5 record for
the Yankees and had looked good in games against the Senators. Robinson had come to the Yankees from the Braves
after a big press build-up, but he never lived up to expecta-
tions. The Senators said no to this Epstein offer.

Meanwhile, Epstein was saying that he would rather be
traded than be platooned by Williams. The Senators didn't
come close to a deal for Epstein in the spring of 1971, and
Mike was disgruntled. He was quoted in the *Washington Star*
as saying that "the Senators don't have anyone in the front
office capable of making a trade." That statement probably
assured him that there would be a deal. It came later in the
season in the form of a multi-player deal with the Oakland
A's.

The Senators' first major deal of the 1970 season sent popular third baseman Ken McMullen to the California Angels
for third sacker Aurelio Rodriguez and outfielder Rick Reichardt. The trade was announced on April 27 at Kennedy
Stadium. It was exactly 27 days from the time the Angels had
come to the Senators with the proposal.

Trade talk can be initiated many ways. It can be started
by the field manager, coaches, scouts, owners who involve
themselves, and, to the horror of most baseball front-office
people, broadcasters and writers. In this particular case, the
Angels had authorized one of their scouts, Carl Ackerman, to
offer Rodriguez and Reichardt to the Senators for McMullen.

He agreed to a clause protecting the status of the lawsuit. The rest of it, he said, was out of the question.

"Then there's no deal," snapped Marvin Miller, chief counsel for the Players Association, who was, of course, party to the negotiations.

Short told Miller he was being foolish. He said, "If you think about it, you'll see that you've got everything you've asked for." Why insist on having in writing what they already had in fact? "Do you think I'm going through all this to trade him? I'd have to be an idiot."

Flood signed a $110,000 standard contract, because Short gave him a verbal agreement, Flood said later. He quoted Short as saying:

"I promise that I won't trade you. And I guarantee you the full year's pay no matter what happens. And at the end of the year, if we don't agree on terms for the following season, I'll make you a free agent so you can work out a deal with another club. But I can't put any of this in writing. And if anybody says that I agreed to such an arrangement, I'll deny it."

Baseball Commissioner Bowie Kuhn gave his blessings to the Short offer, which stipulated that the Phillies could have Goossen just for the right to negotiate with Flood, and that the Phillies would receive two other players should Flood agree to play for the Senators. Maybe Kuhn was quick to okay the proposal because of the possibility that Flood's return to the game might harm his suit against baseball. Maybe the Commissioner just felt that Flood's return as an active player would be good for the game.

But one thing was wrong with the deal. It is not legal to offer a player to a club for the right to negotiate with a player. Shirley Povich of the *Washington Post* was among the first to point out the rules violation. By this time, Short had already talked with Flood and was making headway in his efforts to lure the controversial centerfielder out of Denmark. So the Goossen offer for the right to negotiate was academic by that time. Commissioner Kuhn ruled that Goossen would simply be a part of the three-player package Short would give the Phillies for Flood.

But there were more complications. Short was offering minor-league first baseman-outfielder Gene Martin and minor-league pitcher Jeff Terpko to complete the trade. Martin was acceptable to the Phillies, but they would accept Terpko only on a conditional basis. After looking at him during spring training and the early part of the season, they wanted the right to return him to the Senators if they so desired. If they returned Terpko, the Phillies wanted the Senators number-one draft choice in the 1971 free-agent draft. The Phillies proposal regarding Terpko was acceptable to Short. He was so excited about the prospect of luring Curt Flood out of retirement that he really didn't care what he had to give. Just think of the possible publicity. This would be a coup comparable to his success in getting Ted Williams to manage the Senators.

Commissioner Bowie Kuhn approved the Phillies' counterproposal regarding Terpko and the Senators number-one draft choice. Only one hitch. It developed that trading a draft choice in baseball was against the rules. It is done frequently in football, but it's a "no no" in baseball. Again, Shirley Povich was among those who pointed out the latest rules violation in the Flood deal between the Senators and Phillies. And he roasted Commissioner Kuhn, owner Short, and general manager Quinn for not knowing the rules, or at least trying to bend the rules.

Bowie Kuhn reconsidered the situation and decided that it was indeed against the rules for Short to give the Phillies their number-one draft choice if the Phillies returned Terpko. After more talks between Quinn and Short, it was decided that should the Phillies return Terpko, the Phillies would have the right to select any Senators player not protected on the Senators major-league roster. In other words, Short was willing to give the Phillies the player of their choice from the Senators minor-league system. The Phillies took a look at Terpko and then returned him to the Senators.

Then the Phillies scouted the Senators minor-league system closely. Philadelphia farm director Paul Owens, who succeeded Quinn as general manager in 1972, told me that the Phillies were looking for pitching. The best pitching prospect in the Senators system not protected on the big-league roster was Roger Quiroga. He'd been the Senators number-one draft choice in the regular phase of the free-agent draft in 1971. So the Phillies wound up getting the number-one choice anyway.

Quiroga had not pitched any professional ball and was only eighteen years old. The Phillies had been high on Quiroga in the draft but didn't get a chance to take him. He is a 6-foot, 185-pound right-hander who was a baseball and basketball star at Ball High School in Galveston, Texas. He commands so much respect from the Phillies that he was invited to the Phillies 1972 major-league spring training camp in Clearwater despite his tender age. He was impressive, but the Phillies knew the youngster needed seasoning. He split his rookie season between Spartanburg of the Western Carolinas League and Pulaski of the Rookie League. and showed great promise, despite unimpressive figures.

Quiroga is a flame-thrower who was the first choice of a number of major-league teams. He was the seventh player picked out of 972 selected in the draft by all major-league clubs.

After the Senators drafted him, they went all out to get his name on a contract. The Senators chief scout, Jack Sheehan, was sent to Quiroga's home in Galveston, Texas.

Sheehan met with young Quiroga, his father, who works for the City of Galveston, and Quiroga's high school coach Albert Choate who played minor-league ball in the Dodgers organization before becoming the baseball coach at Ball High. Sheehan was unsuccessful in getting young Quiroga to agree to terms.

The Senators sent their farm director, Hal Keller, to Galveston four or five times to visit with Quiroga before the Senators signed the eighteen-year-old to a bonus calling for $50,000 in cash and his college expenses of $8,000 to $10,000, depending on the actual costs. Quiroga indicated that he would play professionally right away but wanted to obtain his college degree by attending school in the off season.

Bob Short and the Senators kept the signing of the Quiroga boy top secret. Short was pleading poverty and was in the process of trying to obtain permission to move to greener pastures in Texas. There was also the fear that the Senators might lose young Quiroga to the Phillies as final payment in the Curt Flood deal. Their fears were justified.

So Bob Short quietly lost his $60,000 bonus pitcher to the Phillies to complete the infamous Curt Flood deal.

Williams read Flood's book *The Way It Is* in galleys and was irritated at Curt's public disclosure of his exploits with women and his resentment of authority in general. Short was irate too, and forced Flood to delete the actual wording of their verbal agreement, but Flood went ahead and revealed the substance of the conversation with Short, although he did tone it down. When the book came out, Flood quietly passed out copies to his new teammates, then refused to talk about the book, or to promote it at all which might explain why the book did not make a bigger splash on the sports scene.

Actually, the book was more of an exposé of baseball than was Jim Bouton's *Ball Four*. Commissioner Bowie Kuhn was understandably upset over some of the revelations.

Kuhn may have learned a lesson from Bouton's book. His objections and the resultant publicity helped Jim's book become a best-seller. Kuhn didn't utter a public word about Flood's exposé.

Flood wrote that the baseball player's attaché case contains "a portable dispensary of chemicals for the relief of his occupational discomforts." Then he went on to list: "Potions for sleeplessness, tranquilizers for especially hairy days, and pep pills to transform the tranquilized into a competitive tiger." Flood continued, "I know a superstar who spikes his beer with double bourbons and performs erratically." Adding, "I have known a few dozen other players for whom the sport became a way station to abject alcoholism."

Flood went into great detail about the sex life of major-leaguers and advanced the theory that sex for the baseball player was a necessary tranquilizer. He wrote, "Girls are therapeutic. The ballplayer uses them medicinally, like an apple a day." To the horrors of the baseball Puritans, he went into greater detail. "Of the at least 360 major-league baseball players, managers, coaches, and other glamorously uninformed types away from home during the season, at least 300 are randy as minks." And Flood added, "In whatever stadiums baseball is played, and wherever the players sleep, eat, or socialize, avid women swarm.'

Curt seemed to take pride in revealing his exploits with white women, and hinted that more than one black player had been shipped to the minors for consorting with any female that he chose. Curt didn't make any more friends with the baseball establishment when he added, "All this passed rather quickly. Those most protective of the Image of the Game may have realized that it was impolitic to make a big issue of who was screwing whom. Not with adultery as rampant and widespread as it always had been in major-league life."

Flood had been twice married and twice divorced to the same girl. He was, without a doubt, one of the most unhappy players to wear a uniform in 1971. He seemed to find people and life a bore. At times Flood showed great irritation at being asked by a fan to sign an autograph.

By the time Flood was reporting to the Senators after a year layoff, his case had already been defeated on two occasions. First, after testimony by a veritable Who's Who in baseball, Judge Irving Ben Cooper of the United States District Court in New York City upheld baseball's argument that federal anti-trust laws do not apply to the sport. Judge Cooper did say, however, that he was impressed by Flood's arguments and believed modifications in the reserve system should be achieved through negotiations between the players and owners, without court action. Then a three-judge U.S. Circuit Court of Appeals upheld Judge Cooper's decision. "All they did was hold that it is up to the Supreme Court to overrule the Supreme Court," said Marvin Miller after the decisions. "I think everyone knew it would be difficult for a District Court to overrule the Supreme Court." Shortly afterward, the Supreme Court announced it would hear the Flood case.

Then Flood started the longest spring training of his career. Williams had always been skeptical about Flood's capacity to come back. He told me he had reports that Flood had slowed down before he quit and that he had a weak arm. After an examination of Flood, Senators club physician George Resta concluded that Flood had an "old" thirty-three-year-old body. But Williams rooted for Flood because he remembered how hard it had been for him to come back to baseball twice, the second time when he was thirty-six years old himself.

Flood worked hard during the spring. He started off by pinch-hitting in exhibitions and gradually worked into the lineup without causing any raves. If anything, he caused consternation. "He was polite," wrote Merrell Whittlesey of the *Star*. "But his answers were yes and no. He rarely answered a question with an opinion that would lead to another question. He had room service for most of his meals. He wanted no part of controversy and gave the hello-goodbye treatment to the writers following the American League whom he did not know. He also turned down television interviews with the explanation he was afraid of being misinterpreted."

Jack Mann, who knew Flood from his rookie days thirteen years before, wrote in *Look* magazine: "One of baseball's easiest interviews for a decade, Flood was testy this spring. He would say he was 'amused' at charges of ingratitude after he filed his . . . suit against the reserve clause, but he did not appear amused when he said it."

Flood asked Mann, "As long as he isn't hurting anybody else, why can't a man do his own thing? Why do they care so much?"

On Opening Day Flood appeared in centerfield. In the fifth game of the season, Flood made the last out in the eighth inning and when he looked to the bench for somebody to bring his gloves and glasses, he looked in vain. He was being replaced. Flood did not return to the lineup for almost a week.

"This is no big thing," Williams said at the time. "I told Curt we needed runs and we're not scoring them with him in there. He understands. He'll be back."

"He can still do it," said Short with a forlorn look. "But if he doesn't, I'd still make the same move again."

The day before he split the country, the Senators had a respectable ten win-six loss record. Flood had seven hits in the thirteen games he had played, all singles.

When he took off, infielder Elliott Maddox, Flood's roommate, was just as surprised as everyone else. "I had no indication that he would jump the club," Maddox said. "I knew there were some things on his mind, but he never told me what they were. As for his benching, he told me, 'That's okay, as long as we're winning.'"

Mike Epstein, another moody player, was especially stunned by Flood's disappearance. Flood had told Epstein the previous weekend while they were shagging balls in the outfield that "things are closing in on me." Epstein said he tried to talk Flood out of doing anything serious. "I told him life was like baseball and we all went through slumps," Epstein said.

Short and Williams both publicly invited Flood to return, though I sensed an air of relief in the front office. A rotten season by Flood would not make Short's deal look very good. If Flood jumped the club now, it would save Short $55,000 in salary. It was apparent that Flood was not going to draw people to the park the way he was performing. With Flood's taste for drink and women, and his obvious resentment of baseball authority, there was sure to be a clash with Williams and his rather Puritan attitude toward training rules. So the public statements by Short and Williams describing their disappointment at Flood's departure may well have been so much propaganda.

Finally in June of 1972, eleven months after Flood jumped the Senators, the Supreme Court decided, 5–3, to leave baseball's anti-trust exemptions alone—a reaffirmation of the reserve clause and a resounding put-down of Flood's last attempt to vindicate his mixed-up separation from a life of baseball. Flood's own mismanagement of his personal affairs, plus his panic in Washington, make it difficult to elevate him to the level of a martyr to the baseball status quo, although history may very well bear that out. It is important to point out that Chief Justice Warren F. Burger cast the deciding vote despite "grave reservations" and threw the ball to Con-

gress. "It is time the Congress acted to solve this problem."
In effect, too, three other Justices voting to affirm the exemption cited "positive inaction" by Congress as a primary reason for the Court to keep hands off the precedent set by
former Justice Oliver Wendell Holmes in his famous 1922
decision. However, six Justices did disagree with Justice
Holmes' opinion that baseball was just a game. They affirmed
instead that the sport is indeed an "interstate commerce." So
really they just set the scene for Congressional action. Until
then, though, Flood will stay out of sight in Majorca, writing
another book about the suit.

Some Senators said, by the way, that somehow that
Flood's flight in 1972 killed the Senators as a team. If that was
the case, the club never had much life to begin with.

10

IF YOUR NAME IS IN LIGHTS, WE'LL TAKE YOU

Trade talk is just about the cheapest thing in baseball. There will always be outlandish trade rumors. Some are planted by clubs themselves to shake up certain personnel. Some people in baseball like to keep everyone loose. Some trade rumors are started by writers because they need a story. Many trade rumors are legitimate, even though they may later be denied by officials simply because the club was not successful in making the deal.

The science of trading becomes more complicated and sophisticated every season. Clubs trade for many different reasons: to improve themselves for the present, to improve themselves for the future, to unload high salaries, to get rid of troublemakers, and in some cases as favors to other clubs. There have been many times when players were traded to a contending club for the pennant stretch run, only to have the player go back to the original club after the season. Those mystery trades or loans have had much criticism down through the years but still seem to crop up from time to time.

Ted always did a lot of brain picking to gain information and find out how informed other people were. He catalogued information about players who were discussed—not on paper, but in his keen mind. He grilled everybody with whom he came in contact about players and the game in general. They included players, coaches, managers, club officials, writers, photographers, broadcasters, and umpires. In this way, many people acted as scouts for Ted Williams whether they knew it or not. And he gained the information he wanted in a very discreet manner. If he wanted a person's idea about a pitcher, chances are that he wouldn't come right out and ask about that pitcher but about another pitcher on the club. And, before you knew it, the information that Ted really wanted came out in the conversation.

The same principle applies when a club is engaged in actual trade talks. A smart trader won't come right out and make a proposal involving the player he really wants. He'll make a proposal including someone he doesn't want and maybe the counterproposal from the other club will include the player he is really after. It's similar to selling and negotiating in other businesses. The people with the better brains, superior knowledge, and the slickest technique will make the best baseball trades. The clubs with the better scouts and front-office personnel will likely have the upper hand most of the time, whether it's trading, drafting talent, or signing new talent.

Ted Williams knew that he was working under a severe handicap with the type of baseball organization he had in Washington. Many times Ted would say, "Our front office has no imagination or initiative in proposing trades. They are afraid that they will propose something that Short won't like and, if they do come up with something decent in the way of an idea, it's too late and someone has beaten us to it."

Ted and I often discussed trade situations. He liked me to sit with him on flights because I always had statistics and other baseball data at my fingertips. Many times on a flight, he'd lean over and say, "Would you trade this player for that one?" Many times Ted asked me to look up what so-and-so was batting with, say, Boston. Or find out about this minor-leaguer at Oklahoma City. My opinion probably didn't carry much weight and I don't think I ever changed Ted's idea about anything. I always kept trade talk and proposals strictly confidential. It did hurt me in one way. Short had the idea that I had more influence on Ted than he did, and it got to a point where Short and Burke would blame me when Ted disagreed with them on trades or anything else.

I thought the Denny McLain trade was awful and when Ted told me that Short was ready to give Coleman and Brinkman for McLain, I hollered so loud that Short may have heard me upstairs. Never did I dream that Aurelio Rodriguez would be included in any kind of deal like that. There was more to that trade than meets the eye.

Jim Hannan was a Senators pitcher who was also included in that deal. Jim is a very astute fellow, with degrees from Notre Dame and NYU. He holds a master's degree in finance from NYU and is a very successful stock and bonds broker with Reynolds Securities, Inc. in Washington. Jim is completely out of baseball now and recently we were discussing the McLain trade. Jim feels certain that the Tigers gained considerations other than players in the deal. I have talked with many people who feel certain that Short brought a Detroit yes vote to move his club to Texas when he made that McLain trade.

Jim told me how he learned that he had been traded to the Tigers in that infamous deal. He heard it on the radio.

Few traded players learn of their fate in this manner.

Most clubs have the courtesy to make phone calls to the players involved in a trade, and many clubs tell the players in person. But the Senators rarely gave the players that courtesy. Eddie Brinkman learned of his trade when Darold Knowles called him after hearing it on the radio. Brinkman thought Knowles was pulling a practical joke on him when he said, "You have been traded to the Tigers." When Knowles named the players involved in the McLain deal, Brinkman was even more convinced that it was a practical joke. But it wasn't, and finally Eddie realized it. Rodriguez heard about it in Mexico, where he was playing winter ball.

A year later, the Senators were still informing their players of trades in the same manner. Bernie Allen learned of his trade from a WWDC disc jockey, Johnny Holliday, who telephoned him and advised him that he was no longer a Senator and had been traded to the Yankees. Unser learned that he was a Cleveland Indian when Allen called him with the news. Brinkman, Allen, and Unser had all been at their homes and no one tried to call before the trades were announced to the media.

In business manager Joe Burke, Short found a man who was willing to side with him in all trade disagreements with Williams. Time and time again, I have heard Williams tell Burke, "Joe, we are going to have to stick together a little more. We can't let Short do some of these fucking deals that are not sound baseball moves." But the next time Williams and Short would disagree on a player transaction, Burke would side with Short. This was just the kind of man that Short was looking for. He could always come back to Ted and say, "Burke has been in baseball a long time and he agrees with me."

The first trade that Short had a chance to make was with the Atlanta Braves. The Braves were offering Joe Torre for Paul Casanova and Mike Epstein. Casanova, after a good season in 1967, had gone back instead of improving. Epstein had one unimpressive season in the majors and showed a bad attitude to go with his athletic potential. Both had spent part of the 1968 season with the Senators' Buffalo farm club. Torre was a versatile established major-leaguer who could play first base or catch, and as it turned out, could play third base. Short fired Selkirk, nixed the deal with Atlanta, saying that Torre was finished. The Braves then sent Torre to St. Louis for Orlando Cepeda. Torre gained superstar status with the Cardinals in the next three years. In those three seasons, Torre had a composite batting average of .328 averaged 113 RBIs, 202 hits, and 21 home runs per season. He was named the Most Valuable Player in the National League in 1971.

The Senators didn't make many deals during the 1969 season. There were a couple of small transactions during spring training. When Ted Williams started trimming his club to make the twenty-five-man roster by opening day, it was decided to trade outfielder Cap Peterson, a one-time bonus baby with the Giants, to the Cleveland Indians for minor-league pitcher George Woodson. It was not a popular deal with the Washington press and fans, as Peterson had hit three home runs in one game that spring. Of course, the wind was blowing out at about forty miles per hour that day.

The Senators got rid of some of their pitchers early in the 1969 season. Williams kicked Phil Ortega off the club early in the spring because of his bad training habits. The Senators would have given Ortega his outright release if necessary, so they were happy when the California Angels claimed him for the $20,000 waiver price shortly before the season started.

In the middle of May, the Nats sent journeyman pitcher Frank Kreutzer to the Pittsburgh Pirates for pitcher Jim Shellenback. That deal was a good one for the Senators, as Shellenback stuck with the club and pitched some alternately great and awful games. One has to admire Jim Shellenback for just being in the major leagues. He walks with a limp as a result of a serious car accident. On October 1, 1967, Jim suffered a compound fracture of the right leg, rib fractures, a sprained left wrist, tongue lacerations, and internal injuries. Doctors said that he would never play baseball again, but he was back pitching in June of the following year.

Five weeks later, Ted finally convinced Short and Burke that a veteran black outfielder named Lee Maye could help the Senators. The Indians, since spring training, had offered Maye to Washington in deals, but Burke often had trouble being color blind when it came to evaluating player personnel, and believed that Maye couldn't help the Senators. To get Maye, the Senators paid the waiver price.

Lee Maye was an interesting and outspoken person. He often told me that he was unhappy playing for Al Dark, the Cleveland manager. Dark once made the mistake of saying that "black people's muscles are built differently than those of whites." Not too many blacks enjoyed playing for Alvin after he made that statement.

If Ted Williams is considered the most profane person in baseball, Lee Maye and perhaps Denny McLain have to be close behind. Every other word uttered by Maye is "motherfucker." Lee, a sharp dresser who sells clothes in Houston during the off season, is a professional pop singer who may have been the first major-leaguer to have a batting coach and a singing coach. His most successful song was "Halfway Out of Love," which sold a half million copies in 1964. In fact, Lee Maye was never halfway out of love. Ted used to say, "That Lee Maye is the biggest screwer on this club."

Lee Maye never did get along with Ed Stroud, another black on the team. They just couldn't hit it off, and things finally came to a head late in the 1969 season. They were trading insults and vile language in the dugout before a game at Kennedy Stadium when it erupted into fisticuffs. I was seated on the dugout bench when fists started flying right in front of me. I grabbed Stroud from behind, and Mike Epstein grabbed Maye. It didn't last long and no one was hurt. Ted just brushed it off, saying, "It's the result of short tempers near the end of a long season."

The trouble between Maye and Stroud carried over to the next season. Traveling secretary Burt Hawkins was having trouble making up a rooming list that pleased everyone. Players and coaches usually double up in rooms on most clubs. About an hour before the start of the Presidential Opener in 1971, Ted and I were chatting in his clubhouse office at Kennedy Stadium. Hawkins entered and said that he was having trouble with the rooming list because some of the blacks refused to room with one another. Maye and Stroud were refusing to room together, and John Roseboro wanted to room alone.

Ted said, "Damn it, if they want to room alone, charge them the difference between a single and a double and take it out of their pay."

Hawkins added, "The blacks are the only ones I am having trouble with." Ted was upset that anyone was bitching about roommates. He roared, "What the hell is going on with the blacks of this club? I treat everyone the same. Get all the blacks in here right now for a meeting with me."

So Hawkins went out to round up the blacks. Ted said to me, "We'll stop this shit right now. I take pains to see that everyone gets a fair shake regardless of his race or color, and I don't expect any trouble over something like this."

I excused myself, and just as I was leaving, Lee Maye, Ed Stroud, Paul Casanova, John Roseboro, and Dave Nelson paraded into the office. Ted was closeted with them for about twenty minutes. Afterwards, he told me, "I gave it to them pretty good and when I was finished, they all wanted to room with each other."

The Senators bought infielder Zoilo Versalles from the Indians for the $20,000 waiver price. Bob Short remembered him as a player who had sparked the Twins to a pennant and had been voted the American League MVP only four years earlier. Versalles slumped to a .200 batting average in 1967, and the Twins gave up on him, sending him to the Dodgers. Then he went to San Diego in the expansion draft, and was promptly traded to Cleveland. He was batting .236 with the Indians when they dealt him to Short. Bob was sure that Versalles would return to his days of brilliance, but Ted was more concerned with reports that Versalles had little desire to play, and was a troublemaker.

Short paid for back surgery on Versalles during the winter and predicted that Zoilo would be as good as new in the spring of 1970. The infielder recovered from the surgery all right, but reported to Pompano Beach the following spring with a potbelly and an attitude that had deteriorated. It was pretty clear to most of us that Versalles would not go north with the club.

Late in August, 1969, righthander Cisco Carlos was picked up on waivers from the Chicago White Sox. Carlos was reported to have good control and good breaking stuff. But Ted said, "He doesn't throw hard enough to brake a pane of glass." Carlos was a nice fellow, but he never helped the Senators much.

A couple of weeks later Catcher Paul Casanova forced a player transaction when he got drunk, beat up his wife, and landed in jail. Jim French was the only other catcher on the roster, so the club had to activate coach Doug Camilli, who caught the next night in what was to be his last game as an active player. Casanova got out of jail, and his wife dropped the assault charges after club attorney Stan Bregman went to court with Paul. Casanova always claimed that his wife provoked the attack by threatening to kill him.

The year 1969 had been a great season for Washington fans, the most succesful record in over two decades, but Williams knew that the club couldn't stand pat. He wanted to wheel and deal. Ted was having trouble getting Short to let him make a substantial trade.

The annual winter baseball meetings started at Bal Harbour, Florida, and Williams went there determined to make some trades. The first deal sent side-arm relief specialist Dave Baldwin to the Seattle Pilots for veteran George Brunet. The trade proved to be a plus for the Senators, as Brunet had a pretty good season in 1970 before the Senators, late in the season, traded him to Pittsburgh for pitcher Denny Riddleberger and $50,000 cash.

The next day, the Senators, at Williams' insistence, made an even better trade. It was a foregone conclusion that pitchers Barry Moore and Dennis Higgins would be traded after the season. Moore, who possessed a strong left arm and a taste for bourbon, had a good first half of the season in posting a 6–2 won-lost record, but he slumped badly in the second half and finished with a record of 9 and 8, with a fat 4.30 ERA.

Higgins was a tall righthander from Missouri, who could throw hard. But his record of 10 wins and 9 losses, with an ERA of 3.49, was not good for a reliefer. He sealed his fate by throwing wild pitches fifteen times in 1969, more than any other reliefer in the league.

Moore and Higgins were traded to the Cleveland Indians for infielder Dave Nelson and pitchers Horacio Piña and Ron Law. After the deal was announced, Short said that the trade was Ted's, and he was afraid that Moore might win twenty games the next season with the Indians. Moore didn't win twenty games for Cleveland or anyone else. He and Higgins were traded away from Cleveland and both wound up in the minors in 1971. The trade turned out to be a dandy for the Nats. Nelson became a regular, and reliefer Piña had a couple of pretty good seasons with the Senators. Law overcame arm trouble, and posted a record of 11 wins and 6 losses in helping Denver win the American Association pennant in 1971.

The Senators' final player transaction of the season took place on New Year's eve, and it was Short's turn to make a deal. He talked catcher John Roseboro into accepting a $40,-000 contract and predicted that Rosey would be "an important cog in the club's drive for the American League pennant." Rosey was a nice guy, but he had a series of ailments ranging from arthritis to piles, and he had not contributed much to the club when Williams convinced Short that Roseboro should be taken off the active list. John was deactivated on August 19, and finished the season as a coach. But Roseboro was not Ted's kind of a coach and was released from his coaching duties at the end of the season.

Looking back at 1969, I shudder when I think of good trades that the Senators passed up. Williams was ready to wheel and deal, but Short held him back. Ted often told me, "If I had a free hand to run this baseball operation, I would trade and trade."

The first major deal that Williams was willing to make was early in the spring of 1969. Gabe Paul of the Cleveland Indians, now a part owner of the New York Yankees, was always very high on Frank Howard, and he was willing to give a package of players to get the big slugger. But Bob Short held to his superstar philosophy, and there was no way that he was going to let Howard go for any number of players. Howard had reached superstar status the previous season with 106 RBIs and 44 home runs, including an incredible performance of 10 homers in 20 times at bat over a six-game period. Paul was offering outfielder Lee Maye, pitcher Mike Paul, infielders Larry Brown and Vern Fuller, and catcher Duke Sims for Howard. Paul was willing to substitute a promising minor-league catcher for Sims in the event the Senators didn't like the other proposal. He was Ray Fosse, who had batted .301 in 1968 with Portland of the Pacific Coast League. Williams was ready to make either deal. The catcher would have been the key man for the Senators, but Short didn't like Sims and wouldn't listen to anyone about Fosse's potential. Short rejected both proposals.

Gabe Paul didn't give up in his efforts to land Howard just because Short said no in spring training. He kept hounding Short and Williams, making minor adjustments in the proposal. He flew to Washington and talked with Short and Williams in Ted's Shoreham West apartment until several hours past midnight. But there was no way Short was going to part with Howard.

Williams always felt that a rebuilding organization such as the Senators should deal for numbers when possible. Especially Washington, because the organization had not signed many good young players in the past several years. Therefore, Ted had been willing to give his big man for a multiplayer package. Any five-player package including Fosse would have been a good trade for the Senators, for he became the All Star catcher for the American League in the 1970 season.

Short and Williams were rookies in the trading business at that time, and they had not developed an operating procedure when it came to making deals. Their critics say that they never did develop a sound trading policy or procedure. One thing is for certain. Every time Short thought about a deal, he was thinking about what would help at the box office. And every time Williams thought about a deal, he was thinking about what would help the ball club on the field on a long-range basis.

Perhaps the biggest blunder ever by the Senators, excluding the Denny McLain trade, was Short's decision not to trade Brant Alyea during the 1969 season. Alyea, a 6-foot-3-

inch, 220-pound "swinger" from New Jersey, made American League history on September 12, 1965, when he became the first pinch hitter in the history of the league to hit a home run on the first major-league pitch thrown to him. Alyea had a very unimpressive spring training in 1969 and was lucky to go north with the club. In addition, he had the reputation of being a "flake" who thought more about his personal goals and records than he did about the overall team performance. But Williams liked his long-ball possibilities and tended to overlook his lack of speed, average arm, and his butchery in the outfield.

Ted was feeling pretty good about Alyea, but Short was delirious. Short saw Alyea as another Frank Howard-type box-office attraction in the making. Brant hit well the first half of the season. Williams spotted him against left-handers, despite Alyea's baseless claim that he could hit right-handers as well as southpaws. He responded with some lusty hitting, which prompted a trade offer by the Minnesota Twins.

Minnesota's Cal Griffith was looking for some right-handed power, and he felt Alyea might be the answer. He offered Short an obscure infielder-outfielder named Graig Nettles, who was on the Twins roster but spent most of his time on the bench. Nettles had hit with authority in the minors, and many baseball people felt he had potential. However, Minnesota was a contender, and they were willing to let Nettles go for some immediate right-hander power. Bob Short didn't like the offer, and was on the phone with Ed Doherty, ridiculing the Minnesota trade proposal. Short was talking from his offices in the Leamington Hotel in Minneapolis, and I was with Doherty in Williams' executive office upstairs at Kennedy Stadium when the conversation took place. Ted's secretary, Hazel Phelps, and I were listening to Doherty's end of the conversation, and Ed was agreeing with Short that Nettles for Alyea would be an awful trade. After

A startled Frank Howard obliges
Morgana, an exotic dancer who
jumped out of the stands at
Kennedy Stadium opening day of
the 1970 season, ran to home
plate and kissed big Frank.

Frank Howard greets his new
manager at Pompano Beach,
spring training, 1969.

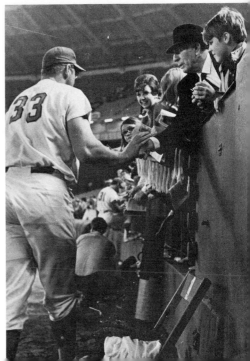

Frank greets some of his fans
prior to his final game in a
Senators uniform. He later hit a
home run which he termed the
greatest thrill of his career.

Denny McLain poses with Ted
Williams soon after McLain joined
the team. The smiles didn't last
long.

McLain berates umpire Art
Frantz in a game at Robert
F. Kennedy Stadium.

McLain meets the media
after being suspended for
the first of three times
during 1970.

Denny appearing on the author's
Sports Round Table.

Curt Flood, Howard Cosell, and Marvin Miller discuss Flood's case against baseball and his decision to attempt a comeback with the Washington Senators.

Flood's uniform hangs in his Kennedy Stadium locker the night he jumped the club.

An unhappy Curt Flood rides the bench in the Senators dugout. This photo, the last of Curt in a Senators uniform, was taken the night before he jumped the team and flew to Spain.

Bob Short dries his beer-soaked head after a fan doused him during a 1972 Orioles-Rangers game at Baltimore's Memorial Stadium. A somewhat amused Jerry Hoffberger, Orioles owner is on Short's right, Joe Burke is on Short's left.

A shocked ball club in the dugout during the first game after Short got permission to move the club.

A hint of the fans' reaction to Bob Short and his move of the franchise.

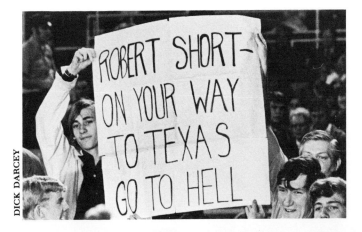

AS RANGERS

CAN BASEBALL LEAGUE

American League President Joe Cronin and Bob Short ham it up with ten-gallon hats in celebration of the Texas move.

Joe Danzansky, unsuccessful bidder for the Senators, George Neuman of the D.C. Armory Board, Shelby Whitfield, and Congressman B. F. Sisk of California, discuss the loss of the Senators on Whitfield's program at Franny O'Brien's Anthony House.

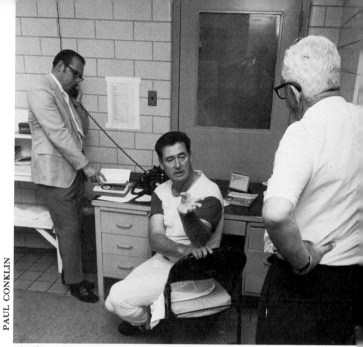

Shelby takes a phone call as Williams talks with
Ed Doherty in Ted's clubhouse office.

Ted with veteran clubhouse man Fred Baxter. After Williams
resigned, Bob Short fired Baxter.

MATTHEW LEWIS/WASHINGTON POST

A happy Bob Short and Ted Williams at a press
conference unveiling Williams as the new
manager of the Washington Senators.

Four years later, Short and Williams at a press conference
announcing that Ted will not return as manager of the Texas
Rangers in 1973.

WIDE WORLD PHOTOS

hanging up the phone, Doherty cautioned me about saying anything to Ted about the trade offer. Ted didn't know anything about the proposal, and Doherty said that Short was afraid that Williams might want to make the trade if he learned about the offer. Williams received this kind of treatment from Short and some of his front-office people from time to time. Ted rarely initiated any trade talk with other clubs, and if Short didn't like a deal that had been proposed to Joe Burke or himself, there was a pretty good chance that the offer never got to Williams.

If you evaluate baseball talent solely on baseball statistics, it's easy to see how Alyea looked better than Nettles at the time. On the June 15 trading deadline, Alyea was batting .306 with six home runs, and Nettles was batting .269 with three home runs. But good baseball men will tell you that such things as attitude, age, speed, arm, and desire have much to do with it, and Nettles had it all over Alyea in these departments.

Alyea collapsed almost totally on the field during the second half of the season. At mid-July, Alyea was batting .311, with 10 home runs and 31 RBIs in 118 at-bats. In his next 119 at-bats over the final half of the season, Alyea batted .186, with only 2 home runs and 9 RBIs. Williams tried to shake him out of the slump every way that he could think of. He played him against the weaker pitchers. He used him in the better parks for hitters. On occasion, Williams encouraged and pampered Alyea, and there were times that he would try to fire him up by needling him in front of his teammates with comments about his poor hitting. But nothing Ted tried seemed to help.

After the 1969 season, the Senators were determined to get rid of Alyea in view of his being a "high risk" on and off the field. Finally, they did unload him to the Minnesota Twins on March 21. Washington received Joe Grzenda and

Charley Walters, a couple of little-heralded pitchers. Grzenda was a journeyman left-hander who had an unimpressive record of 5 wins and 5 losses in the majors. He had spent much of his fifteen-year professional pitching career in the minors. Walters was a sore-armed pitcher with little chance of making the majors. Williams was the only one who saw any potential in Grzenda. A thirty-three-year-old skinny, frail-looking person, he was nonmuscular, and his teammates called him Shakey.

Walters was shipped to the minors, but Grzenda stuck with the Senators and posted an unimpressive season record of 3 wins, 6 losses, and an ERA of 4.98. Joe was not impressive the following spring and few gave him a chance to make the club. But Williams' faith and patience paid off, and Grzenda had a 5–2 record with a brilliant 1.94 ERA in 1971. It was by far his best season in baseball. So the Alyea trade turned out pretty well for the Senators, even if it didn't look so good the first year.

Short committed a colossal mistake in 1969 when he refused to permit Williams to trade first baseman Mike Epstein. Short was of the firm belief that Epstein would be a superstar, but Williams was more realistic in his evaluation of the big, moody athlete. Mike was not the average major-league ballplayer. An articulate, 6-foot-4 inch 225-pounder, Epstein took pleasure in looking down on the other players and placing himself on an intellectual pedestal. He was addicted to using big words. Mike's tastes included classical music and heavy reading, two nonfavorites with most major-league ballplayers. It's either hard rock or country and western with most of the jocks. Williams and Epstein were not compatible in many areas, but they could relate in their mutual interests in guns and hunting. Ted recognized that Epstein could not hit many left-handed pitchers, so he got the most out of Mike by using him against right-handers and spotting him against the weaker lefties. Mike has to make his mark with the bat, as his fielding capabilities are limited and first base is the only position he can play. Epstein had a sensational minor-league career in the Orioles farm system, and when Baltimore elected to play Boog Powell at first base instead of him, Mike was mad. He demanded that the Orioles play him or trade him, and refused to return to the Birds Triple A farm club at Rochester. He said that he would quit the game and go into public relations before returning to the minors. The Orioles with their astute baseball organization recognized that Mike was no Boog Powell, so they dealt the discontented Epstein to Washington. The trade included pitcher Frank Bertaina and Epstein for pitcher Pete Richert. There is no doubt that Williams helped Epstein as a hitter. During the '69 season, Mike upped his batting average 44 points to .278, and increased his home-run production from 13 to 30.

But during that 1969 season, Williams often told me, "We are getting everything that we will ever get out of Epstein, and we'd be smart to unload him." Ted had tried all of the different approaches on the former University of California fullback and decided that the best way to get through to Mike was with the fatherly advice, soft-sell approach. But it was often hard for Williams to stomach. Frequently Epstein did not respond to Ted's advice, except with a surly sneer. But Epstein was a politician, and he made it a point to get close to Short and club attorney Stan Bregman.

With Epstein having a good year in '69, and with some people predicting that he would become a superstar, it was natural that there would be some trade offers. The California Angels made perhaps the best offer of all. The Angels were willing to deal outfielder Jay Johnstone, catcher Jose Azcue, and pitcher Clyde Wright for Epstein.

Following the 1969 season, the Yankees offered left-

The Senators were breaking camp in Florida and had stopped in Tampa to play an exhibition game with the Cincinnati Reds.

After the game, I went to the press room with Cincinnati broadcaster Jim McIntyre to enjoy a beer. While we were there, we were joined by Angels scout Ackerman, who asked me what I thought of an offer of Rodriguez and Reichardt for McMullen.

"What's wrong with Rodriguez and Reichardt?" I asked. "Do they have some kind of terminal illness?"

"No. They're fine."

"Then you can't be serious about making that trade offer, are you?"

"Yes, we have offered the Senators the deal, but Short and Burke don't want to make it. I'm here to see if I can work on Williams. We think we can win the pennant this season if we land a power-hitting veteran like McMullen."

After we finished our beer, I told Ackerman that he should talk with Ted at his earliest convenience and added that I might say something to him.

The next morning, when Ted arrived at Lakeland, I cornered him in the dugout and told him about the Angels' proposal.

He immediately said, "God, I like that one, don't you?"

"I sure as hell do," I replied.

As we broke out of our huddle, Senators coach Del Wilber came up and said, "Wait until you hear what Carl Ackerman of the Angels just proposed to me."

"I don't know what he proposed, but I sure would like to give 'em McMullen for Reichardt and Rodriguez," Ted replied.

The three of us were as excited as kids with candy. Williams bubbled, "Oh, baby! Do I like that one! We'd better get some scouting reports on Rodriguez and Reichardt. Knowing our fucking system, the reports probably won't be worth a damn. Shelby, you know some people in Los Angeles. See what you can find out about Rodriguez and Reichardt."

Ted wanted to make the deal immediately, before the Angels backed out. But Short strongly opposed it, and again Burke agreed with him. All of the Washington coaches were in favor of the trade, and no one could understand Short's refusal to give his approval. Short felt that McMullen could be a superstar, and he was being stubborn about giving his approval. Finally, Williams decided that he had to assert himself in a stronger manner if the trade were to be made. He went into Burke's office, pounded on the desk with his fist, and said, "Goddamn it. We've got to make this deal. Tell Short that we can't afford not to make this trade."

With that, Ted left the room to give Burke a chance to grab the phone and report to Short about Ted's outburst. When Short learned that Williams was getting heated up about the trade, he told Burke to call Angels general manager Dick Walsh and tell him the Senators would make the deal.

When Williams greeted Rodriguez and Reichardt in his Kennedy Stadium clubhouse office, he was as happy as could be. Mister Ballgame was convinced that it was a hell of a deal. Short was back in Minnesota, but Burke was there at the press conference, acting as though the deal had been his idea from the beginning.

Rick Reichardt was as happy as could be to get away from Lefty Phillips and the Angels. He had some unkind things to say about the Angels, and he was soundly booed every time he appeared in Anaheim the remainder of the year. Rick felt that going to Washington with the chance to play under Williams might be the thing that would really get him untracked. Ted elected to platoon him, and even though Reichardt did have a pretty good year, Ted was disappointed in him.

The muscular Reichardt had a pretty good year playing on a part-time basis. He collected 15 home runs, 47 RBIs, and batted .251 in 283 at-bats. But he hated to be platooned.

Rick's healthy $52,500 salary was resented by the Senators front office. Soon after being traded to Washington, Reichardt went to Burke and demanded that the Senators fulfill an agreement he had with the California club. Rick had negotiated a deal that would entitle him to free telephone calls totaling $7,500. Reichardt was insistent that he not lose the benefit simply because of a trade.

Rick was never a problem for Williams when it came to attitude. And he was an adequate fielder. He played all three outfield positions and did not butcher the outfield, as predicted by his critics in California.

Aurelio Rodriguez, a flashy Mexican, and Williams hit it off great, and Ted was saying that the Senators could forget about third base for the next ten years. Aurelio displayed a pleasant disposition in Washington and failed to live up to his reputation of being a "moody" player. His teammates liked him and referred to him as Chi Chi. He made fans quickly and became one of Washington's favorites. I called Aurelio the Señor from Sonora, and Latin fans in Washington would come to the park with signs calling Rodriguez El Gato (the cat). It was mainly because of Rodriguez and his bright future that baseball people all over the country were hailing the McMullen-for-Reichardt-and-Rodriguez deal as a great trade for the Nats. Aurelio stole the hearts of Washington fans with his sensational fielding and steady batting. The surprising thing was that Aurelio developed into a power hitter. He slammed 19 home runs and drove in 83 runs while posting a .249 average. He feasted on fast balls, and will become an even better hitter once he learns how to handle the curve with more regularity. Rodriguez enjoyed playing under Williams, as well as with a fellow countryman, Horacio Piña. Both were happy-go-lucky types with infectious smiles, and they enjoyed rooming with each other, at home and on the road.

The only complaint that Ted had about Rodriguez was that he tended to tire late in the season. Williams and his coaches felt that this was because Aurelio played winter ball in his native Mexico. He was a national hero in Mexico, and the winter season meant a lot to him. Williams was not able to convince Rodriguez that he should pass up winter ball, but after his trade to the Tigers, Aurelio became convinced that it would be to his benefit to rest during the winter.

At the end of the 1970 season, there was little doubt that the Senators had had the best of the trade with the Angels. McMullen batted just .229, with 14 home runs, while Rodriguez and Reichardt had much better seasons with Washington.

Bob Short proceeded to give away Rodriguez and Reichardt. He included Aurelio in the McLain trade and then sent Reichardt to the White Sox for pitcher Jerry Janeski. Right-hander Janeski had posted a record of 10 wins and 17 losses with a poor Chicago club in 1970, and his acquisition by the Senators was applauded by the Washington media. But Janeski didn't do much for the Senators. After posting an unimpressive 1 and 5 record with a fat 4.94 ERA, he was farmed to Denver.

The next deal for the Senators was with the Milwaukee Brewers. During the second week of May, it was announced that outfielder Hank Allen was going to Milwaukee for outfielder Wayne Comer. In addition, the Brewers would receive Ron Theobald, a minor-leaguer from the Senators farm system.

Comer batted .212 with the Senators and didn't hit anything close to a home run. Williams couldn't understand it, as he was counting on Comer for additional home-run punch. Comer had hit 15 homers the year before when the Brewers played in Seattle. Reflecting on Comer's abysmal performance in a Senators uniform, Ted would shake his head and say, "It just shows you how figures can lie sometimes and how a little bandbox park like Sicks Stadium in Seattle can mislead you."

Hank Allen was the older brother of Richie Allen, the much-traveled and controversial slugger. Hank spent one season with the Brewers, batting .222 before he went down to the minors. Ted always said that "Hank could have been a better major leaguer, but lacked the necessary drive and motivation." He could run and throw, and the season before, under the direction of Williams, he raised his batting average from .219 to .277.

Allen had critics who felt that he was militant and the misdirected leader of the blacks on the club the season before Ted Williams arrived on the scene. Teammate Bernie Allen once told me, "Hank Allen controls all of the blacks on the team."

There had been reports that, from a racial standpoint, all was not well with the Senators in 1968 when Jim Lemon was manager. Black outfielder Ed Stroud once told me: "That man Lemon called us monkeys." When Hank Allen would run after a fly ball, according to Stroud, Lemon would say: "Look at that monkey go."

Williams always felt that he could help most of the black players in the league. He had an excellent rapport with blacks and believed that many of them had not been handled or treated properly. As a matter of fact, Williams thought that the Senators front office did not have an objective outlook when it came to evaluating black players and he told this to Short. Most of the blacks who played for Williams responded to his fair treatment by giving 110 percent all the time. It was Williams who got the ball rolling for the admission of old-time blacks into the Baseball Hall of Fame at

Cooperstown, New York. Ted's comment when he was inducted into the Hall of Fame in 1966 was that he hoped some way would be found to honor Negro greats like Satchel Paige and Josh Gibson who never had a chance to prove themselves in the majors. Paige saw some action in the "bigs" in the twilight of his career, but never got a chance during his prime. Williams was delighted when Paige was voted into the Hall of Fame in 1971. Later in 1971, Howard University, held a luncheon in Williams' honor in appreciation for the part that Ted played in opening the doors of the Hall of Fame to old-time black greats.

Ted was far from happy about the trading situation in Washington. He said, "Other clubs are making moves and we are sitting still."

There are some players in the league that Ted wanted so badly he could hardly stand it. Bobby Murcer of the Yankees was the one Ted coveted the most. During the 1969 season, when Murcer batted .259, Ted frequently told me that Murcer would become one of the top hitters in baseball. Again, in 1970, when Murcer was on the way to a .251 season at the plate, he reiterated that Murcer would become one of the game's best hitters. It was late in the 1970 season when Ted came to me and said, "Do you think the Yankees would give Murcer for Mike Epstein and Rick Reichardt?" I said, "I don't know, Ted. They are supposed to like Epstein, but how do they feel about Reichardt?" He said, "Well, I don't know, but they just claimed him on waivers and we withdrew him. God, would I like to make that deal." The Yankees didn't like it and Murcer rewarded their confidence in him in the 1971 season by batting .331 with 25 home runs and 94 RBIs.

There were times when other clubs in the league would put players on waivers and Williams would not learn about it. Short and Burke would keep the information from him. That pretty well stopped when Ted blew his stack over an incident late in August, 1970. Williams noted in the newspapers that relief pitcher Paul Doyle of the Angels had cleared waivers in the American League and had been signed by the San Diego Padres in the National League. "Goddamn it, I wouldn't have wanted to claim him, but I deserve the courtesy of being asked about anyone on the waiver list." It was amazing that Short and Burke were shutting Williams out of this part of the operation, especially since there was no general manager.

Ted came up with the idea of unloading pitcher George Brunet to one of the contenders in the National League. Ted saw a chance to pick up a player for the future. The Pirates came up with the best offer. They were willing to give $100,-000 for Brunet, but Ted insisted that the Senators get a player in the deal. The player was pitcher Denny Riddleberger, who appeared in 57 games as a Senator the next year. That was more appearances than any other Washington pitcher made.

Short was happy to get $50,000 in cash to complete the deal. Short was about to start his poor-mouthing in earnest, and a few weeks later he claimed that he needed that $50,000 to meet the club payroll the final month of the season.

Lee Maye's career with the Senators came to an end the second week of September, 1970. The Senators were thinking ahead to a youth program and had placed Lee on waivers.

After the Senators closed out the season with a 14-game losing streak and solidly entrenched in last place, Williams was in no mood to go to the league playoffs or the World Series. Ted just wanted to get away from it for a while, to visit with the wife and kid in Vermont, and to unwind with a little woodchuck hunting in New Hampshire.

Meanwhile, Short was intent on trading for his playing idol, Denny McLain. The Senators owner had a flair for the sensational and he hoped to pull off this headline-making deal in time to upstage the World Series. Short and Williams had discussed guidelines for a McLain trade in detail before Williams left for New England. Short knew that Ted didn't like the deal. Short was in a race against time if he was to complete arrangements for a McLain trade in time to make the announcement at a big press conference before the World Series started in Cincinnati. He and Tigers general manager Jim Campbell agreed to the bizarre terms on an airplane between Minneapolis and Baltimore. Then Bowie Kuhn had to give his blessings to that deal and had to agree to lift the McLain suspension. Ted told me that Short finally leaned on him in phone conversations until he said, "Oh hell, Bob, you're giving up too much, but if you are going to make the deal, I can't stop you." If the trade had not come at the close of a long, frustrating season, a last-place finish, and a 14-game losing streak, Ted might have fought Short a little harder.

And Short was right on schedule. There was a big press conference in Cincinnati to upstage the World Series. Short had ruined the makings of a pretty good ball club in one grandiose spectacle. It boiled down to Joe Coleman, Aurelio Rodriguez, and Eddie Brinkman, three outstanding major-leaguers, for a suspended Denny McLain. Jim Hannan, Don Wert, Elliott Maddox, and Norm McRae were all secondary figures in the deal. Short publicly called the trade "a gamble" but told Oscar Molomot it was "a stroke of genius." The reaction by baseball people was almost uniform. "The worst trade in the history of the game" was a phrase frequently heard around World Series headquarters. People could not understand the deal unless there was more to it than had been revealed. Had Short received several hundred thousand dollars in cash? The Tigers Jim Campbell said no.

Bob Short expressed surprise at the almost unanimous criticism of his Denny McLain trade, but it's difficult to understand how he expected anything else.

The last deal the Senators made in 1970 was the purchase of switch-hitting outfielder Richie Scheinblum from the Cleveland Indians. Williams had always liked Scheinblum, even when he went 0 for 30 at the start of the 1969 season. He could run and throw and was an adequate fielder. Ted always said that Richie should be able to hit. The Senators purchased him in a waiver deal and gave him an opportunity to make the starting lineup at the start of the 1971 season. But Richie collected just 7 hits in 49 trips to the plate for a .143 batting average.

In May of the 1971 season the Senators decided to send Scheinblum and weak-hitting catcher Jim French to the minors to make room for two rookies, pitcher Mike Thompson and first baseman-outfielder Larry Biittner.

The move touched off an angry blast by French, who was the club's player representative. The little catcher claimed that he was being sent down because of personal reasons and not because of his .146 batting average. Jim had made only 6 hits in 41 trips to the plate. Jim claimed that he was being sent down because Williams had soured on him. Denny McLain had been requesting that he be caught by French instead of Casanova and French thought Williams felt that he was responsible for McLain's making the requests. Ted says that was not the case at all.

Additionally, French claimed that Williams was mad at him because of an incident that happened in Minnesota on the last road trip. The slump-ridden Senators had lost their sixth game in a row when McLain was beaten by the Brewers on May 5 in Milwaukee. The next day was an off day in Minnesota and Williams scheduled a workout for the team at Metropolitan Stadium in Bloomington. Some of the Senators resented the workout on the off day, and the players organized a boycott of the team bus to show their displeasure. All of the players took cabs to the ball park, leaving a practically empty bus in which the manager and coaches rode from the hotel to the practice session. French claimed that the bus boycott had been organized by McLain and that he had nothing to do with it. Williams told me that he didn't hold French responsible for the incident.

Short and Burke had been looking for ammunition to use in getting rid of French. They both had claimed that French, at best, was nothing better than a Triple-A ballplayer, but Williams had always come to the defense of Frenchy.

Jimmy was unhappy and was making a lot of noise. And the Washington writers loved every minute of the criticism of Williams by a disgruntled player. They played it up big. Ted told me, "Look, I wanted to keep the little guy on the club, but Short, Burke, and everyone in the front office were for sending him out. What can I say when he is hitting .146 and we have lost ten of our last eleven games? Short is pressuring me to make room for Biittner and Thompson." When Ted and I were on the air that night with "The Ted Williams Show," I asked him about French's complaint. "No one likes to be farmed out to the minors and that's understandable," said Ted. "But I can tell you this: I *know*— I *know*—we have been fair to Jim French and I will promise him right here, publicly, that we will call him back at the end of the season to give him the thirteen days he needs to qualify for the pension."

The Senators took French off the Denver roster and placed him with the Atlanta Braves farm club at Richmond.

True to his word, Ted made sure that French was called up at the end of the season to get the thirteen days of active major-league duty to give him four years in the majors and qualification for the pension plan.

It didn't seem right that Williams and French would wind up their relationship on a sour note. Ted really liked French's spunk. French would needle Ted, and Williams would get a big kick out of it. Ted jokingly would say, "French, where do you plan on playing next month?" And French would reply, "Right here. Where do you plan on managing next month?" And Williams would laugh.

During their final year in Washington, the Nats continued to make trades, at the insistence of Williams. Ted wanted to try everything possible to improve a club that had been all but wrecked by the Denny McLain deal the previous winter. At the start of the season, the Senators sent outfielder Ed Stroud to the White Sox in exchange for outfielder-first baseman Tom McCraw. Ted was reluctant to give up on Stroud, but he had always wanted to acquire McCraw and was happy to make the trade with the White Sox. McCraw proved to be a bitter disappointment. After a fast start, he faded at the plate and joined the group of malcontents who seemed more interested in knocking Williams than improving their performance on the field. He would up batting .213 for the Senators, a few points worse than his .220 average for the White Sox the previous season.

The Senators made their biggest trade of the 1971 season on May 7. Mike Epstein and Darold Knowles went to the Oakland A's in exchange for first baseman Don Mincher, pitcher Paul Lindblad, catcher Frank Fernandez, and $300,-000 in cash. The Senators players didn't know about the cash at first, and Epstein and Knowles, seemed insulted that they would be traded for the three Oakland players involved. Epstein, who had always been able to get sympathy from Bob Short when he went to the owner to complain about Ted Williams, said that he hated to leave Washington because Short had treated him like a son.

Williams was happy when Mincher hit about as well as Epstein. Mike batted .234 with 18 homer and 51 RBIs in an Oakland uniform, while Mincher batted .291, hit 10 homers, and drove in 45 runs with the Senators. Ted thought that Mincher was a much better team player.

Catcher Frank Fernandez never did much with the Senators, and they traded him back to Oakland during the month of August. Short received some cash and a minor-league infielder named Jimmy Driscoll, who was sent to Denver where he helped the Bears win the American Association pennant. Driscoll made the major-league club in 1972 when the franchise was switched to Texas.

The big trade with Oakland was a good one for Short and the Senators, primarily because of the $300,000 in cash. Short took half of the money and signed hard-throwing right-hander Pete Broberg off the Dartmouth campus. Broberg became a sensation in the American League. People all around the league said that Broberg threw as hard as any pitcher in the game. Ted Williams said that Broberg would never see a day in the minor leagues. It's ironic that Short would give Broberg a $150,000 bonus from money he received from Charley Finley in a trade. It was Finley who had offered Broberg a bonus of $175,000 when the pitcher graduated from high school, only to have Pete refuse it in favor of attending college.

One thing that must be said for Short. He was generous when it came to bonuses and salaries for his players and manager. He personally handled most of the salary negotiations the first couple of years, but after the novelty started wearing off, and once he realized that the salaries were getting out of hand, he let Joe Burke, the club's business manager, do the talking with the players. That is not to say that Bob Short was not still running the show.

Ted Williams may have obtained the best contract ever negotiated by a major-league manager.

Frank Howard is famous for his holdouts and dislike for spring training. He had some storied salary hassles with Short and Hondo came off pretty well every year. Frank signed for $97,500 in 1969, $110,000 in 1970, and $120,000 in both 1971 and 1972.

The Senators had to be the highest-paid fifth-place club in baseball in 1971. Short raised Mike Epstein from $15,000 to $40,000 in two seasons, despite the fact that Epstein dropped from 30 homers in 1969 to 20 homers in 1970.

Relief pitcher Darold Knowles was raised to $40,000 after his 2–14 record in the 1970 season. Short didn't help himself any at the bargaining table when, months earlier, he went around calling Knowles a half-million-dollar pitcher.

Short didn't balk at paying a fading Camilo Pascual $47,-000 in 1969. Other Senators received nice raises under Bob Short in Washington. Dick Bosman climbed to $35,000, Ken McMullen and Eddie Brinkman hit the $30,000 mark, and Del Unser advanced to $25,000.

Short may not have been good to the fans of Washington but he was good to many of his players. He gave *all* the players a raise in 1969. He recognized the need to sign players in the draft, and he was never hesitant to shell out big bonus money.

One much-heralded bonus baby was Jeff Burroughs, who was signed out of a Long Beach, California, high school for a bonus of $88,000. Burroughs was the number-one draft pick in the entire country in 1969. After watching him work out at Anaheim, Williams stated that he hit the ball as far as anyone in the game today with the exception of Frank Howard.

Williams was very high on another bonus baby named Bill Fahey. He's a great catching prospect who signed for $50,000 while attending the University of Detroit. The Baltimore Orioles were very high on Fahey and tried every way they knew to get him in a trade.

The first bonus baby signed by Short was Joe Lovitto, who made the club in 1972 and opened the season in centerfield for the Texas Rangers. His bonus money was $55,000. After watching Lovitto hit for the first time at Pompano Beach in

1969, Williams compared him to Carl Yastrzemski at the plate.

Frank Howard's name was always popping up in trade talk during the Short-Williams era in Washington. The Senators had another good chance to trade Frank to Cleveland at the start of the 1971 season. The Indians were offering infielder Larry Brown, infielder-outfielder John Lowenstein, and pitchers Mike Paul and Phil Hennigan. Williams was ready to make the deal. Williams argued that Brown could play shortstop. Lowenstein was a promising player with a good hitting record in the minors and he could play just about any position. Hennigan had posted a 6 and 3 record as a relief pitcher with Cleveland the previous season, and Ted had always been high on lefty Mike Paul, despite the fact that Paul had never been a big winner in the majors. Short once again vetoed the trade of the big man.

Williams knew that the longer the club held onto Howard, the smaller his trade value became. By the start of the 1971 season, Ted was ready to peddle Frank for a good pitching prospect. Williams got excited about a tall right-handed pitcher with the Milwaukee Brewers, Bill Parsons, and wanted to trade Howard for him, even up. Bob Short almost had a fit. "Who, pray tell, is Bill Parsons?" Williams had seen him pitch just once but he liked what he saw. Short nixed any chances of offering Howard for Parsons and the tall pitcher went on to post a record of 13 wins, 17 losses and a fine ERA of 3.20 in his rookie season.

Del Unser was a fine player, an excellent fielder with a great arm. He was also a good hitter, the best bunter on the club, and he possessed good speed. But Unser wasn't Ted's type of hitter. Occasionally Unser would go into a slump and lose his coordination at the plate. When he did that, Ted would say, "Unser looks to me as if he is afraid of the baseball." Ted had told me that every batter should have respect, maybe even a little fear for the ball. But Williams felt that Unser respected the ball to the extent that he sometimes wouldn't stand in and take his rips. And Ted knew that Unser was not exactly a Ted Williams fan. Knowing the full background, I wasn't surprised when Ted unloaded Unser to Cleveland.

Much has been said about the fact that Cleveland Manager Alvin Dark has engaged in performance incentive-clause contracts with Indians stars Sam McDowell, Vada Pinson, Hawk Harrelson, and Graig Nettles. Commissioner Bowie Kuhn first learned of the illegal contracts when *Cleveland Plain Dealer* baseball writer Russ Schneider broke the story. Kuhn took action by fining the Indians $5,000, giving Dark a written reprimand, and writing new contracts. But it was not generally known that three of the players who went to the Rangers in the trade had special clauses added to their standard baseball contract in 1971, and all three were signed by Al Dark. Mike Paul would receive a $2,000 bonus if he appeared in fifty games and won ten games during the 1971 season. Rich Hand devised a points system, whereby he would receive a $5,000 bonus if he earned 20 points, and Ken Suarez would receive a $2,000 bonus if he remained with the club for the entire season.

Incentive contracts are legal in the National Football League, but are not permitted in baseball, and with good reason. Paul didn't come close to making his bonus goals in 1971, but he would have come very close had he had the same arrangement with Texas in 1972. With Texas, Paul won eight games and appeared in 49. So it's easy to see where a manager could let his use of the player be dictated by his bonus arrangements, either helping or hurting the player, whichever the manager wanted to do.

The trade of Bernie Allen was another sure bet. Allen had been outspoken in his bitter criticism of Williams. The 1969 season went fine for Bernie Allen, but the Senators traded for Dave Nelson before the 1970 season and Allen was urged to retire as an active player and become manager of the Senators farm club in Denver. Williams and Short made the offer shortly after Allen had reinjured his knee playing a charity basketball game for WWDC. Allen rejected the managerial offer, as he thought he still had some good major-league ball left in him. The former Purdue quarterback alternated with Tim Cullen at second base after Nelson fizzled and was shipped to the minors. Then, in the 1971 season, Williams started looking at young second baseman like Len Randle and Tom Ragland, and Allen became even more disenchanted with the manager. It's no surprise that Bernie was the Imperial Wizard in the Williams Underminers Club. He was dead serious in his resentment of Williams and a number of his teammates even openly called Allen "Wizard."

When he was traded to the Yankees, Allen put the blast on Williams, calling him the most egotistical man he had ever met. Bernie added that "Williams ran a concentration camp and did not communicate with his players."

Ted told me that he was going to clean house and get rid of the troublemakers. Sure enough, Williams' critics Denny McLain, Bernie Allen, Del Unser, Tom McCraw, and Tim Cullen were gone by the start of the 1972 season.

Bob Short and Joe Burke were finally successful in getting Ted Williams to agree to peddle Paul Casanova, the off-the-field dynamo. He was traded to the Atlanta Braves for catcher Hal King. The trade turned out to Atlanta's advantage. King spent much of the season in the minors, and Casanova was the number-two catcher for Atlanta all season.

Williams always kept a close watch around the league to see who might be unhappy with management. Ted believed that you could get a player for less than his value if he happened to be in the doghouse. When outfielder Reggie Jackson was having trouble with Charley Finley in 1970, Ted kept bugging Short to make a solid offer for Reggie. Mike Epstein and Darold Knowles had big seasons in 1969 and Ted thought Finley might let Jackson go for the pair. And Ted would have been willing to sweeten the pot.

Perhaps Ted's biggest fault in evaluating baseball talent was his tendency to make judgment too quickly. He had a habit of getting excited, particularly about young players, at first sight. The first time he saw the Dodgers young left-handed hitter Bill Buckner, Ted exclaimed, "There just may be the next .400 hitter!" Buckner may never be a .400 hitter, but it appears that he will be an outstanding major-league hitter. Buckner had seasons of .344, .315, and .335 in the minors. In 1971, he batted .271 in his rookie year with the Dodgers, but in 1972, he batted .319 and was one of the top hitters in the National League. Williams made his evaluation of Buckner before the player saw any action in the majors.

It irritated Ted Williams when Short thought in terms of making trades with nothing but the box office in mind. Bob believed that people would pay money to watch Denny McLain and Curt Flood regardless of their performances. They were faces to Short, and he often said, "People will pay to watch Flood strike out or McLain give up home runs." Nothing could be farther from the truth. People will pay money to watch competitive baseball, especially winning baseball. After the first couple of starts, the novelty wore off and there wasn't any appreciable increase in attendance simply because McLain was pitching. And it's doubtful that Flood, with his lackluster, abbreviated stay with the Senators, brought any additional fans to the stadium. Superstars like Sandy Koufax, Bob Feller, and Willie Mays surely brought extra fans to the park, but there is no evidence that McLain and Flood pulled additional attendance.

The club continued its strange trading after the official

move to Texas. Short's first deal there sent relief pitcher Joe Grzenda, who had just completed his best season, to Saint Louis for vetaran infielder Ted Kubiak. Grzenda had an off season with Cardinals. After batting .213 in 46 games with the Rangers, Kubiak was sent to Oakland in a multi-player trade.

Kubiak and veteran Don Mincher, who was leading the Rangers in RBIs, with 39 after 61 games, went to the A's for minor-leaguers Vic Harris and Steve Lawson plus journeyman infielder Marty Martinez. It was a funny deal, because veterans like Mincher and Kubiak were just what Finley ordered for pennant insurance, and Short needed cash, not to mention the need to get rid of the salaries of Mincher and Kubiak. Their salaries totaled about $80,000 for the season. Kubiak played some good ball down the 1972 pennant drive, and Mincher got a big hit in the World Series.

In a deal before the end of the season, the Rangers sent veteran righthander Casey Cox to the New York Yankees for pitchers Jim Roland and Rich Hinton.

In another of his many deals with Charley Finley, Short sent pitcher Paul Lindblad back to the Oakland A's for minor-league infielder Bill McNulty and a player who was to be named later, plus $150,000 in cash. The player turned out to be former Senators outfielder Brant Alyea, who was assigned to the Rangers minor-league system.

And then, Short and Finley pulled the shocker. Moody Mike Epstein was traded to the Rangers for pitcher Horacio Piña in an even-up trade. Epstein was going from the World Champion Oakland A's to the lowly Texas Rangers. It was like going from the penthouse to the outhouse. At first, Epstein was shocked, and indicated that he might not report to Texas. But he later changed his mind and said that he was happy to be rejoining his old buddy, Bob Short. After all, Ted Williams was no longer around.

That brings up the question: did Short make a loan-trade

of Epstein to the A's, with the understanding that he could get him back once Williams was out of the picture? After all, Short always wanted to keep Epstein, and it was Williams who insisted that he be traded. And how about those players that Finley sent to Short's club who later went back to Finley's A's? Don Mincher, Paul Lindblad, and Frank Fernandez, the three players whom the A's traded to Short in 1971 all wound up back in Oakland. One has to wonder about that kind of player and cash shuffling. With that kind of public dealing, what goes on in private?

11

GAMES THAT
PEOPLE PLAY

The Player agrees to perform his services hereunder diligently and faithfully, to keep himself in first-class physical condition and to obey the Club's training rules, and pledges himself to the American public and to the Club to conform to high standards of personal conduct, fair play and good sportsmanship.

Section 3 (a) of Uniform
Player's Contract

Like Babe Ruth, the mythical Ted Williams managed to "pledge himself to the American public" without losing his own personality in baseball's manic and sometimes hypocritical Puritanism. As a manager, he often even seemed to assume the role of enforcer of that kind of baseball morality exemplified. He maintained a strict $500 fine for any player

200

caught with a girl in his room on the road. I once witnessed him kick a player off the team when Ted discovered the guy's sex life was not only outrageously public but also the wrong kind. His rule against drinking more than three beers on a flight angered many, especially Frank Howard. Williams frowned on excessive drinking during the season and continually pestered the players with questions about the extent of their drinking. I don't think Ted worried about these things in order to protect the image of baseball as much as because he feels those rules helped make him a successful ballplayer.

The best example is Ted's unrelenting crusade against smoking. He is against putting any kind of smoke in one's lungs, be it tobacco or marijuana. I remember once in the visiting club's dressing room at the Oakland Coliseum in May, 1970. Ted was telling one writer how he could get his wife to stop smoking those damn cigars.

"Just go outside and ask the equipment man for some snuff," he said. "It's fermented tobacco. Tell her to put a little bit of it under her tongue. She'll never want to smoke anything again. It'll cure her."

It bothered Ted to be around smoke so much he would rarely tolerate it. Part of the reason could be that his bronchial and upper respiratory system were often highly sensitive to smoke due to a bad case of bronchial pneumonia suffered while in Korea. Ted feels so strongly about young people smoking that he'll often approach a young lady or teenager smoking in public and say, right out of the blue, "Does your mother know you are smoking?" With this in mind, one can imagine Ted Williams' reaction if he knew some of his own players, like others throughout baseball, occasionally smoked marijuana.

It's really no secret. Erstwhile Washington third baseman Joe Foy, who came to the Senators with a marijuana history, told freelance writer Jack Mann in the spring of 1971, "How many young people in New York do you know who *haven't* smoked grass?" Washington *Daily News* sportswriter Tom Quinn, who occasionally covered the Senators in 1970 and 1971, claims to have smoked marijuana with "professional athletes of four major American sports, including professional baseball."

And Short exploited these whispers. After his famous debacle of a trade with Detroit, Short tried to justify getting rid of third baseman Aurelio Rodriguez by telling writers like Roy Blount of *Sports Illustrated* that Rodriguez smoked "pot" and by intimating that the Mexican ballplayer probably smoked it with that "goddamned hippy Quinn." Since Quinn, who had just spent four years in South America, spoke fluent Spanish and Short could never understand what he was saying to Rodriguez and Horacio Piña, who spoke little English, Short assumed they talked only about dark deeds in that strange tongue. "None of that was true," Quinn told me later. "Rodriguez and Piña were always more wary of me since I spoke their language. The fact is, I never really got to know them and, of course, I never tried to smoke any *cannabis* with them. I did smoke pot with a couple of other Senators' players."

Actually, marijuana in baseball is no big surprise. I personally discovered marijuana in organized baseball in 1956 when I was broadcasting games in the Class B Southwestern League. When Ponies pitcher Gene Armstrong remained in Plainview, Texas, for one road trip because of an injury, we spent some time together and he told me about the great wonderweed called marijuana. Gene, who was a pretty good pitcher (but never made the majors), tried to describe to me the feeling he and his girlfriend got when they took off their clothes on cold nights and smoked on California beaches. He never felt the cold or the wind.

If people like Armstrong were smoking marijuana as far back as 1956 when many still considered it the killer weed, one would be naïve to think it's not happening in professional baseball right now. "For better or worse, the everyday life of a baseball player is particularly conducive to the use of marijuana," Tom Quinn has told me. "What easier thing to fill those long stretches of tedium in a hotel room than light up a joint in private and listen to music or goof on the television or just simply drift off into one of those naps."

Quinn smoked marijuana with Senators players Jim Shellenback and Paul Casanova. He and Casanova got high on pot in the hotel in Kansas City on a road trip, and Quinn remembers Casanova going to the window, looking out, and saying, "Life should always be like this." Quinn tells me that he once traded Casanova three joints of marijuana for a dildo. Now there's a trade that must be a first in baseball.

Quinn said, "I got the impression talking to different players that blowing pot was a more common practice in the National League up until 1971, when apparently marijuana spread everywhere. It is still a fairly clandestine thing among the players in 1972, but those who do smoke seem to know who their counterparts are on other teams. Marijuana smokers in baseball seem to have a kind of underground communications grapevine to identify their own ilk." Casanova claims that a pitcher for the California Angels even grows his own.

Not all players smoke pot, and it should be pointed out that some players actively participate in programs designed to combat drug abuse. Wes Parker, Jim Lefebvre, Carl Yastrzemski, Reggie Smith, Byron Browne, and Larry Bowa are among those who have been acclaimed for their part in these programs.

I applaud Baseball Commissioner Bowie Kuhn's efforts to educate players about drug *abuse*—especially the misuse of amphetamines, the so-called "greenies." I never saw any of the Senators pop greenies the three seasons I was connected with the club, even though it may have happened. The only time I ever knew of one being suggested for a player occurred during the 1970 season. Outfielder Tom Grieve had been called up from the minors, and joined the Senators at Yankee Stadium. Grieve reported just before game time, and I was with Ted Williams when Ted asked him if he would be available to pinch hit if Ted needed him. Grieve said, "I guess so, but I am pretty tired since I traveled most of the night and didn't get much sleep." Ted said, "Well, take one of those little green pills. That will perk you up." I don't know if Grieve actually took the pill, and Ted may have been kidding.

It was common knowledge on the club that the Senators had some of their pitchers on the controversial anabolic steroid drugs in an effort to beef them up. These are the drugs taken by some football players, many weight lifters, and some weight specialists (shot put, discus and hammer throwers) in track and field. The drugs are designed to add weight and muscle to athletes, but they can also harm the sexual organs. Taken in excess, the drugs actually have a rotting effect on the testicles. Many doctors claim that the anabolic steroids can be beneficial if used properly. The Senators program was properly administered under the expert advice and care of Dr. George Resta, the Senators club doctor and an expert in the field.

Most players still prefer the more conventional means to get high and relax. Beer is everybody's favorite "replenisher of body fluids" in the clubhouse and booze seems to fit the national pastime a lot better than marijuana probably ever could.

I'll never forget the time that the thought of a couple of post-game drinks scared the dickens out of Papa Short. In the

1970 season David Eisenhower was traveling with the team as a statistician. David was good at it and he seemed to have a love of baseball like that of his grandfather, and an affinity for detail like his father-in-law. Everyone in the organization seemed to want to treat him as if he belonged to a more fragile existence than the real world. Maybe it was because he often wore dark pinstriped suits to the pressbox where he would work diligently and silently until the seventh inning, when he would stand up for the traditional seventh-inning stretch and ask a pressbox attendant for a cup of ice cream (and everyone else asked for beer and sandwiches). In Detroit one night, two Washington players, Darold Knowles and Jim French, invited David out for a couple of drinks after the game. They told the rest of their teammates they were going to get David drunk and laid. That seemed to be a particularly mischievous thought since David was married to President Nixon's daughter, Julie. Short saw them all getting into a taxi together outside Tiger Stadium, and he turned pale and screamed at them to be careful. The next day David told me they just went to a neighborhood bar for a couple of drinks, but Knowles recalled that David downed seven whiskey sours. Other than that, nothing happened and the joke, it turned out, was more on Short and Burke than anyone else.

I do remember one time when David Eisenhower was, well, nonplussed. On this flight he was seated right in the middle of the players (baseball's airplanes are segregated: brass, coaches and writers up front and then the proletariat) when they decided to select one of their freak all-star teams. I was introduced to these mythical teams the year before when I was elected Ugliest Broadcaster on the All-Ugly team. (Ted Williams, Ugliest Manager; George Susce, Ugliest Coach; Russ White, Ugliest Writer; Ugliest Players included Andy Etchebarren, Joe Grzenda, Tom Matchick and Bob Priddy.) As usual, the Knowles-and-French Comedy Team were the ones behind some of these teams. On this particular flight, I just managed to hear them propose an "all-pecker team" and caught the look on David's face. It was a blanch with shock. But the players showed no appreciation of David's embarrassment, and they went on to name the finalists: Frank Robinson, Minnie Minoso, Ralph Terry, Paul Casanova, and the Captain of the team, Orlando McFarlane. McFarlane? Casanova protested.

"You guys don't know nothing," Casanova said. "And you're my teammates! You should *know.*"

"Yeah, yeah, man," Ed Stroud butted in. "It's got to be McFarlane. They had to strap that man down when he ran the bases to keep him from tripping over himself."

The results were not announced over the plane's speaker . . . out of respect for the stewardesses.

George Brunet, who changed teams thirty-one times in an eighteen-year career in professional baseball, passed through Washington in 1970 between Seattle and Pittsburgh. He came to the Senators in Pompano Beach with the nickname Brew-master and a reputation to go with it. It didn't take him long to prove it either. Early in spring training Brunet went on a self-pity drunk, finally blubbering to the traveling secretary, Burt Hawkins, that he wanted to be traded and wouldn't have a chance with the Senators. The next morning Ted Williams invited Brunet to his thatch-roofed bungalow at Pompano's Municipal Field, convinced him he would pitch for the Senators, and warned him to stay out of trouble.

Brunet went on to have a good season for Ted until Short traded him to pitcher-poor Pittsburgh in the midst of a pennant run for Jim Shellenback and $50,000. Short claimed he needed the $50,000 in order to make the September payroll with the Senators in 1970. However, Brunet will be remembered in at least the twenty-three cities he has played in, and maybe even farther and wider, not for his pitching but for a funny little fact revealed in Bouton's book, *Ball Four.* Brunet, wrote Bouton, does not wear any underwear. Well, neither did Ted Williams on occasion. Sometimes he didn't even wear a jockstrap under his uniform. I would cringe every time I saw Ted pull those scratchy flannels over his bare fanny. I guess the Senators led the league in personnel without underwear in 1970.

The Senators also led the league in bankruptcies, with those of Denny McLain and Paul Casanova. Casanova was a regular consumer-out-of-control when Short talked him into declaring bankruptcy in 1970. Especially, he couldn't resist gadgets. He'd buy them on whim and play with them like a kid. He bought a camera with a timer so he could set it up to take a picture of himself. Except Casanova would pick up a photogenic gal in bars at home and on the road and then set up pornographic pictures of both of them. For a while, he carried a projector around with him on road trips and showed stag films. He'd also lug around his own stereo cassette tape recorder loaded with hard rock and latin music. I recall Ted remarking, when he saw players carrying attaché cases and music machines on road trips, "The fucking times have really changed. I used to carry my fucking bats. Now they carry everything except something that deals with baseball."

Broken marriages are not uncommon among the players in the majors. I suppose the ratio was no higher with the Senators than with any other group of prima donnas in society. Here were a group of men who felt so removed from the everyday world that some often referred to baseball fans disdainfully as "brownbaggers" or "nine-to-fivers." Most of them never had to work outside of baseball. It takes a long time for some men to mature in this artificial environment, like plants trying to grow under the neon.

Brant Alyea, Casey Cox, Dick Billings, and Paul Casanova all split with their wives while with the Senators. Barbara Billings, Carol Cox, Iva Watt (formerly married to Eddie Watt of the Orioles) and Gloria Bertaina have formed a Washington Area Ex-Players' Wives Club. Carol Cox actually had her husband arrested at the end of the 1971 season on a complaint of nonsupport. She claimed Casey walked out on her at the beginning of the season, so she hired a detective to follow him. She finally divorced him in March, 1972. A tell-tale sign of a baseball hubby who is fooling around, Carol Cox advises, are receipts for unaccounted-for clothes from Milt Goldberg, a wholesale ladies' clothing store in Boston frequented by the entire American League. "And I would recommend to baseball wives to get a detective if they have any suspicion whatsoever," Carol Cox told me.

She also said that baseball-wife friends of hers usually express concern about the supposed availability of stewardesses for the players. "Most of the stews don't care," Carol Cox said. "The players are fair game for stews." And I'll have to admit Rick Reichardt, Joe Coleman, Jim Hannan, Dick Bosman, and Brant Alyea all married stewardesses they met in Washington.

There was one player-chaser who not only admitted it, she tried to make it a career. Her name was Morgana Roberts, a stripper billed simply as Morgana. She made her debut on a cold, damp April afternoon during the Presidential Opener at RFK Stadium in 1970 when she climbed over the railing on the third base side, dashed onto the field and gave Frank Howard a kiss while he stood at home plate looking befuddled. I mentioned on the air that it was a wonder she didn't get frostbite in a micro miniskirt so short at first I thought it was a mod belt. Later that season, Morgana nailed Billy Cowan of the Angels in Anaheim and Wes Parker of the Dodgers in Los Angeles. I thought it was significant that she always went for the home team. But Morgana obviously over-stepped her bounds when she tried to get to Pete Rose at the All Star game in Cincinnati. That time police were waiting for her, and NBC censored her exposure (if that's the right word) when they refused to put the cameras on her. I don't know what they told her, but it convinced her she couldn't kiss baseball players without their permission. She never made another baseball appearance, which is sad because she had a great first half before the mid-July break.

There are plenty of young lovelies who make the rounds of spring training camps. One of the first outrageous stories of this nature I ever encountered was at Vero Beach in the spring of 1969. Ted Williams and Short always admired facilities like Dodgertown and Astrotown at Cocoa Beach, where Houston trains. Both clubs have barracks-type complexes which permit close scrutiny of the players by management. Ted always felt that plush resorts like Pompano Beach and Fort Lauderdale presented too many diversions for the players and few methods of checking up on them. That's why it was ironic that Dodgers officials were whispering and media people were laughing that day about a breach of security in Dodgertown the night before. It seems that some of the Dodgers had smuggled a Playboy Bunny into their barracks and she spent the night making Dodgertown a happier place.

Later that same spring Brant Alyea was visited by a couple of admirers at the Surf Rider Hotel there. Alyea at the time was a carefree bachelor whose clothes were as loud as he. Continually bragging about his lovemaking ability, he agreed to prove his point by putting on a show for some teammates. So on this night he arranged for the two girls to stay in a room in a hotel wing across from the players' housing. Then he left the drapes open so his pals could watch the show. Apparently several players were duly impressed and, of course, Alyea was incorrigible for months afterward.

Later that year, July 7, Alyea was arrested by the Fairfax County, Virginia, Police and charged with attempted rape. The warrant was issued on a complaint by a girl whom Alyea had been dating. He was released on bail after being booked, but he never stood trial because the girl later dropped the charges. Club lawyer Stan Bregman and the Fairfax County Prosecutor, Robert F. Horan, both contend that no money changed hands and that the girl dropped the charge of her own will. Bregman and Mrs. Louise Carmalt, the resident manager in the River Towers Apartment, where the incident allegedly happened, both say they felt the charge was trumped up.

The River Towers apartment complex was a favorite of the Senators players. Frank Howard usually stayed there until his family arrived in town after school let out each season. A lot of other professional people lived there. There was a heavy concentration of stewardesses, and that likely made it a more attractive place for the single Senators. The River Towers appreciated the prestige of having a number of ballplayers living there, and the resident manager said they were good tenants.

One of the saddest cases I ever ran across in baseball was a Mexican-Yaqui, mestizo-American named Filomeno Coronado Ortega. Everyone called him Phil. In fact, the Senators called him Firewater Phil because he couldn't drink whiskey very well but he couldn't turn it down either. Phil was signed by the Dodgers out of Arizona for a bonus of around $70,000 but the six-foot-four, two-hundred-pounder never lived up to his promise. He knew he would have to fight for a job with the Senators under Williams in the spring of 1969. Ted tried to get Ortega to throw more breaking balls. I remember the pitcher remarking after one session that he hadn't thrown so many breaking balls in a month. The pressure was surrounding Ortega then—and not just the pressure of baseball. Baseball writer Russ White always told me that Phil had an identity problem, that he was confused about whether he was an Indian or a Mexican or simply an American. Ortega was driven to break curfew and drink. One night, he got drunk and cracked up a rented car by slamming it into the back of another auto stopped at a stoplight. Police found out he played for the Senators so they brought him to the Surf Rider Hotel and reported the incident to Burt Hawkins, the traveling secretary. Hawkins told Ortega to go to bed but Ortega wandered around looking for an eighteen-year-old rookie, Jim Mason, who was away from his Alabama home for the first time. Mason told me the next day that Ortega wound up pounding on his door, begging him to let him in while Mason yelled at him to go away. The commotion woke up some coaches, who shooed Ortega away, presumably to his own room. But Ortega, who was fond of Mason, was persistent.

The next morning the whole team, including Ortega, was on the bus ready to go to West Palm Beach when Ted was first apprised of what had happened the night before. "Get his ass off that bus," he told Hawkins. "And get his ass out of camp." None of this was picked up by the press at the time. All Ted would say was that Ortega wasted a lot of potential.

Even though Ortega then caught on with the California Angels, his season of 1969 continued to go wrong. Late that April Ortega missed the Angels' team bus from Milwaukee to Chicago and had to pay a taxi $62 to take him the ninety miles in time. Eighteen days later he was badly beaten in a fist fight at 2 A.M. in the Casa Escobar Restaurant in Anaheim. He was hospitalized that time for a broken jaw and concussion, as well as cuts and bruises. California put him on its disabled list. Ortega got off the list in June, but in the first week in July, on a trip to Kansas City, a house detective caught him in the lobby of the Muehlbach Hotel, where the

Angels stayed. Ortega was dressed only in his undershorts. Manager Lefty Phillips fined the pitcher $500 and called Ortega "a disgrace to the ball club and to himself."

Ortega did not appear in another Angels game after the beating in Anaheim. And shortly after the incident in Kansas City, the Angels dropped him to the Hawaii farm club, the same thing they did to Bo Belinsky when they decided he was getting too outrageous. As a bonus baby, Ortega was a flop. He squandered his bonus so fast the money seemed to do him in.

A temperamental but still very promising Bob Short bonus baby is Jeff Burroughs, who got $88,000 in 1969 at the age of eighteen, right out of high school in Long Beach, California. Burroughs celebrated his twenty-first birthday in spring training of 1972 with some spirits and companionship in his room. Apparently he was not too discreet and word got back to Williams, who called Burroughs in for a chat. He asked Burroughs if he would like to go to Plant City, the Rangers minor-league camp. Well, Burroughs blew up at Williams and said he had taken enough "shit" from general manager Joe Burke and Williams and was ready to leave camp. Then he stormed into the clubhouse, ripped his uniform off, cursed Williams, and vowed never again to play for Williams. "He thinks he's God," Burroughs raged. "Well, I've had enough of him. I'm going home." Clubhouse man Fred Baxter asked Burroughs' friend Joe Lovitto to try and calm Jeff.

Meanwhile, Williams and the rest of the club had boarded the team bus for a short ride to Fort Lauderdale and an exhibition game against the New York Yankees. Irritated at waiting for Burroughs, Ted gave orders, "If he doesn't get on this bus, it's a $1,000 fine." Burroughs refused to board the bus and did not show up for workouts the next two days. The Rangers did a remarkable job keeping Burroughs' absence without leave out of the press. In the meantime, Short and Burke got in touch with Burroughs, and after some pleading and promising, got the "bonus baby" to rejoin workouts.

It was Burroughs' birthday celebration and the aftermath that set the stage for the most serious falling-out between Short and Williams later in the season. Most people in the Rangers camp seemed to side with Burroughs in the birthday celebration dispute. After all, he was a rich baseball player who could afford a little celebration, and even the most typical young men elect to celebrate their twenty-first birthdays.

Burroughs was not the typical eighteen-year-old bud of youth who signs for an enormous baseball bonus. Even as a recent high school graduate he insisted that Short draw up a special contract for him so that his parents would *not* get a nickel of his bonus money.

Burroughs was not a hero with the maids at the Surf Rider Hotel in Pompano Beach. He had a habit of sticking his gum on the headboard of the bed when he retired each evening. The maids objected to this and left him a note asking that he stop it. One of his teammates found the note and penned a postscript which read, "Go fuck yourself." The maid who found the note didn't appreciate the humor, and called the note to the attention of the Senators front office. It was reported to Williams, and there was old Teddy Ballgame, perhaps feeling much like a counselor at a boys' school, having to call in bonus baby Burroughs to scold him for sticking gum on the bed and for writing nasty notes to the maid.

Jeff may have been juvenile in some ways, but he was precocious in others. During the 1971 season, Williams told me, "Burroughs is sleeping with a forty-five-year-old broad here in Washington. He must be able to screw better than he can hit the curve."

It was apparent late in the '71 season that Williams and Burroughs were going to have some personality problems.

Jeff had a tendency to get a little heavy, especially in the fanny. Ted remarked, "I had a dream last night. I dreamed that Burroughs got so fucking fat that his ass was six ax handles wide." One of the writers heard the remark, cleaned up the language and wrote it in his game story. Burroughs didn't appreciate it, and I was in Ted's clubhouse office when Jeff came in to ask about the remark. Ted laughed it off, and told Jeff that he was just kidding, and couldn't believe that anyone would print the remark.

After the big altercation at Pompano Beach the following spring, things went downhill for Burroughs. He developed a bad back and went on the disabled list early in the '72 season. When he got back in the lineup, he had trouble hitting the curve and was farmed to Denver. And the fact that Burroughs was letting his hair grow to near-shoulder length didn't endear him any to closely cropped Ted.

12

TEXAS—OR BUST

Short was so greedy to take his team to Texas that his Washington Senators actually debuted in Dallas in 1969 before they did in the District of Columbia. Nobody should have cared at the time. The team was filled with the TW-BS "Whole New Ballgame" that first year, and the Presidential Opener was just two days away after a long, long spring warm-up. But strangely, eerily, we all seemed to notice.

Joe Burke had made out the 1969 exhibition schedule and he filled in the last two days with games against Pittsburgh in Louisville, Kentucky. Not only was Louisville a good traditional choice for major-league exhibitions, but it was also Burke's hometown, where he got his start in baseball management. The games would give Joe a good excuse to visit his relatives.

215

However, Senators groundskeeper Joe Mooney went to Louisville to inspect the playing field and returned with word that the field was flooded. "Can't play there," decided Short instantly. "We've got to play them in Dallas."

Dallas? Immediately *Washington Star* writers Merrell Whittlesey and Morris Siegel gave Short the third degree about the switch. Did this mean Short was threatening Washington even before the community had a chance to respond? Short coolly denied any premeditations whatsoever on the last-minute change and everyone let it go. Or rather, the Presidential Opener right after the series crowded the incident out of everyone's mind.

Both Senators exhibitions drew poor crowds of under 5,-000 in Dallas-Ft. Worth and I can remember the nervous joking by Burke, Hawkins, and the writers about the "bush-league turnout." One piece of trivia stuck in my own mind: the Senators had never played exhibition games in Dallas before. This was the first indication to me that Short indeed was flirting with Texas. The next year Short officially scheduled exhibitions there. That does not mean much until you fit the fact into the rest of picture.

For instance, at the outset Short refused to include in the franchise contract a clause that would obligate him to keep the ball club in Washington. James Lemon especially tried to get Short to agree to at least a short-term commitment but Short said no. Another pointer came early when, in 1969, Short refused a Vince Lombardi proposal to install artificial turf in Kennedy Stadium, the cost to be split three ways among the Senators, the Redskins, and the Armory Board, the stadium landlord. Short conveniently claimed that he was opposed to artificial turf because Williams preferred real grass. Throughout his three years in Washington, Short would continue to avoid investing a penny in modernizing the stadium. Even when he got improved lighting and fencing on the parking lots around the stadium, for more night protection, the government paid for it, not Short.

I became more suspicious during Short's second season, when I had interested Ted Williams in buying a home in the Washington area. I knew that Ted, being such an outdoorsman, might have felt more comfortable living in a wooded country-club surburb with plenty of waterfront—such as Tantallon on the Potomac adjacent to Fort Washington National Park. Ted liked the idea too and he got quite excited at some of the plush $80,000–$125,000 homes in the area. People were willing to knock $10,000 off the price of a home just to get Ted Williams into the development. Since Short was paying $15,000 a year to maintain an apartment for him at the Shoreham West, Ted thought it might be a better investment to put the money in equity on a house. Short said no! Short also dissuaded Mike Epstein and Del Unser from buying homes in the Washington area.

In addition, when radio and TV contracts ran out the end of 1970, WWDC radio wanted a one-year contract for 1971 with an option for 1972. Short would not agree to the option and, to me, that meant the club would not be there. This was all but confirmed when Short countered WTOP-TV's proposal for a three-year contract with a special clause rendering the contract void if he moved the Senators.

By the middle of the 1971 season, I was becoming convinced Short would move at all costs, but WWDC station manager Bill Sanders did not agree. He did say, however, that WWDC might not pay the $200,000 net fee Short was asking for the Senators radio rights the next year. I told him that I had a plan to buy the air time from the station and sell the advertising myself, perhaps making enough to pay the ball club a $300,000 net fee for the rights. Sanders asked me to take the proposal to Short and I did so around midseason.

Short's reaction confirmed all my impressions. There was

no way he would operate in Washington after 1971. He said maybe I could make the offer to whomever the new owner might be if he didn't get permission to move.

Short knew that his selling price of $12.4 million was inflated. He said, "All I want is the $9.4 million I paid for the club, plus the $600,000 I lost the first year, the $1 million I lost last year and what I've lost so far this season."

"Short's demand has been equated with the curious logic of a man who paid $9,000 for an automobile, mishandled and maltreated it, paid $3,000 in repairs, and says, 'Now I've got a car that's worth $12,000,'" wrote Shirley Povich in the *Post*.

Suddenly in late 1971, frustrated Washingtonians began to come awake to the Short Game, a version of the old Charley O. Finley shuffle. Finley showed in Kansas City that a little loathing can take you a long way. Breed it and the fans will practically pay you to leave.

Short started with tickets and seating. As soon as he took over in 1969, Short raised the prices of all seats and converted much of the regular grandstand into reserved seats. Despite those measures, 918,106 paid to see the Senators at RFK Stadium that year—the second highest attendance in the seventy-one-year history of baseball in Washington. But the next year he raised prices again, giving Washington an average rise of between 50 and 100 percent on tickets over two years, as well as the distinction of having the most expensive seats in baseball. Even so, over 825,000 fans turned out that second year, and Short would brag to me that he would take in more money than the Orioles, who brought in over a million attendance. Indeed, the Orioles unreserved grandstand seats sold for 85 cents compared to Short's $2.25. Moreover, Baltimore had special 55-cent prices for kids but Short never permitted that. The only way underprivileged kids, or groups, would get into a ballgame was if some businessman bought tickets and donated them. At a front-office meeting at Kennedy Stadium, April 11, 1969, it was determined that, "There will be no free admissions or discount tickets, regardless of the circumstances. We will approach businessmen in the area for funds for the poverty areas."

The kids were not the only people who received shabby treatment at RFK Stadium. At the close of the 1969 season, Jack Anderson used his syndicated column to reveal how Short and company were treating wounded Vietnam veterans and other hospitalized soldiers who wished to attend Senators games. In past years, the Senators management had handed out complimentary box-seat tickets to the wounded and sick veterans. However, Short, through Molomot, informed Washington's Walter Reed Army Hospital that box seats would no longer be given to patients. The Senators did make general admission tickets available, and all during the season, veterans in bandages and with crutches were obliged to hobble to the top of the great stadium to watch games from the highest bleachers. Because the soldiers in wheelchairs couldn't make it, they were allowed to park their wheelchairs precariously on the ramps.

Explained Molomot to the Jack Anderson people, "We are a business, not an eleemosynary institution. Seats are our stock in trade like coats on the rack in a clothing store." Anderson closed out his column by saying, "Although he couldn't afford to let wounded veterans sit in the box seats, he offered this column free tickets for next season."

As soon as the announcement about ticket price increases and the changes in the location of general admission seats were announced, the Senators were flooded with letters of protest. Many were senior citizens who had been used to sitting in good general admission seats on ground level. Many were retired, and the price increase made a severe dent in their budgets. Since Short made all the general admission seats upper-decks seats, it presented the physical problem of climbing several steep ramps. The protests were discussed at that same front-office meeting on April 11, but the minutes of the meeting state, "Discussed the situation of old-timers having to sit in the upper deck because the general admission seats were moved. Decided that these people would just have to pay more for a reserved seat or sit in the upper deck."

Short resented doubleheaders, the old fan bonus of two games for the price of one. In 1968 under the ownership of James H. Lemon, the Senators scheduled six double-bills. The first year Short managed to cut them back to four. In 1970, Short had just two doubleheaders and the following year, just one. In his first season in Texas, Short scheduled only two doubleheaders. Thirteen other major-league clubs played at least four; six clubs played six or more.

All along Short had alienated the Washington fans with big things such as ticket prices and little things such as a refusal to permit televising of the Presidential Opener any of his three years in D.C., despite the fact the game was always a sellout! Short went so far as to threaten to sue the Baltimore Orioles for televising a few Orioles games from RFK Stadium in the 1970 season.

His greatest failure with the fans had to be the farcical trade for Denny McLain with Detroit. If the man was not stupid, people figured, he was at least indiscreet. Fans identified with Ted Williams' rage with Short over that one. But a year later some of these same outraged fans began to think that Short had to scuttle the team a little in order to create the kind of Finleyesque disgust that would make it easier for Short to pull out. Short purposefully was alienating the press, fans, advertisers, and civic officials just so he could prove to the other owners: "Look! No support! Let me go!"

Finally that last year, Short unleashed an insupportable barrage of unrealistic demands and claims. "I thought that owning a major-league club would be fun," he said. "Well, I've put in more time and money and had more headaches

in baseball than in my trucking and real estate combined.
. . . I thought I could do something in this town. A fresh
outlook, promotion, Ted Williams managing—that sort of
thing. If I could roll back these three years I would under no
conditions buy this club . . . Washington, except for a few
loyal people, is a bad baseball town. . . ."

He was as full of lawsuit threats as a scorpion is full of
poison. He threatened to sue us broadcasters for second-
guessing TW; to sue WTOP-TV and WWDC over minor
policy disagreements; to sue Pompano Beach, Florida, for
better training facilities; to sue the landlord and the Washington Redskins football team for playing on wet turf and
churning up the field. ("Ya' know what that's like?" he asked
rhetorically about the Redskins. "That's like inviting someone into your home and having him shit right on the car-
pet.")

Some of the squabbles that Short would get into were
petty and funny. He started the practice of giving away au-
tomobiles from time to time in lottery drawings after the
games. Oscar Molomot and Ted Rodgers worked a deal with
the Lustine Chevrolet people in suburban Maryland for several cars at half-price of dealer cost to be given away by the
club. Part of the agreement was that Lustine would provide
a bullpen car to bring in relief pitchers, and this car would
be painted with signs advertising Lustine. All was well and
good until the Armory Board, which controlled the stadium,
informed Short that the advertising was illegal, since the
stadium contract stipulated that the only advertising within
the stadium would be that purchased on the scoreboard billboard.

Short told Armory Board officials, "To hell with you. If you
don't like it, sue me." So the bullpen car, complete with
advertising, was used for the next two seasons, since the
Armory Board didn't elect to sue.

The Lustine people must have thought they would never

get paid anything for the cars. They received no money from the club for the cars given away in 1970 until well into 1971.

But they were in the same boat with dozens of creditors. When the 1970 season began, one of Short's veteran employees remarked, "Now you are going to find out how Short operates. He will not pay his bills and will scream poor mouth."

The prediction was absolutely correct. Not only did he not pay any stadium rent for the 1970 and 1971 seasons until after he had moved his franchise to Texas, but other creditors had to wait almost as long.

Dozens of letters came through the Senators promotions office, wanting to know when payment would be made for items that had been purchased for premium giveaways to fans. In other words, when the kids of Washington were playing with bats, balls, etc., and were wearing buttons, hats, and tee shirts, given away by the Senators, creditors were wondering if they would ever be paid for those items.

The capper came at the close of the 1970 season when I answered a telephone at the stadium. It was the C&P telephone company, saying that if the Senators didn't pay their long overdue bill, service would be discontinued.

When I would confide to close associates and friends regarding the fact that the Senators weren't paying any bills, and were being hounded by creditors, the response would be utter astonishment. After all, wasn't Short a multi-millionaire, and didn't he fly his personal jet around all the time?

His use of the private Lear Jet was the one thing that seemed to outrage Washingtonians the most. He was screaming poor mouth, about to go bankrupt (belly-up is the way Short always said it), and yet, here he was, with a pilot and co-pilot flying him all over the country in a private jet.

The $700,000 plane was owned by Gopher Aviation, which in turn was owned by Short. He once told me that it cost him at least $750 to put it in the air for any kind of flight.

But the actual cost varies, depending on the lease agreement and the number of hours the plane is used. The average operating cost for a Lear seems to be about $400 per hour, a lot more than conventional commercial airline travel.

Maybe the worst symptom of neglect on Short's part was his own front office. One of his first deeds as owner was to buy up general manager George Selkirk's contract, and to make it obvious he either wanted to take charge himself or he wanted *nobody* in charge. Usually, it was more like the latter. No one knew where authority stopped or started. Ed Doherty, former PR man with Ted in Boston and former general manager in Washington, was brought in, presumably because Ted wanted a familiar face nearby. But his presence accomplished even more confusion. Short's personal promotion man, Oscar Molomot, took away one of Burt Hawkins' three titles, Public Relations Director, and Doherty took away another, Press Relations Officer, which left Hawkins with the mere label Traveling Secretary. That made Hawkins mad and nervous. It also made John Welaj jittery when Molomot commandeered his own title, Director of Promotions and Advertising. Naturally, a petty, catty front-office power struggle developed among the four.

And before spring training was over in 1970, Ed Doherty was demoted to a scouting position and asked to travel all over the country. It was heartbreaking and ultimately health-breaking for the old man who just a year prior had been the one who sat with Short in the owner's box at games. He and Burke both wanted to be general manager, both wanted to represent the team in meetings for general managers. It was an ironic situation; Doherty was the man who had hired Burke and approved the hiring of Hawkins, and they were the two who convinced Williams and Short that Ed was not needed. Hawkins was happy to get back his title as press relations chief when Doherty left.

Half a season later Doherty had suffered a stroke and

could not speak well. As a favor, I met Ed at National Airport the day before the 1970 World Series started in Baltimore. Ed had to write out everything he wanted to communicate. I drove him to Baltimore for his last World Series. I couldn't believe that people like Joe Burke and Burt Hawkins were treating Doherty like he had the plague. But I guess I shouldn't have been surprised.

Ed deserved a better ending in baseball. His first wife had died, and he had remarried during the 1969 season. He was a spry seventy, and wanted to continue in baseball for several years. But his demotion to a traveling scout in 1970 broke his heart, and a man who had devoted his entire life to baseball suffered a stroke in a demanding traveling job. He deserved a better fate. It made me sick when Burke represented the club at Doherty's funeral in 1971.

There is little use in going into all the detail about the misorganization of Short's front office. The handwriting was on the wall when he fired George Selkirk and announced that he would run the club as an absentee owner. Another key mistake on his part was his refusal to give a valuable person in the farm department a token raise. Marjie Smyth had been in the farm department for almost a decade, and there were those who felt she knew more about it than farm director Hal Keller. She had been long overdue for a raise, and was going to ask whoever bought the club for it. Keller knew she deserved one, but there were many rumors in print that he was going to be replaced, so he wasn't about to make any recommendation to Short which would cost the new owner money, regardless of how little it might be. When Short visited the minor-league spring training base at Plant City, Florida, Marjie hit him up for a raise. He gave a negative reply, and she indicated that she would have to find other employment.

"I'll have to give two weeks' notice, Mr. Short, because I must have more money."

"No, you won't," Short replied. "If you can't work for me in two weeks, you can't work for me now. You're fired."

The very same day, Marjie called the Chicago White Sox to inquire about employment and was hired on the spot at the salary she wanted. Short lost a good employee.

Marjie's replacement was Mary Corado, a honey of a blonde. After the 1970 season, Mary told the Senators she had to have more money. Again, the answer was no, and she too left for a much better-paying job.

Two other cases in point were the loss of the team trainer and the groundskeeper after the 1970 season. When Short wouldn't give them raises, Joe Mooney left to become the groundskeeper at Fenway Park in Boston, and trainer Tom McKenna left to become a trainer with the New York Mets.

But why worry about a front office if you have plans to move the franchise? Many employees would not want to make a move somewhere else because of homes and roots in the Washington area. Besides, if he moved to Texas or Toronto, he would have to work a few local people into the front office.

Williams often said, "Damn, I wish Short had the money to hire the scouts we need to be competitive. We need scouts in South America. The successful clubs have them there. That alone can be the difference in being a winner and a loser in the league." Ted even had some Latin scouts in mind. He wanted to hire Minnie Minoso and Camilo Pascual among others. But Short always pleaded no money, and the scouting system was not improved.

In spite of the good turnout of 918,106 fans at Short's inflated ticket prices in 1969, Short claimed that he was losing money, and needed fresh capital to continue operation. Many people, including some front-office personnel, didn't see how he could have lost money in 1969. There were front-office whispers indicating that he must be putting some of the ball-club cash flow into his other businesses, which were floundering. He never opened his books to the public, so it's impossible to really know if he was pumping ball-club money into his other businesses. Regardless of what was happening to the money, Short needed more.

The first place that most baseball clubs go when they need cash is to the Emprise Corporation, an outfit which employs 40,000 people and does $125 million worth of business annually. The chief subsidiary of Emprise is Sportservice, which caters at all types of sports arenas, airports, theaters, and other outlets in the United States, Canada, and England. It also operates parking lots, sells books and news materials, programs, and advertising space at sports sites.

Emprise has long been baseball's "angel," extending interest-free loans to floundering franchises in exchange for favors such as long-term concession contracts. Bill Veeck borrowed money from Emprise when he operated clubs in Milwaukee, Cleveland, Saint Louis, and Chicago. Connie Mack borrowed $250,000, interest-free, when he was having money troubles with his old Philadelphia A's in 1951. More recently, Emprise has loaned $200,000 to the Chicago White Sox, $500,000 to the Detroit Tigers, $2 million to the Montreal Expos, $2 million to the Seattle Pilots, and when the Pilots became the Brewers and were switched to Milwaukee, Emprise put another $500,000 into the organization. Needless to say, these loans reaped some benefits. Sportservice has the concessions for the White Sox, Brewers, Expos, and Tigers. The fat loans to the Montreal and Milwaukee franchises returned special plums. Sportservice has an exclusive ten-year concessions contract with Montreal, with an option to renew. The concessions contract with Milwaukee is for twenty-five years.

In all, Emprise, under the name of Sportservice, handles the concessions for seven major-league baseball clubs, eight professional football teams, five professional basketball clubs, fifty horse and dog tracks in the United States and Canada, plus ten more in England and Puerto Rico.

It's easy to see how baseball and sports in general were embarrassed on April 26, 1972, when the Emprise Corporation, along with two Mafia figures, was convicted by a federal grand jury in Los Angeles on charges of criminally conspiring to obtain secret ownership of the Frontier casino-hotel in Las Vegas. *Sports Illustrated* reported in its issue of May 29, 1972, that Anthony Zerilli and Michael Polizzi of the Detroit Mafia were convicted along with the Emprise Corporation. Emprise is subject to a maximum $10,000 fine.

Emprise had long been under fire from several lawmakers in Washington who claimed that the Emprise organization had turned into a front for the mob. Emprise officials denied this and claimed that if they did business with the Mafia, they didn't know it. It came as no surprise when in May of 1972, the Jacobs brothers came in for much grilling before the House Select Committee on organized crime in sports, chaired by Claude Pepper, a Democrat from Florida. Congressman Sam Steiger, a Republican from Arizona and a longtime critic of Emprise, charged before the committee that "the Jacobs brothers did business with the Mafia, bribed, intimidated people, and used hidden money." The Jacobs brothers again denied the charges.

Some people in Washington were surprised to learn that Emprise had the concessions at Kennedy Stadium, as well as the restaurant and cocktail lounge at Washington National Airport. The Washington *Daily News* headlined its story about the hearings, May 10, 1972, "MAFIABURGERS AT THE OLD BALLPARK."

Had Bob Short had control of the concessions at Kennedy Stadium, there is a good chance that the Senators would still be in Washington. He often said that if he could gain control of the concessions, he would obtain a huge interest-free loan from Sportservice, in exchange for a long-term concessions contract. He needed something in the neighborhood of $7.5 million to pay off his notes on the Senators franchise. That is the figure which he later received from the Arlington Park Corporation in Texas. But there was little hope that Short would gain control of the concessions at Kennedy Stadium. With its being a government-owned and publicly financed stadium, the Armory Board, an agency of the D.C. government, was insistent that it keep a good share of the concessions since the stadium was a white elephant, and the Armory Board had a hard time meeting interest payments on the stadium bonds. *None* of the principal on the stadium bonds had been retired since the stadium was constructed a decade before. The Redskins also came in for a share of the concessions.

Short thought that his chances of gaining control of the stadium concessions were slim. Besides, his stadium contract, which controls things like the rent and concessions, was not up for renewal until the end of 1971, and he needed cash now. Therefore, he was not in a position to qualify for the Emprise interest-free loans which were so readily available to financially troubled owners. To further complicate any Emprise possibilities for Short, Sportservice was already in Kennedy Stadium, so any loan reward for them would have to be in the form of a long-term extension of the concessions contract.

At the end of 1972, Sportservice unexpectedly and without explanation dropped its contract with Kennedy Stadium. The fact that a baseball club didn't return to Washington for the 1973 season may have been a factor. The $23 million-dollar stadium stood vacant most of the time, and with the limited use, perhaps Sportservice felt that the contract wasn't worth the trouble. However, critics point out that the Stadium is within eyesight of Capitol Hill, and feel that the 1972 investigation into Emprise may have made it uncomfortable for Sportservice.

It had already been tough for Short to borrow the $9 million a year earlier to purchase the club. Money was tight, and the prime interest rate was at an all-time high, about 9 percent. But never underestimate Bob Short's ability.

Short somehow managed to obtain a loan fund of $2,-200,000 from the Fruehauf Corporation in Detroit. He had done business with Fruehauf through his trucking interests, but the fact that he was able to obtain that type of loan under the existing tight-money conditions is difficult to understand. Some, including at least one player who was involved in the Denny McLain trade with the Detroit Tigers, feel that the Tigers assisted Short in obtaining the loan, thereby setting the stage for the one-sided trade between the Senators and Tigers. While Short and the Tigers deny this, if the Tigers did assist Short in obtaining the loan, it's easy to see how he would be indebted to them and would be in a compromising position when it came to making player trades.

Short borrowed $1 million dollars from the fund on January 1, 1970, and it became apparent that he was talking with the Tigers about a McLain trade a short time later. As a matter of fact, at the Welcome Home, Senators, Luncheon in early April, he sat next to Tigers manager Mayo Smith, and when Short made his remarks to the audience, he revealed that he had been talking with Mayo about a possible trade for McLain, even though McLain was suspended from baseball for his part in an alleged bookmaking operation. Short said, "I have every hope that McLain will be with the Senators by the first of July." That was when Denny would come off the suspended list.

If Short did receive help from the Tigers in obtaining the big loan fund from Fruehauf, he certainly didn't receive the most favorable loan conditions. Short was to repay any amount drawn from the fund within 60 months together with interest at 9.75 percent a year. That is about the same interest that he contracted when he bought the club a year earlier. The loan fund with Fruehauf was secured by means of a grant to Fruehauf of a security interest in 521 of Admiral-Merchants' trailers.

The Fruehauf loan was actually made to Admiral-Merchants, a trucking interest owned by Short, but it was clear that he obtained the loan primarily for the Senators. When he borrowed the $1 million from the Fruehauf fund the first of January, the money was transferred from the Marine Midland Grace Trust Company in New York to his Admiral Merchants account with the First National Bank of St. Paul, Minnesota, and then to the Washington Senators account with the American Security and Trust Company in Washington.

In making this loan, Short may have violated the Interstate Commerce Act (Title 49 U.S. Code), and section 10 of the Clayton Anti-Trust Act. Both of these laws state that carriers, such as Short's Admiral-Merchants outfit, cannot engage in financial transactions with other companies that have interlocking directors or officers, such as Short's Washington baseball club, unless the arrangements have been made pursuant to competitive bidding. Short was the president and senior officer in both Admiral-Merchants and the Washington Senators, and there was no competitive bidding connected with the loan.

When Senator J. Glenn Beall of Maryland became aware of Short's questionable loan from Fruehauf, he demanded an investigation by the Interstate Commerce Commission. Actually, the ICC was already investigating the matter, but it was a hush-hush affair. The investigation began in June of 1971, about four months before Short was granted permission to move the franchise to Texas. Many observers felt that had the Interstate Commerce Commission elected to take Short to court, it would have prevented the switch of the franchise. Baseball's chief counsel in the office of Commissioner Bowie Kuhn, Sandy Hadden, was advised of the possibility of legal action against Short, and it was then reviewed by the baseball bigwigs. Finally, it was decided to let the franchise move go through unless the government brought legal action against Short. If that happened, baseball would reconsider the feasibility of the franchise shift, under the circumstances.

After its investigation, and a typical bureaucratic delay of almost a year, it was decided that the ICC would not prosecute. In a letter to Senator Beall, ICC Chairman George M. Stafford expressed his deep concern over the possible ramifications which might have resulted from the loan arrangement involving Admiral-Merchants and the Washington Senators.

However, he was not positive of winning a case against Short in court, and, therefore, elected not to prosecute. He did indicate his desire for Congress to change the reading in the Interstate Commerce Act to insure successful prosecution in future cases of this nature.

Stafford came in for criticism from Tom Dowling in the *Washington Evening Star* for his failure to take Short to court, who quoted an ICC source as saying, "Short shouldn't have got away with this." The headline over the story read "ICC LET SENATORS GET AWAY. FACTS OF SHORT'S ILLEGAL LOAN BARED."

People within the Interstate Commerce Commission have told me that for some unknown reason, the agency whitewashed the Short loan matter and handled it all in a very secretive manner. In my efforts to discover why, I learned that, like most agencies, the ICC is supposed to be operated in a bi-partisan manner. But like most agencies in government, politics seem ever-present. I discovered that Commissioner Stafford, even though a Republican, was appointed to his post by President Lyndon Johnson, at a time when Bob Short was treasurer and chief fund-raiser for the Democratic Party. When I suggested to ICC officials that this fact might be the basis for a whitewash job on Short's loan transaction, I naturally received a denial.

Again, Bob Short had proved himself astute at operating with someone else's money. And how was he going to pay back that Fruehauf loan? With some money from Texas, naturally. On November 19, 1971, the Arlington Park Corporation, using taxpayers' money, drew a check for $1,181,-458.23 payable to Admiral-Merchants and Fruehauf with the notation "payment of invoice per approval of Washington Senators, Inc. in accordance with terms of indenture." This check drawn on the Republic National Bank of Dallas satisfied the $1 million loan to the Senators, plus the absurd interest.

But what happened to the remainder of that loan fund? Short was given credit for $200,000 with the purchase of 350 new trailers from Fruehauf at the time the $2.2 million fund was established. That left Short with $1 million in available credit in the fund, but with the ICC investigation, plus subsequent publicity, the heat was on too much to borrow any more cash under the existing arrangement. Short requested and received permission from Fruehauf to convert the balance due to an Admiral-Merchants equipment obligation, thus the nature of the remaining balance due was changed. On December 31, 1971, the $209,348.43 which Short owed for the 350 trailers was added to an existing equipment obligation, bringing the total obligation to $791,340.26 to be repaid over approximately 80 months.

Short continued to add new trailers to his empire, buying 20 more from Fruehauf in 1972, with an equipment obligation at an interest rate of 8.5 percent.

Despite the fact that he received a $7.5 million advance on his radio-TV rights for the Texas Rangers when he moved to Arlington, apparently, Short continued to have money problems with his business. In September of 1972, the ICC discovered that Short was negotiating with the First National Bank of St. Paul, Minnesota, for a $500,000 revolving credit loan at 1 percent above the prime interest rate.

Bob Short was well aware that his franchise shift to Texas would have to be done with precision planning and timing. He opened the 1971 season with two new gate attractions in Curt Flood and Denny McLain and with renewed promises that he would give Washington a pennant, but at the same time he was advising Del Unser not to buy a home in Washington because "we may be somewhere else next season." When Flood jumped the club and McLain started his losing and troublemaking act, it became apparent that the Senators were doomed for another last-place finish, and that many fans would show their resentment over the McLain trade by staying away from the park. Maybe that's what Short wanted.

It was full speed ahead for Short and his plans to leave Washington. It wouldn't be easy. It would take many threats, some agitation, a lot of deception, and a lot of politics.

In June *The Sporting News* made public the fact that Short was not paying his stadium rent or any other bills. The next month, the Armory Board threatened to shut off the stadium lights and lock the stadium gates unless Short or his representative would arrange a rent-payment schedule. That was exactly what Short wanted. When people in Washington decided they had enough of his game, and started making threats, he would have them where he wanted them. "Look, this town doesn't want me. You can't make me go broke in Washington. Nobody wants to buy it. Let me go to Texas where they will appreciate me."

Things were falling in place for Bob Short. Now Bowie Kuhn and the American League were concerned. A special "highly confidential" meeting was called the last day in June in Detroit. Short presented all his alleged problems to the owners. Things that he called lack of civic support, lack of competitive media contracts, the unwillingness of city officials to give him a sweatheart contract.

Baltimore Orioles owner Jerry Hoffberger, never a fan of
Short, tried to get Short to show his hand by asking if he
planned to ask permission to move, now or in the future. But
Short played it cagy.

Knowing that no one would buy at his inflated asking
price of $12.4 million, his official stand at that point was, "The
club is for sale." Short's plan was progressing smoothly. The
secret Detroit meeting ended with the American League
owners adopting the following resolution: "The president of
the league should be authorized . . . immediately to consider
the urgent Washington matter discussed today by studying
all possible solutions and further that the president . . . report
the results of each study and make recommendations to the
league with an appropriate solution or solutions."

It wasn't long before news of what happened at that secret Detroit meeting started to leak out. Short had threatened the owners with a lawsuit, if they didn't let him move
his franchise. But he stopped short of making a formal request to move. He needed nine votes to move, and many
people didn't feel that he could get them. However, Shirley
Povich of the *Post* did a private survey and learned that Short
might well have the votes, even at that early date.

As would be expected, and perhaps as Short wanted, the
Washington media people really started to give him hell for
his threats to move, his failure to pay his rent and other bills,
and his off-season trade for McLain, which had become the
baseball joke of the century. Short continued bad-mouthing
D.C.

Meanwhile, Bowie Kuhn and Joe Cronin were working
together to see if they could save the franchise for Washington. Kuhn grew up in Washington and had been a scoreboard
operator at the Griffith Stadium. He thought Washington was

a good baseball town, and he knew the bad spot baseball would be in if Washington were left without a franchise. Short didn't think highly of Kuhn's efforts to prevent his move. He never liked Kuhn, and practically every time Kuhn's name would come up in a conversation between Short and myself, he invariably described him as "that idiot."

When Short kept on bad-mouthing Washington, Kuhn finally told him to keep his mouth shut about the situation. This became public when I asked Short to come on my talk show out of Fran O'Brien's to discuss the baseball situation in Washington. Shirley Povich and several other writers were to join me on the program. But it was with some embarrassment that Short told me that Kuhn had muzzled him and wouldn't let him discuss the matter publicly until a solution to his problems was found.

Bowie Kuhn beat the bushes in an effort to find someone who would pay Short's inflated asking price, he even talked with several corporations, but had no luck. Short's plan was working perfectly. Short liked his chances of getting the votes needed to move when the time came to ask. He knew he had the Milwaukee vote. After all, he was a vocal leader in the move to switch the Seattle franchise there, and that made him a hero in Milwaukee.

And how about those clubs that might want to move later on? Short correctly felt that they would be reluctant to vote against his move if there was a chance they would come back with a move request of their own. Vern Stouffer was in financial trouble in Cleveland, and was courting New Orleans. Charley Finley had moved once, and might want to do it again. The Yankees were talking about a move to New Jersey, should the city of New York not come up with an improved Yankee Stadium lease, plus a bundle of cash to refurbish the old ball park. Cal Griffith in Minnesota was Short's biggest supporter for a move. After all, Griffith had moved the original Senators out of Washington and hated the city. Another franchise move out of the nation's capital would only make him look good for having moved a decade earlier. It's ironic that Griffith's club in Minnesota has drawn under a million fans in each of the last two seasons, and his franchise is now in serious financial trouble.

So Short felt that he had yes votes from Detroit, Milwaukee, Minnesota. Cleveland, Oakland, and New York, giving him seven votes with his own. He knew he couldn't count on Baltimore and Chicago, two clubs who were solidly aligned against him. So Boston, Kansas City, and California appeared to be the undecided clubs, and Short needed two of those three votes for the necessary nine votes. Short had some plans to apply some pressure on Williams to call Boston owner Tom Yawkey and try to talk him into voting with Short. Short well knew that Yawkey had worshiped the ground Ted Williams walked on for over thirty years.

Ted really didn't relish calling Yawkey, but Short kept after him, and I was with Ted in his clubhouse office when Yawkey returned his call. Ted and his former boss exchanged small talk for several minutes, and finally Ted made his pitch to Yawkey. Ted used the soft sell on the Red Sox owner. He said, "Short just has too many problems here that he can't overcome. I hope he gets permission to move." Yawkey replied that he would consider all the facts, and would enter the meeting with an open mind. I frankly was surprised when Yawkey went along with Short.

Ted hadn't put the phone down for more than twenty seconds when Short was calling from upstairs.

"Did you talk with him?"

"Yeah, I did. I had his good ear, and he said that he would go into the meeting with an open mind." Ted added, "I don't think you will have any trouble with him."

Ted felt that Washington had great baseball fans, but

Short had pretty well persuaded him that there were some problems which were insurmountable. Ted was ready for a change of scenery. He was sick of the Washington writers, and Texas would be like starting all over.

The move action seemed to be the only outcome Short worked toward. Every other alternative was a red herring thrown to keep the Washingtonians and prospective buyers off-track.

Short's brow-beating and angry blasts at the D.C. Armory Board were resulting in some pressure on the board to make the concessions that Short was demanding, if not making them meant loss of the franchise.

So the board, which had been holding many meetings trying to combat Short's plan to move the franchise and leave them with an empty stadium, did meet a number of his demands. On August 19, A.J. (Dutch) Bergman, a former great football coach in Washington with Catholic University and later with the Redskins, but at the time, Armory Board chairman, revealed a number of concessions to Short.

The board would bend over backwards to meet his demands, even if they couldn't afford it. Let's face it, Dutch Bergman, who suffered a heart attack and passed away in 1972, and the other Armory Board members didn't want to be the ones blamed for the loss of Washington's baseball team.

Short could have the "sweetheart" deal that he was demanding. The Armory Board would give him his free rent on the stadium for the first one million admissions; Short would have the right to name the concessionaire; he could operate the concession stands during football and baseball seasons; and he would receive revenue from billboard and other stadium advertising during the baseball season. It was a deal that was hard for Short to turn down. But he did. He labeled it as coming too late, even though it was in mid-August. Then it became more apparent than ever that Short did not wish to remain in Washington and was going to move to Texas come hell or high water.

Five days after Short rejected the new stadium rental proposal, City Council Chairman Gilbert Hahn filed suit against Short for failure to pay back rent, and against the Armory Board for failure to collect the rent. At the time, Short owed $136,847.93 in unpaid rent over the last two seasons. While one can appreciate Hahn's desire that the rent be paid, he had played right into Short's hands. He could tell the American League clubowners, "Look, even the head of the city council is suing me in that damn town. How can I operate there?"

The move action would rule out the alternative that some Washington interest might save the team and buy Short out. But Short contacted people he knew were not interested in buying the club. He listened half-heartedly to offers from Washington grocery-store-chain magnate Joe Danzansky, former club owner Bill Veeck, former home-run slugger Hank Greenberg, and former Saint Louis Browns owner Fred Saigh. Danzansky's offer seemed to be the most serious. Danzansky with Marvin Willig and Dr. Robert Schattner as partners, had $10 million ($9 million purchase price and $1 million operating capital). Danzansky naïvely thought that the owners would force Short to sell at his $9 million purchase price to avoid the scandal of taking the national pastime out of the nation's capital. Ironically, of Danzansky's $10 million, $3½ million was solid cash and the rest would come from four area banks, making his financing stronger than that of any of the last three Senators owners.

Danzansky was the bidder that Short feared most. He knew that Danzansky wanted to save baseball for Washington, and Short knew that he would have to discredit his offer and convince some of the other owners that his offer was not legitimate. Short also feared that the *Washington Post* would join forces with Danzansky to buy the club.

Short went to the September 21 meeting at the Sheraton Plaza Hotel in Boston as confident as he could be that he had the necessary votes to move the franchise. Yet he kept up his act publicly right until the time for the meeting. "The ball club is for sale. I really think someone will come up with the money. I don't think I will have to move it."

It wasn't cut and dried after all. Short discovered that the Angels and Athletics had joined the Orioles and White Sox in opposing a move. Finley's opposition was a surprise to some. His critics said that he was just trying to keep the Dallas market open for himself, for a later move.

Joe Danzansky made his pitch to buy the club, but either he didn't do a good job of selling the owners and Short did a good job of discrediting his offer, or too many owners feared Short's threatened lawsuit and were not going to insist on a sale, regardless. Short never made a request to sell the club. And he knew that his fellow owners couldn't act on a franchise sale unless the owner made a formal request to sell.

He did make a formal request to move to Texas. This was no big surprise to me, as I knew that he had everything all set in Texas. He and Joe Burke had made numerous trips there to finalize plans for the move, even though they were denying this to the media.

The first vote on Short's request to move was 8 to 2 in favor of the move; Baltimore and Chicago had voted no, and Oakland and California had abstained. That left Short one vote short of the necessary three-fourths' majority he needed. Short was plenty nervous at this point, and so was the Texas delegation, which was headed up by Arlington Mayor Tom Vandergriff. The Mayor had led the fight for major-league baseball in his area, and he had made an impressive presentation to the club owners. But Charley Finley thought he could come up with a last-minute owner. He wanted to contact Ed Daly, the chairman of the board of World Airways, Inc.

All club owners were present with the exception of Gene Autry of the California Angels. The former western movie and cowboy singing star was hospitalized a few miles away at Leahy Clinic, where he was undergoing eye surgery. He had instructed his representative at the meeting, Bob Reynolds, to vote against a move of the Senators. Proponents of the move persuaded Reynolds to take a cab to the clinic and explain the deadlock to Autry. Meanwhile, Finley had contacted Daly, who said the he wouldn't make a snap decision about buying the club. So Finley said that he would vote for approval. Then Reynolds came back from the clinic with the word that Autry now favored the move of the Senators.

Joe Cronin called for another vote, and approval of the move was given by a vote of 10 to 2.

Bob Short had done his thing. He and the Texas delegation were jubilant. Joe Danzansky and the Washington delegation were heartbroken.

Bowie Kuhn was shaken and disappointed. He had fought against the switch, and didn't think permission would be granted. He underestimated the ability of Bob Short to accomplish things with threats, arm twisting, and back-room politics. Commissioner Kuhn reportedly turned to his lawyer, Sandy Hadden, and said, "Can I veto this?" He knew he had the power, but apparently he was looking for reassurance. He didn't get it. Hadden reportedly said, "Yes, but I wouldn't advise it." In other words, it wouldn't set well with ten of his bosses, who might have mustered enough support in the National League to fire the Commissioner because of such a highhanded indiscretion.

Like most people in Washington on that infamous day of September 21, 1971, Ted Williams and I were eager for any information from the meeting in Boston. We knew that the owners had been in session all day. Ted and I recorded a program before the game, and then we speculated about the Boston outcome. I had been predicting that Short would get the approval to move, but few people in town seemed to agree with me. That night, we watched Dick Bosman pitch a meaningless 9 to 1 win over the Indians. But our thoughts were in Boston.

I saw Ted briefly after the game that night. The first thing he said was, "Have you heard anything from Boston?" I indicated that they were still in session. We said a hasty good night and we both headed for our homes to await the "word from Boston." Ted got the first news of the move off Channel 4. I received it at the same time off Channel 7, and will never forget it. As the Commissioner and the clubowners left their meeting room for the news conference which had been set up in a nearby room, Len Hathaway asked Bowie Kuhn, "Mister Commissioner, will Washington have a baseball club next summer?" The Commissioner moved his head in the negative. That's the way many Washingtonians learned that the capital was without major-league baseball for the first time in seventy-one years. Channel 7 sports director Steve Gilmartin summed up the feelings of many when he immediately stated on the air, "That fink has moved the club to Texas."

Short called Williams immediately after the press conference and told Ted of his "happy" news. Short had convinced Ted that Washington was too close to Baltimore and that the media contracts and the rental agreement were unfavorable for the successful operation of a club in Washington. Ted always maintained that the Washington fans were "great," but his loyalty was to his employer.

The next night, dozens of reporters swarmed around Williams at Kennedy Stadium before a game with the Indians, and Ted did his best to defend Short's move. I filmed a television interview with Williams for ABC, discussing the move of the club to Texas, and the network carried parts of it that night on the evening news. Williams again cited the closeness to Baltimore, the stadium rental agreement, and unfavorable media contracts as reasons that Short could not make a go of it in Washington.

On the face of it, Short seemingly had an excellent case. I sometimes felt that Short was sincere and had really tried to make a successful effort in Washington. But more frequently, indications would point to a well-laid plan to create conditions in Washington which would make it impossible for him to operate the club. I respected Ted as a man of strong conviction, and Short certainly had him convinced that he had done everything possible to succeed in Washington. Sometimes, Ted would be so sincere in passing the Short "line" along to me that I caught myself feeling sorry for poor old Bob Short. But I would always come back to reality when I remembered some of Short's methods of operation.

Washington reaction to the Boston decision was disbelief, anger, and renewed resentment of Short and baseball owners in general. Shirley Povich dubbed the Boston meeting the "Boston Tear Party," and called it a "Night of Infamy."

Few people in Washington felt that the baseball moguls would dare take major-league baseball out of the nation's capital. After all, Washington was a charter member of the American League, and the Senators had fielded teams for seventy-one consecutive years. The more or less consistent ineptitude of the Senators was almost a part of baseball. "Washington, first in war, first in peace and last in the American League," went the old joke.

Because of the weight of tradition, then, baseball fans in general—Washingtonians in particular—were sure that other owners would not give in to the threats of Bob Short.

They felt the risk of alienating Congress, which had granted baseball its attractive anti-trust exemptions and tax shelter, was too prominent a consideration.

Besides, wasn't the man in the White House a big baseball fan? And everyone knew he was a friend of Ted Williams and often attended Senators games. Many felt that Nixon did not take a stronger stand against the threatened move of the club because it was the eve of an election year. After all, sports and politics do reflect each other eerily and Texas is a key state with 26 electoral votes, while the District of Columbia has only three. The day before the club owners met in Boston to consider Short's request to move the franchise, President Nixon told newsmen that it would be "heartbreaking" if the franchise abandoned Washington. But obviously the President's avowed broken heart meant nothing to the owners.

The vote by the league owners to let Short go touched off angry bi-partisan protests from lawmakers on Capitol Hill.

Perhaps Senator William Spong, a Democrat from Virginia, was strongest in his criticism of Short. "Mismanagement should not be rewarded," fired Spong. "Short got the club with the purpose of trafficking with it. He did the same thing with the Lakers. Short was a man who knew little about sports and did a very poor job. The owners possess and savor immunities and privileges. In recent years, the game has taken on the aura of big business first and the interest of the fans second."

Senator John Tunney, a Democrat from California, saw a wider significance in Short's action. "I think the move has created a tremendous amount of interest in the baseball anti-trust exemption. It has focused on the cavalier way owners move franchises around the country. There's a fans-be-damned attitude on the part of owners. They are playing one city off against the other. A disregard for public interest was shown in the move."

The reaction in Washington seems to have touched off hard scrutiny of baseball's special anti-trust exemptions. One Washington columnist wrote, "Incidentally, just as Cornelius Vanderbilt's 'public-be-damned' attitude set the stage for Congress' first control over pure capitalism, Bob Short's own . . . disdain for both the sport and its public will assure him a place in history along with the other robber barons. Short's uprooting of the Washington baseball franchise caused a lot of legislators to review this giant industry called professional sports."

The lawmaker leading the battle to wipe out these special legislative favors to pro sports is Senator Sam Ervin, a Democrat from North Carolina, who said in reaction to Short's move: "Professional sports club owners treat clubs like private playthings . . . If the owners ask to be treated as a monopoly, they should expect government regulation."

Senator Ervin is chairman of the Senate Committee that conducted hearings into a possible merger between the National Basketball Association and the American Basketball Association. Strangely enough, those hearings were scheduled to begin on the very day after Bob Short obtained permission to move his team. The impact of such timing may affect pro sports for years to come. Both Abe Pollin, owner of the Baltimore Bullets NBA team, and Earl Foreman, owner of the ABA Virginia Squires, appeared on my talk show later and both decried Short's move as the "worst possible thing that could happen to our merger plans."

Congressman Wilmer Mizell, a Republican from North Carolina, is better known in baseball circles as Vinegar Bend Mizell. He played professional baseball for twelve years, in fact. Exactly one month after Short got his move vote, Mizell made a speech before the House of Representatives, saying, in part: "I strongly oppose permitting a baseball team to be moved for the sole purpose of reaping a pot of gold for the owners. It seems obvious to me that this is exactly what happened in the case of the Washington Senators. If the fast dollar is the number-one criterion for baseball owners today, on what grounds can they plead exemption from anti-trust laws?" Mizell went on to characterize Washington as a great baseball town with a history of loyal fans over seven decades.

By the end of 1971, thirteen bills aimed at stripping baseball of its anti-trust exemption had been introduced in Congress. It looks like Short stirred up a hornets' nest and lawmakers may do more than simply "deplore" the situation.

One of those bills was sponsored by Congressman B. F. Sisk, a Democrat from California. The day after Short got his permission to move, Sisk introduced the bill. Sisk later became chairman of a committee of Congressmen and civic leaders dedicated to returning a major-league franchise to the capital. He led a delegation of nine concerned Washingtonians to Phoenix on December 2, 1971, to discuss the chance of getting another club with the leaders of baseball.

Washington's major-league schedule in 1972 was restricted to a pair of charity exhibition games. The town responded with major-league turnouts on both occasions. Over 38,000 turned out to see the Orioles and Pirates play in May, and over 32,000 attended a game between the Mets and Red Sox in August. The first game attendance was in spite of threatening weather, and the second game was played in the middle of the baseball and football overlap in a town that is Redskins-crazy.

With typical brashness, Bob Short put his ten-gallon Stetson hat on and played the part of the hero and honored guest at a November 23, 1971, luncheon attended by 800 Dallas-Fort Worth businessmen. The line was familiar. He proclaimed to the Texans, "We'll pay whatever is necessary to acquire the needed talent." And Short okayed the printing of bumper stickers which read, "World Series, '72, Arlington,

Texas." It all seemed very, very similar to those pennant and World Series promises we got in Washington.

To the astonishment of most Washingtonians, Bob Short let it be known that he would like to come back to Washington and tell his side of the franchise shift in a speech before the National Press Club.

Sam Fogg, a baseball writer for UPI when the Senators were here and still a UPI staffer, as chairman of the board of the National Press Club, drew the chore of introducing Short. Fogg began: "To make our speaker of the day feel at home, I am making the following announcement: The board of governors has just sold him the charter of the National Press Club. Therefore, the price of the lunch is immediately increased to $10 a person except for the last row of the balcony. The entire active membership is forthwith transferred to the Elk's club in Arlington, Texas."

Then Bob Short started his prepared speech, and I could hardly believe my ears. He went through the same line he had been singing for three years, but he had added some new verses. Short repeated his charges that Washington was a lousy sports town, was a lousy radio-TV market, had awful civic support, and had an unfair, antagonistic, ungrateful press. His public profession about the press being unfair and ungrateful was new for him, even though he had often privately said it. His most amusing charge was that the stadium was unsafe and that people were afraid to attend the games at night. He left himself wide open with that statement. Why did he switch his Saturday afternoon games to Saturday nights if it was so unsafe? After stammering around, Short finally conceded that the question was a good one that he could not easily answer. Finally, he said that his Saturday afternoon crowds were so poor that he felt he just had to try something else.

Short also charged that there was not a legitimate offer

from anyone to purchase the Senators, not even Danzansky. He tried hard to make this point.

The Washington press analyzed Short's last Washington appearance. George Solomon, then with the *Daily News,* and now with the *Post* said, "Bob Short is a master of distortion. He uses people's fears. He cuts into well-meaning individuals who oppose him."

Shirley Povich, in the *Post,* wrote, "Short was a charmer, selling his snake oil with a virtuoso performance and telling just enough truths to win some credence."

13

THE FLOP
OF THE CENTURY

After twenty years of seeking major-league baseball, Dallas was anxious to get a foot in the door—no matter whose door it happened to be—when Bob Short popped up and offered his Washington Senators. The Senators became the Texas Rangers in 1972. The name "Rangers" appeared on the new team uniforms with Robert Short's initials capitalized: RangerS.

Arlington mayor Tom Vandergriff, the sparkplug of the effort to get a major-league franchise, met with Short and his representatives first in secret in 1971, then openly to guide Short to the Southwest. The key to the deal was Vandergriff's offer of an immediate $7.5 million to Short in exchange for ten years of radio-TV rights. Short used the money to pay off debts incurred in Washington and to put the ball club on a more or less solid basis.

The irony was that Texas press and fans did not truly welcome Short and his Rangers even after all the fuss to get them there. "Even if our people were enthused, which they don't seem to be, it's too damned hot to go to a ball park," wrote Dallas *Times-Herald* sports editor Blackie Sherrod. He added, "I wouldn't say the people here are apathetic, although they may be. I'm more inclined to think they've got to be shown." Even more critical was *Dallas Morning News* sports editor Sam Blair. Blair wrote a series of unfavorable articles about Short. When I spoke with him recently, he said, "I have made a study of Bob Short's method of operations, and I don't think we are getting any bargain in him."

It was not surprising that few Texans actually turned out to see the Worst Darn Team in Baseball. Though Short was already haranguing ("We've got to have 800,000 to break even here."), only some 660,000 fans passed through the turnstiles in 1972, despite Short's having taken 20 percent off his league-leading prices in Washington. After the season, Short sheepishly admitted, "Well, I never said we'd draw a million." The actual attendance in 1972 was about *half* what Arlington Mayor Vandergriff had predicted for the team's first year.

"It's a real hard thing promoting baseball in the Dallas-Fort Worth area because that's college and pro football country. Second-rate baseball means nothing," said the club's announcer, Bill Mercer, late in the season. Mercer and his broadcasting partner, Don Drysdale (Drysdale left after the '72 season), were fortunate that Short was not in a position to exert as much control over the broadcasters as he was in Washington. When the Arlington Park Corporation advanced Short $7.5 million for the radio-TV rights for the next ten years, he forfeited any hopes of exercising direct control of the announcers.

Because of the poor attendance, the Rangers delayed plans to add a second deck to Texas Stadium, increasing capacity from 35,815 to 48,000. "I still think it's a tremendous area," said Commissioner Bowie Kuhn. "And I don't think there is a time limit for them to produce. This year you have to look at it from the standpoint that the team is in last place in the standings and the nearest other team to Arlington [Houston] is doing well."

The team drew poorly despite a story-book beginning in Texas. Overnight, it seemed, the minor-league stadium had been revamped from 10,000 hard seats to 35,000 seats all with backs. And despite a traffic jam that clotted the flow into the stadium, some 20,105 went to the Texas debut, the second biggest crowd of the season as it turned out. The stadium was half filled with fancy Stetsons, and Vanessa Vandergriff, teenage daughter of the mayor, sang the national anthem. Ted Williams had been presented with a pair of cowboy boots. The fans were excited that Texas was finally in the major-league standings. Then Frank Howard made the debut unforgettable by smashing a 450-foot homer in the first inning far over the green fence in dead center field. When Howard hit the first Texas homer, thousands of balloons were suddenly released and the huge Rangers scoreboard flashed in bright red lights for two minutes. The game was typical of the Rangers that season except for one thing—they won. But they didn't win, 7–6, until after blowing a 6–1 lead over the California Angels, with four errors.

The Ranger home park was situated next door to a man-made recreation park called Seven Seas, described as "the world's largest inland sea-life park." But even the killer whale, roller-skating penguins, and dancing porpoises of Seven Seas were not enough to attract interest in the spike-shoed knicker-wearers next door. The Texas apathy was such that Vandergriff's people were having trouble selling radio and TV games to sponsors. Bill Knobler, an executive for the Dallas advertising agency contracted to sell the Rangers games, admitted that the first exhibition game had to go on the air without a single sponsor. A spokesman for the Arlington Park Corporation, which had bought the air rights from Short, pointed out that the Rangers "sponsor package" was hard to put together because of the late move of the franchise. They didn't have a full load of sponsors even when the team opened the season. In mid-February, 1973, the Rangers broadcast network, consisting of 25 radio stations and 10 TV stations, was dissolved by the Arlington Park Corporation. The substantial losses in the '72 season were cited as the reason for the network's collapse.

The attendance situation got so desperate in Texas that halfway through the season, Short called Oscar Molomot in from Minnesota, where he had been assigned to promote Short's hotels. Oscar immediately counted all the left-over helmets from Washington, had a "T" painted over the "W" and staged a "Helmet Night." Molomot announced afterwards, "We gave out 5,000 helmets, and if my memory serves me right, that's more than we ever gave away in Washington." He added, "It's easier than in Washington because so many people and businesses want to help here. And I don't think we'll have as many peaks and valleys in attendance." Despite Molomot's free panty hose and bats and hot pants contests, attendance was ruinous the rest of the year. He was right about the consistency—just one long flat Texas prairie of an attendance chart.

There were basic reasons for some of the apathy, naturally. All the seats were out in the open, directly under the sun or exposed to showers, and the stadium was notorious in the area for its poor toilet facilities. In Texas they like their baseball with plenty of beer, and beer and baseball don't quite go well together if you don't have a handy "john." There was also bad luck: when the club promoted "Dallas Night," a record crowd appeared but many departed in the first inning when it began raining. And when there wasn't rain, there was plenty of heat—so much, in fact, that the steel girders would expand in the sun and give off what fans described as "a sound like a gunshot." And a sound like that is liable to make you nervous in Texas.

There seemed little doubt that Texas Stadium needed some sort of cover to protect fans from the blazing sun. There were the usual bugs that go with every new stadium. The players complained about the glaring sun during day work-outs and games, and there was considerable trouble getting the lights adjusted so that at night there wouldn't be a blinding glare. It appeared that some of the Rangers might favor another player strike when they learned that there was no hot water in the clubhouse after an early season game at Texas Stadium.

The fans were annoyed with the traffic jams, which seemed to occur with the smallest of crowds. When 11,000 showed up for a special Ball Day game, cars were jammed up for eleven miles on the turnpike. It cost 30 cents to drive the turnpike each way, a little inconvenience that Short did not have to contend with in Washington.

One thing about Texas baseball which seemed to appeal to the media people was the pressroom that Bob Short maintained for media types. It was catered by Walter Jetton, the famous barbecue man whom Lyndon Johnson used so frequently for barbecues in Washington and Texas.

Texas had a 15-game losing streak at the end of the year, which gave them the worst percentage (.351), the least number of wins (54), and put them farther behind their division leader (38½ games) than any other team in baseball. They were the only team in the major leagues to lose 100 games. In the final statistics, Texas had the fewest home runs, doubles and triples in the American League.

The Rangers pitching was no better. The club had the

highest earned run average in the majors, a gaudy 3.53. And they also had the lowest number of games completed by pitchers in the history of major-league baseball: eleven.

The Rangers were consistent. In addition to having the worst hitting and pitching in baseball, they were last in fielding. Texas committed the most errors in the majors, 166, and had the lowest fielding percentage, .972. Short had turned the franchise from one of the best fielding clubs into one of the worst. The only thing the Rangers seemed to be able to do was run—and they led the league in stolen bases with 126, thanks to 51 steals by Dave Nelson, 20 by Elliot Maddox, and 15 by All Star reserve shortstop Toby Harrah. Too bad they couldn't steal first base, too.

The high point of the season was when Texas swept a four-game series from Baltimore, of all people, in the middle of the pennant race! "It was like we had won the World Series," Williams was quoted. "I hope the cry isn't going up: 'Break up the Rangers!' " After that, the Rangers lost three games to the Tigers.

Another club to lose four in a row to the Rangers was the California Angels. General Manager Harry Dalton said that that series loss to the lowly Rangers was the low point of the year for the Angels. He added, "That series will haunt me the rest of my life."

Even the Rangers who were performing halfway decently were not getting many breaks. Typical was pitcher Bill Gogolewski, who finished strongly in Washington in 1971 and had been counted on to win 15 games for Texas. But Go-Go got off to a bad start. He was still in a seven-game losing streak by mid-September when he came within four outs of a no-hitter, blanking the Angels, 3–0. Wearing Number 13 resolutely all year, Go-Go lost three out of four despite giving up only 16 hits and 6 earned runs in 31 innings (a 1.97 ERA).

At least Washington fans got some psychic relief the first time the Rangers came into the area to play Baltimore. Typically, Pete Broberg pitched masterfully but lost a two-hitter, 1–0, when his catcher Ken Suarez stepped on a bat while attempting to complete a double play, lost his aim, and hit Brooks Robinson on the back of the head. That allowed Merv Rettenmund to score the winning run.

At least 600 "hard-core" Washington fans had made the trip to Baltimore and when they discovered that the Villain Bob Short was there, too, well, the party was just beginning. First they chanted, "Short is a bum! Short is a bum!" Then a former usher for Senators games at RFK Stadium, "Baseball Bill" Holdforth, had a Baltimore vendor take Short a hot dog and beer "compliments of the Washington baseball fans." But Short refused to accept their gracious offer. Then Holdforth sidled up to Short with a dummy effigy of the baseball owner, stuffed with old copies of *The Sporting News* and dressed in a Senators hat and pennant. Everyone in the crowd of 6,000 seemed to enjoy Short's moment of humiliation.

The worst came in the seventh inning. A woman broke through the minimal protection around Short's special box behind the visitors' dugout and dumped a cup of beer over BS's bleached-blond mane. The lady protested that she had slipped, but as she was being ushered out of the stadium, she admitted to George Solomon of the *Washington Daily News,* "I'll tell you something, I didn't slip. I purposely poured a cup of beer over that bum Short's head. And I'd do it again."

Perhaps the nadir of the season was a game that didn't even count. People had been disparaging the Rangers all year by comparing them to a Triple A ball club. Oakland A's pitcher Blue Moon Odom commented after the Rangers suprisingly defeated him, "I can't pitch against that Triple A club." John Welaj, a Senators-Rangers front-office employee, went even further. "This is the worst team I've seen in the major leagues," Welaj said. "It's not even a good Triple A club. It's Double A." Anyway, maybe that is why the Rangers chief farm team in Triple A, Denver, slaughtered the parent club, 11–4, in a mid-season exhibition game at Mile High Stadium. Five Denver pitchers limited Texas to six hits, while Denver hitters got 14 hits. Of those, catcher Bill Fahey collected a homer, a triple, and a single and then was called up to Texas for the rest of the year.

Soon afterwards, Denver general manager Jim Burris said the team wanted to replace its affiliation with Texas as the major-league parent club. Burris explained that reports that Bob Short was seeking to sell the organization to Texas interests made the working agreement insecure.

This was the first public indication that Short was proceeding just as he had done with the Lakers in Los Angeles. Move, then sell at a profit. According to his master plan, Short should sell the Rangers by the end of the 1973 season, which marks the end of a five-year depreciation claim for tax purposes. Thus he can depreciate the club for the full $9 million purchase price—and then get out. He'll probably ask for $13 to $14 million for a handsome capital gain. And likely, he'll get it from rich and provincial Texans. (The New York Yankees were sold for $10 million in 1973.) Short may even be able to avoid paying tax on such a capital gain if he can show enough paper losses. Otherwise, he may ask that the capital gain be deferred over several years so that the bite will be light.

Ted Williams can make a chunk of that too. Williams still holds an option to buy 10 percent of the club at the $9 million price. If Short sells at, say, $14 million, Williams stands to make about $500,000 overnight.

I wonder, though, if all the ugliness was worth the money. Short may have won his battle and undermined all of baseball when he eradicated the ball club from Washington and left behind a Congress of angry men. Since the Supreme Court has recently ruled not to touch baseball's historic anti-trust exemption, the ball is back to Congress, which has the power to take that exemption away from baseball and all sports.

Williams suffered through the dratted Texas heat, which rose to 115 degrees during the July 16 game with Cleveland and precipitated a change in the starting time for Rangers games from 5:30 to 7:30 P.M. And the heat was no worse than the ability of the players, and the raps. Said Brant Alyea, who was traded in 1970: "That was a good club in 1969, 10 games over .500, then they traded guys like Ken McMullen, myself, and Frank Bertaina. We were good for morale and people don't realize how important that can be. I guarantee that I'd be leading the Rangers in RBIs and homers but they'd rather play guys like Lovitto, who aren't ready. No, I think Williams was a good manager but Jesus Christ couldn't win with that club." Rapped Mike Epstein, "The team was on the upswing, it had confidence. Why make a trade you didn't have to make? There were more changes and no one knew where he stood." Added Cleveland's Tom McCraw, another former Senator, "As it is now, that team needs a builder. Williams is a perfectionist. You have to stay with the kids, you can't platoon them." Tim Cullen, released by the Rangers in spring training, later to catch on with Oakland, said, "Williams does not have enough patience to be a manager. That's why every one of the old gang [1969 team] except Dick Bosman has gone. Most of those kids they have now should still be in the minors."

Meanwhile, the "old gang" was making contributions elsewhere. Cullen himself became an important addition to the World Series-bound A's. The A's also had Mike Epstein, who hit 26 homers that season, Kubiak and Mincher. The latter had a big hit to help win a game in the World Series of 1972.

But the team which really owned Short a round of thanks was Detroit in 1972. When Detroit finally vaulted into first place at the end of the season it was on the strength of a homer and two run-scoring singles from ex-Senators third baseman Aurelio Rodriguez. Rodriguez also made defensive plays so spectacular that his manager, Billy Martin, said, "As a fielder, Rodriguez is there with Brooks Robinson as the best I've ever seen. The kid has an arm, too, and unlike others who can throw, but can't aim, he's accurate." Martin added that he most valuable player on that team had to be shortstop Ed Brinkman, another ex-Senator, who committed only seven errors all season, the fewest by a shortstop in major-league history. Included was a 72-game string without an error, a major-league record. That was not all. Brinkman established two more new major-league records, as he handled 331 consecutive chances without an error, and established a fielding percentage of .990. Brinkman missed the American League playoffs because of a back injury. He underwent surgery following the season, and while he was still in the hospital learned that his teammates had voted him the Most Valuable Tiger of the year. Billy Martin was quick to stress that it wasn't a sympathy vote.

Another Bob Short contribution to the Tigers was Joe Coleman. The hard-throwing right-hander, who won 20 games his first season after leaving the Senators, added 19 wins in 1972 and pitched a great game in the playoffs against Oakland. And Short's other contribution to Detroit, Frank Howard, won at least one game for them with a homer during the final pennant stretch.

And so manager Ted Williams turned in his uniform after a four-year try.

When he announced his decision to quit as manager, there was an air of relief at every stratum of the Rangers organization, beginning with Williams himself. "Managing was a great experience, one I'm glad to have had," he said at the end. "Winning as a manager is the most exhilarating feeling in the world, but constant losing produces the exact opposite. I think this club has reached bottom. There is no way to go but up. It has tremendous potential and in some ways I'm sorry I won't be around to see it jell. Many of these fellows have had only 3-4-5 years, and experience dictates it takes a team of players with 5-6-7 years to be at peak effectiveness. We need to plug some gaps, add hitting. That's been my biggest disappointment this year—the hitting. I thought it would be better. But I'll be glad to help in any way I can. Short has ruled out only about one thing for me next year—hunting and fishing for the whole season. I'll probably work with hitters in spring training [as he formerly did for the Red Sox] and scout major-leaguers and free agents. I think I can contribute something that way or I'd leave right now . . . Who knows? I might even make a few banquets. I've been pretty good at skipping them in the past, even one at the White House, but I want to help in any way I can."

A couple of weeks after the World Series, when Williams was in Canada fishing, Short got around to naming a new Texas manager. Short went out of character and ruled out a "name" manager. Short called a press conference at Arlington, Texas, and revealed that Whitey Herzog would be the new Texas manager. From the statements at the press conference, it was obvious that Short went after a man who agreed with his baseball philosophy.

The new manager of the Texas Rangers would have to be considered a surprise selection. Herzog was an outfielder who averaged appearances in only 79 games per season the eight years that he bounced around the major leagues. The forty-one-year-old Herzog came to the Rangers from the New York Mets organization, where he had been head of player development in the minor leagues. Herzog said that he felt he could handle and develop the younger Texas players. He explained that the young players today are so much different than they used to be. Herzog made a point of saying that he would not platoon.

It didn't take Herzog long to feel the pinch of Bob Short's lack of operating capital. The Rangers' owner limited Herzog to a three-man coaching staff in the majors for the 1973 season. Williams had insisted on a five-man coaching staff and, on occasion, operated with six coaches when people like John Roseboro, Del Wilber, and Al Zarilla were carried as coaches for parts of some seasons.

Herzog named the youngest coaching staff in the majors; thirty-three-year-old Jackie Moore, thirty-four-year-old Chuck Estrada, and thirty-seven-year-old Chuck Hiller. Maybe the young, inexperienced coaches were selected with the young Rangers club in mind, but the fact that they didn't command large salaries may have had something to do with it.

So the Ted Williams era as a manager of the Senators-Rangers ended with differences between Short and Williams becoming more apparent. Bob Addie of the Washington *Post* spoke with Bob Short at the 1972 World Series, and then reported that Ted would be "phased out" of the Rangers operation. Ted will still draw his salary for the final year on the contract, but as Addie reported, "Ted's activities will be limited to giving hitting instructions during spring training and a token banquet appearance or two in Texas." Williams would be happy to exercise his option and sever his Texas ties.

Ted once thought that he would move into the front office as general manager when he decided he had had enough of managing. But I knew that once Short named yes-man Joe Burke general manager in 1972 Ted would never hold that position, or any other front-office position of authority where he might butt heads with Short.

Short made a big point at the press conference revealing Ted's resignation as manager of stressing that, "Ted is my dear friend, and this decision is completely his. I'll always be indebted to him for coming back to baseball."

It was apparent to everyone that the Short-Williams relationship had cooled considerably. On August 3, 1972, Ted reacted to an article written by David Fink of the *Dallas Times-Herald*. Fink had written that Short was playing a strong hand in force-feeding the youth movement on the Rangers. Ted exploded: "As long as I'm running this fucking ball club, I'm running it on the field. Everyone in the front office knows it. Short, Burke, everyone knows it. I want that understood. There was one thing right in that column, though. They called me a millionaire. I am a fucking millionaire."

Outside of the McLain trade, the force-feeding of young players was Ted's biggest difference of opinion with Short. Ted claimed they needed seasoning, but Short claimed they could develop in the majors, and he felt that fans would pay money to see them develop. Williams was right. The use of kids who were not ready only resulted in the loss of games, shattering of the youngster's confidence, and a strained relationship between the player and the manager.

I can't help wondering what Williams would have done as a manager had he had a club with more talent; had he been with a club that had some operating capital, and a front office with some baseball savvy. Maybe what Ted Williams had to contend with during his managerial days was best expressed by veteran baseball writer Russ White at the 1972 World Series when he suggested, "Bob Short should be named the Minor League Baseball Executive of the Year."

Bob Short's last deed of 1972 was to fire clubhouse man Fred Baxter, who had been with the franchise for four decades. Baxter started with the Senators as a bat boy forty-one years ago when Walter Johnson was manager. Fred was clubhouse man for the visiting clubhouse from 1932 until he succeeded his brother Frank as Senators clubhouse boy upon the latter's death in 1949. Baxter was the franchise's oldest employee in terms of tenure, but that didn't stop Short from canning him. Fred told me, "I'm in good health, and am working just as hard and doing just as good a job as I ever have in my forty-one years with the club, and want to continue as a baseball clubhouse man for another eight years until I am 65." The Rangers claim they let Baxter go because he wouldn't move his off-season home from Washington to Texas.

Baxter feels the real reason was his loyalty to Ted Williams. He says that Joe Burke and Williams were in a power struggle, and that Burke resented Fred's having worked closely with Ted, and talked Short into firing him. One month after Ted announced his resignation as manager, Short authorized Burke to send Baxter a note telling him that the new manager would select the clubhouse man, and that he should feel free to look for other employment. Baxter contacted Whitey Herzog when he was appointed the new manager, and Herzog told Fred that he wanted him as the clubhouse man. A couple of weeks before Christmas, Baxter got the final thrust of the knife, when Burke sent him another note saying that he was out.

Baxter was deeply hurt, for in addition to being out of a job he had no pension. Fred said, "Equipment men-clubhouse men are not included in the pension plan, so after forty-one years, all I have left are memories."

Short couldn't have claimed that Baxter was costing him too much money, as his base salary for the seven-month job was an unbelievable $4,200. The players gave Baxter more in tips than the Rangers were paying him. Baxter was making $4,200 with the Rangers only because Williams went to bat for him the previous year and got him a raise.

With Short's finances close to the vest, and his five-year

tax shelter running out in 1973, it seems even more likely that Short will have to sell the franchise. Texan Paul Richards, who was fired from the Atlanta Braves organization, is trying to put together enough Texas money to acquire the club from Short. Richards was attempting to join the Rangers in some capacity in 1972. Williams wanted it, but Short and Burke were opposed to it. And there are reports that Short's finances are such that he is trying to refinance the Texas club.

As it turned out, Ted Williams, despite his early praise of and constant loyalty to Bob Short, couldn't have selected worse conditions under which to prove whether he could be a successful major-league manager. Perhaps he, too, is among those who were happy to Kiss It Goodbye!

INDEX